The Jack the Ripper Suspects

The Jack the Ripper Suspects

Persons Cited by Investigators and Theorists

STAN RUSSO

Foreword by CHRISTOPHER-MICHAEL DIGRAZIA

McFarland & Company, Inc., Publishers
Jefferson, North Carolina, and London

LIBRARY OF CONGRESS CATALOGUING-IN-PUBLICATION DATA

Russo, Stan, 1972–
The Jack the Ripper suspects : persons cited by investigators and
theorists / Stan Russo ; foreword by Christopher-Michael DiGrazia.
p.   cm.
Includes bibliographical references and index.

ISBN 0-7864-1775-7 (illustrated case binding : 50# alkaline paper) ∞

1. Jack, the Ripper.   2. Serial murders—England—London—History—
19th century.   3. Serial murderers—England—London—History—
19th century.   4. Serial murder investigation—England—London—
History.   5. Whitechapel (London, England)—History.   I. Title.
HV6535.G63L667   2004   364.152'3'0922421—dc22   2004008624

British Library cataloguing data are available

Cover image: ©2004 Photodisc

Manufactured in the United States of America

McFarland & Company, Inc., Publishers
Box 611, Jefferson, North Carolina 28640
www.mcfarlandpub.com

For Stanley Russo
My Grandfather

whose name I carry
but whose actions
rather than merely a name
I wish to exemplify

Acknowledgments

Special thanks to Chris Costa and Michelle Reid, without whom this book might never have reached the final stage.

Thanks also to Stewart P. Evans, Christopher-Michael DiGrazia, Martin Fido, Christopher T. George, Larry S. Barbee, and Nick Warren, whose help was and is deeply appreciated.

Table of Contents

Table of Contents

Foreword

by Christopher-Michael DiGrazia

In the beginning, there is the name. There are others, of course, that send a shiver down the spine—Manson, Zodiac, Son of Sam—and they are names that are representative not just of bestiality but also of random terror: the unexpected blow, the sudden shock, the cold dehumanization which transforms victims from people into prey. They are names that have found lasting attention among true-crime buffs, each spawning their own cottage industry of theories, websites and controversies. They are names that are symbols of horror. But before long, we return to *the* name.

Jack the Ripper.

Ever since a befuddled P.C. Neil stood over the bleeding body of Mary Ann Nichols in the grey dawn of August 31, 1888, professional and amateur sleuth alike have laboured to put a name to the phantom who lurks forever through the foggy London night. Some have struck wide of the mark, while others have seemed tantalizingly close to a final solution, yet for all the ink spilled, all the words penned and all the pages bound between covers, every case has disappointed, proving hollow at the core. And so, because there is no satisfactory ending, each year sees a new candidate put forward as a sort of Grand Guignol tailor's dummy, to be fitted with the crimson mantle of Jack the Ripper. Whether the name is that of a previously unconsidered suspect, such as quack doctor Francis Tumblety, a resurrected favourite like painter Walter Sickert or a complete nonstarter, such as Lewis Carroll (yes, even the gentle storyteller of *Alice in Wonderland* is not safe from posthumous slander), the mystery of the Whitechapel Murders is so compelling that even the most outlandish claims are given a respectful hearing in the hope that this "first and greatest of murder mysteries" might yet be solved.

But why? Erase the evocative name, remove the storied locale and blast away the encrustations of myth surrounding the Ripper murders, and what is left? Five prostitutes, each in the last stages of alcoholism and disease, brutally slaughtered by a maniacal killer. Both the calling and the crime are as old as Babylon and have been sadly repeated down through the ages. So why do we still remember? Why do we care? Why, in fact, does this book you are holding exist at all?

1

Some of it, surely, is due to the dramatic circumstances that surrounded the murders: They took place in the most populous city of the greatest empire the world had seen; they were eagerly seized upon by sensationalist newspapers out to increase sales; from the outset they were an enigmatic puzzle, and their chief actor was graced—if we may call it that—with a stage name so horribly apposite that not even a century's passing has managed to entirely quell its dread fame. But part of the continued fascination with the Ripper crimes is, I would argue, their very familiarity. Anyone who reads about the case soon comes to see that, despite the alien world of hansom cabs and gaslight, our grandsires were not so very different from ourselves. They, too, were frightened of an unknown killer stalking silently through the night; they were astonished that their prosperous country could contain such desperate outcasts as the Ripper's victims; they, too, tried to pit their wits against the Ripper; and they were just as ready to grab at straws to bring a killer to justice.

One example will suffice. "Catch the Ripper" is a game almost as old as the murders themselves. One of its first practitioners was a customs clerk named Edward Larkins. Pondering the Ripper's depredations, he quickly convinced himself that no true Englishman was capable of such savagery. He decided that because some Portuguese peasants during the Peninsular War had committed atrocities that resembled the Ripper mutilations, it must be a Portuguese man responsible for the crimes; specifically, it must be a man traveling on the cattle boats which ran between London and Lisbon. Perusing ships' lists, Larkins pronounced that Manuel Cruz

Xavier was his man. When it was pointed out that Xavier was out of the country during the murder of Annie Chapman (the Ripper's second "canonical" victim), a lesser man might have retreated into silence. Not our Larkins. He simply rummaged through his lists again and circled the name of another seaman, Jose Laurenco, pronouncing him Xavier's partner.

In all, Larkins named three Portuguese sailors (none of whom, I dare say, ever knew the small part they played in this criminal drama) as a tag team of killers. He wrote constantly to the Home Office with his theory, becoming more and more convinced as the years went by and no official acknowledgment was made of his genius. It was obvious that a jealous Scotland Yard would never admit they had failed where Larkins had succeeded. No matter. Who cared that Sir Robert Anderson, Assistant Commissioner of the Metropolitan Police, might dismiss him as a "troublesome busybody?" The world might mock, but Larkins knew. The mystery of Jack the Ripper was no mystery to him. He had solved the case. He had also become the first in a long line of a particularly annoying breed of Ripperologists: the one who throws over the rules of evidence. It is not enough that *he* believes his theory correct; he demands *you* prove his theory wrong!

And so the unintentionally comic figure of Edward Larkins brings us, at last, to this book. Within its pages, Stan Russo has named close to one hundred men (and women!) who have all, at some point, been accused of being Saucy Jack. But this is no mere accumulation of names; Russo has not only shown why these people were suspected, but *how*, tracing the books, pamphlets, magazines and files which some of the world's finest—as well as most hapless—scholars have used to press their arguments. If the supporting evidence is insubstantial, he makes no bones about saying so, but equally, he encourages research on promising candidates. If, after reading this book, no one can advance Vassily Konovalov or Prince Albert Victor seriously, the mystery which still clings to the sad, lonely figure of Montague Druitt may yet encourage some intrepid investigator to come to grips with this failed barrister so cruelly smeared with the name of the 19th century's greatest monster.

Is the true name of Jack the Ripper somewhere in this book? I believe it is, even as I admit that it is just as likely he lies mouldering in some lost graveyard, unknown and unmourned. But the thought that one of these entries might hold the solution to the Great Victorian Mystery excites me, as it must any lover of the bizarre and unknown.

The search for the Whitechapel Murderer has thrown up useful research, as well as a boatload of rubbish best left to decay. To wade through that great festering cargo in order to create a compendium of suspects is a daunting task, but Stan Russo has accomplished it with grace and clarity. This book belongs at the bedside of anyone whose imagination has ever been fired by the world of danger, darkness and mystery evoked by the name of Jack the Ripper.

Christopher-Michael DiGrazia is the editor of Ripper Notes, *the premier American magazine devoted to research of the Whitechapel Murders, and is a consultant on Jack the Ripper, specializing in press coverage of the crimes. He has been interviewed on The History Channel, NPR, BookTV and the BBC, and served as a consultant to the Johnny Depp film* From Hell. *He is co-author of* The News from Whitechapel: Jack the Ripper in the "Daily Telegraph" *(McFarland, 2002). He is currently researching the Charley Ross kidnapping case.*

Preface

Jack the Ripper murdered and mutilated as few as three, perhaps more than ten, women between the years 1887 and 1891 in the East End of London, England. The mysticism behind his name has attached legendary status to this case. There has been no conclusive answer as to who Jack the Ripper actually was, and the debate has raged for over a century.

This book has been designed to provide a detailed and unbiased account of the men and women who, it has been suggested, terrorized London, England, during the autumn of 1888. The origins and known history of each suspect shall be discussed. Each suspect's particular connection to the Jack the Ripper case will remain the primary focus, encompassing the major facts and theories, theorists and research that have contributed to that suspect's positive or negative candidacy as a viable suspect. A basic analysis of these elements shall be offered on individual suspects. The central goal is to enable future researchers to use this work as a fundamental source for potential research, analysis and theory on the Jack the Ripper case.

Over the 115 years since the murders began, more than 100 suspects have been proposed as Jack the Ripper. In the autumn of 1888, a number of people were suspected of having perpetrated these horrific atrocities. They included John Arnold, Nikaner Benelius, Jack Irwin, John Langan, Douglas Cow, John George Donkin, Alfred Gray and, most notably, John Pizer. Arnold, Benelius, Irwin, Cow, Donkin, Gray and others like them were examined on suspicion and subsequently cleared of the murders during the investigation. Outside of the introduction, they shall not appear within this book due to their obvious lack of guilt in connection with the Jack the Ripper murders.

John Pizer is a similar case. Sergeant William Thick arrested Pizer on September 10, 1888, in connection with the Ripper murders. Pizer appeared at the September 11 inquest into the death of Annie Chapman. In response to the opening question Pizer clearly declared that he was "Leather Apron." Sergeant Thick, who had known Pizer for many years, stated that when a resident of the neighborhood spoke of "Leather Apron," they were referring to John Pizer. Pizer was able to produce alibis for the August 31 murder of Mary Ann Nichols and the September 8 murder of Annie Chapman. He was immediately released from custody and cleared of all charges. Despite the work of researchers, who continued to question the guilt, not only of John Pizer, but also of the suspect, "Leather Apron," Pizer shall not be discussed among the group of suspects within this reference book.

This work deals with 71 suspects, all of whom were mentioned in books on Jack the Ripper well after the murders ended. These suspects are included because their innocence has yet to be fully established, with the exception of four who have been irrefutably cleared of any connection. Regarding those four, however, theories have arisen that attempt to refute documented evidence of innocence. For that reason these four suspects have been included.

Certain suspects, such as "the father of G. W. B." (historian Colin Wilson's preferred suspect at this time) and the "Jewish slaughterman" (proposed by theorist Robin Odell), and certain theories, such as the "brother's-officer" theory suggested by author Harold Dearden, shall not be discussed outside of this introduction. No name—not even a pseudonym—has been offered for these suspects. Therefore, until further research reveals added elements of these particular suspects' stories, they shall languish within this introduction.

The main source book for research on the case is *The Jack the Ripper A–Z.* Originally published in 1991, this book is the most comprehensive encyclopedia on the Jack the Ripper murders ever written. It has undergone two revisions, in 1994 and 1996, with each edition adding and adjusting the known information on the case that has been unearthed by meticulous research. The A–Z provides an overview of the entire case, including policemen, witnesses, in-formants, theorists, researchers, documents and, of course, suspects. Details specific to a suspect's connection to the Jack the Ripper case are focused on here, which approach differentiates this work from *The Jack the Ripper A–Z.*

Even as this book comes to print new suspects are proposed as Jack the Ripper. On Stephen P. Ryder's "Casebook: Jack the Ripper," online participants are free to discuss elements within the scope of the case. Five new suspects who have been recently suggested are Arbie LaBruckman, Julius Lipman, John Anderson, "Mary" Pearcey and Constance Kent. Research is currently commencing into these suspects' histories to gather an insight into their viability as true suspects.

My own personal history with the Jack the Ripper case began in the autumn of 1998, when I purchased my first book on the subject, Bruce Paley's 1995 work, *Jack the Ripper: The Simple Truth.* Paley put forth an exquisite look into the degradation and squalor of life in the East End of London during the latter part of the 19th century. Paley's choice for a suspect was even more intriguing: Joseph Barnett, the lover of the possible final victim, Mary Kelly. Paley depicted an almost silent villain murdering amongst his own. I was hooked. I read book after book on the Jack the Ripper murders, and I was on my course to solve the unsolvable.

This book is a first step. My own research into this mystery continues. Perhaps one day an unassailable theory on who committed these murders will be released, including the secret identity of the most notorious serial killer of all time. Until that day....

Introduction

London, England, in the latter part of the nineteenth century was the epicenter of the industrialized world, as well as an extremely diverse city. Artistic culture flourished in the West End, where the likes of James Whistler and Oscar Wilde roamed the streets and created art and literature that would serve as models for the twentieth century. Meanwhile, the East End of London, only a few miles away, was a million miles removed in terms of civilization. In slums packed with more than eighty thousand people, those who could not crowd into tiny tenements were forced to sleep on the streets. Noted businessman-turned-sociologist Charles Booth created a poverty map of London that drew attention to the horrors of life in the East End, and mystery writer Jack London brought the area to life in his *People of the Abyss*, describing the time he spent there during 1902.

On August 7, 1888, the body of Martha Tabram was found in the East End, punctured with thirty-nine separate stab wounds. No one was caught or charged in connection with her murder, proving how easy it was to eradicate an individual in so densely populated an area.

On August 31, 1888, the body of Mary Ann Nichols was found. One week later, on September 8, another body, that of Annie Chapman, was found with similar wounds. At this point, the police joined the murder investigations of Tabram, Nichols, and Chapman into one.

On September 27, the Central News Agency received a letter claiming to be from the murderer. Although considered to be a hoax, this letter gave a new twist to the case: It provided the newspapers with the moniker Jack the Ripper. The letter warned of future murders.

On September 30 two women, Elizabeth Stride and Catherine Eddowes, were murdered in similar fashion. Because the wounds on Stride were slightly dissimilar to those of Nichols, Chapman and Eddowes, many future researchers would exclude Stride as an actual Jack the Ripper victim. At the time of the murders, however, Stride was considered among the Ripper's victims, as was Tabram—likewise later discounted by many researchers—and another victim named Emma Smith, murdered in April of 1888.

The murders of Nichols, Chapman and Eddowes had occurred at one-week intervals, but following Eddowes's murder the pattern was broken, and Jack the

Ripper did not reemerge until November 9, when he committed his most brutal murder and the only one committed indoors. The victim was Mary Jane Kelly, the only woman under forty years old murdered during the ten-week span. Kelly's murder has led many researchers to speculate that her death had special meaning and that the background of this Irish immigrant may hold the key to solving the mystery. As of yet, that speculation has yielded no results.

Through the years, dozens of identities have been suggested for Jack the Ripper. Occasionally, a new discovery or theory has stirred enough interest to merit its own name, which then becomes a part of Ripper lore. An example is the so-called MacNaghten Memorandum, a document discovered in 1959 among the secret papers of Assistant Chief Constable Melville Mac-Naghten. The naming of three suspects in this memo provided researchers with years of clues to track and trails to trace. In 1970, crime historian Dr. Thomas Stowell created a public frenzy by implying, without actually naming names, that Prince Albert Victor, the Duke of Clarence, son of King Edward VII, was Jack the Ripper. That story evolved into the Royal Conspiracy Theory, which

held that as few as three and as many as twelve Freemasons were involved in committing the murders attributed to Jack the Ripper, to cover up a secret marriage between Prince Albert Victor, or Price Eddy, and a commoner. Serious historians and researchers have shown that the Royal Conspiracy Theory, outlined by Stephen Knight in 1976, has no basis in fact. However, new versions of the Royal Conspiracy Theory continue to emerge.

The latest theory to excite public interest is mystery crime novelist Patricia Cornwell's "discovery" that British Impressionist painter Walter Sickert committed the murders. Cornwell advanced Sickert—not a new suspect, having been previously mentioned as far back as 1970—on the basis that he was a psychopathic woman-hater. Thus, Cornwell buys into the long-standing premise that Jack the Ripper's murderous propensities would have been visible as obvious mental illness, rather than hidden below the surface of a seemingly ordinary man.

Although many new suspects have been proposed and examined, research has left us no wiser as to the true identity of the most infamous serial killer of all time.

THE
SUSPECTS

FREDERICO ALBERICCI

Of the numerous books written about Jack the Ripper, only two books mention Frederico Albericci. The second of these books is the foremost reference work, *The Jack the Ripper A to Z*, an encyclopedia that encompasses the entire scope of the case. A mere nine and one half lines are dedicated to Albericci in this important work. That is because Frederico Albericci may never have existed.

In an advancement of Stephen Knight's 1976 Royal Conspiracy Theory, author Melvyn Fairclough's 1991 book, *The Ripper and the Royals*, announces a number of new co-conspirators involved in different aspects of the Royal Conspiracy. Frederico Albericci is one of these.

Fairclough implicates Albericci (described as a "pickpocket") in at least two murders and another attempted murder. The first is the April 1888 attack and murder of Emma Elizabeth Smith. According to Fairclough, while searching for their intended victims—Mary Ann Nichols, Annie Chapman, Elizabeth Stride and Mary Kelly, known collectively as the "canon"—Albericci and John Netley questioned Emma Smith as to the whereabouts of these women. Realizing that Smith now represented a danger to them, Netley and Albericci threatened her and then beat her up, shoving something into her vagina in the process.

Emma Smith was attacked on the night of April 2 by three youths. They robbed her and raped her. During the rape, a blunt instrument was forced into her vagina, tearing her perineum. The perineum is the area behind the genital region and in front of the anus. Smith was taken to London Hospital, where she died three days later of peritonitis.

The officer in charge of the police investigation on the ground was Inspector Frederick George Abberline. In 1988, Joseph Gorman Sickert, the original proponent of a Royal Conspiracy, revealed that he had possession of three diaries written by Abberline. Abberline's diaries are the major source material for Fairclough's 1991 book. The three youths that attacked Emma Smith, said to have been members of a local street gang, are reduced to Netley and Albericci, as the diaries reveal that Abberline believed Smith was an associate of both Mary Ann Nichols and Annie Chapman, two positively identified victims of Jack the Ripper. The diaries have not stood up under close scrutiny; therefore the material contained within cannot be accepted as fact until further proof is found.

The second murder attributed to Frederico Albericci is that of his own accomplice, John Netley. Joseph Gorman Sickert, who is the self-alleged son of British impressionist painter Walter Sickert and grandson of Prince Albert Victor Christian Edward, told Fairclough that his father stated that Albericci was given the task of murdering John Netley.

There are major problems with this theory, the main problem being that Netley remained alive until 1903, eleven years after the murder attributed to Albericci took place and thirteen years after Albericci's "master," or boss, Dr.

William Gull, had passed away. The 1892 murder attributed to Albericci can only be of a man named "Nickley," who was not the same as the hansom cabbie, John Netley.

According to the Abberline diaries, the attempted murder involved the team of John Netley and Frederico Albericci. Their intended target was Prince Eddy. The head conspirator or "boss" in this attempted murder was Lord Randolph Churchill, who was also implicated for the first time in the Royal Conspiracy in Fairclough's 1991 book. Albericci and Netley pushed Prince Eddy over a cliff at the Royal Scottish residence purchased by Prince Albert of Saxe-Coburg, Balmoral Castle. Prince Eddy survived the fall, and Netley and Albericci undertook no further attempt on Prince Eddy's life. This specific piece of information comes directly from a notebook in the possession of Joseph Gorman Sickert, allegedly written by John Netley. This notebook, along with the Abberline diaries, has had the stigma of forgery attached to it.

One further reference to Albericci occurs in a poem written by Abberline, contained within one volume of his diaries. The poem reads, "Tinker, Tailor, Soldier, Sailor, Richman, Poorman, Beggarman, Thief." The "Thief" is sup-posedly a direct reference to the Italian-American pickpocket known as "Fingers Freddy," or Frederico Albericci.

The two murders attributed to Frederico Albericci do not fall under the scope of the Jack the Ripper murders. In that technical sense, Albericci can be dismissed as a candidate for Jack the Ripper. On the other hand, the murders of Smith and Netley are connected in a roundabout way to the murders committed by Jack the Ripper. Nevertheless, there is no proof as to the existence of anyone resembling the co-conspirator first described in print by Melvyn Fairclough in 1991. Albericci was depicted as a "footman," or an outdoor servant for Dr. William Gull, a major player in the Royal Conspiracy Theory, in the early 1880s. Doubts within the research community persist as to whether Frederico Albericci existed. A name that can now be added to this group of doubters is that of Melvyn Fairclough.

Begg, Paul, Martin Fido, and Keith Skinner. *The Jack the Ripper A–Z* (1996).
Clayman, Dr. Charles B. *The American Medical Association Encyclopedia of Medicine* (1989).
Fairclough, Melvyn. *The Ripper and the Royals* (1991).
Knight, Stephen. *Jack the Ripper: The Final Solution* (1976).

ALBERT VICTOR CHRISTIAN EDWARD OF SAXE-COBURG, DUKE OF CLARENCE

In November 1970, Dr. Thomas Stowell published an article in *The Criminologist* announcing a new suspect. Stowell gave his suspect the pseudonym

"S," after his own surname. Details regarding this suspect showed that it was more than likely Prince Albert Victor, the Duke of Clarence and heir presumptive to the throne of England. This was not the first time Prince Albert Victor, known as "Eddy" to his friends, was linked to the Jack the Ripper murders. After the Stowell article, however, Prince Eddy would forever be intertwined with the legend of Jack the Ripper.

He was born Albert Victor Christian Edward, son of Albert Edward, the Prince of Wales, who would become King Edward VII in 1901, and Princess Alexandra, formerly of Denmark. The year of his birth was 1864. Eddy was born two months premature and weighed only three and three-quarters pounds, but was recorded as an otherwise healthy baby. A brother, George, would follow the next year. George would also be born premature but healthy. The brothers would grow up and spend their entire childhood and adolescence together.

Prince Eddy's childhood was marred by a difficulty with learning. His tutor, John Neale Dalton, described Eddy as having a dormant mind. Dalton also stated that Eddy could not keep a focused attention. Upon telling this to Princess Alexandra, she instructed Dalton to focus on the teaching of good social behavior and moral skills above academics. Dalton always asserted that George was by far the smarter of the two. There are a number of possible reasons for Prince Eddy's learning disabilities. From Dalton's statements it appears obvious that Eddy had what is known today as ADD, Attention Deficit Disorder. Prince Eddy also suffered from partial deafness, a hereditary trait that was passed on by his mother. Difficulty

of hearing might also explain why he fell behind in his studies.

Researcher and theorist Michael Harrison has suggested that Prince Eddy may have suffered from a specific form of epilepsy that resulted in seizures so subtle as to be almost unnoticeable, characterized as petit mal seizures. There are a number of causes for epilepsy, including head injury, brain infections, such as meningitis and encephalitis, brain tumors, alcohol and drug withdrawal, inherited predispositions and birth trauma. The last two symptoms may apply directly to Prince Eddy. His mother, Princess Alix, passed on a hearing defect to him, so it is not illogical to suppose that she may have passed on a form of childhood epilepsy to her son as well. The latter cause for epilepsy is of utmost importance concerning Prince Eddy, as he would be introduced to a doctor later deeply connected to the Jack the Ripper murders.

Eddy's premature birth could easily be construed as birth trauma and could have aggravated a predisposition to epilepsy. His lack of focus and attention could have been symptomatic of petit mal seizures. These would appear to the average person as a lack of attention, or daydreaming. They occur in children and are generally grown out of by early adulthood. Petit mal seizures may be characterized as momentary lapses of awareness, which are often apparent in children who are currently classified with attention deficit disorder.

There may also be a simple answer to why Prince Albert Edward and Princess Alexandra were not at all alarmed by Dalton's description of Prince Eddy's lack of attentiveness and difficulty with learning. In 1871 the Prince of Wales had contracted typhoid fever. This affliction had killed his father, the Prince Consort, Albert of Saxe-Coburg, ten years earlier, and the outlook did not seem good. Princess Alexandra had brought in Dr. William Gull, who nursed the Prince Albert Edward back to health. Gull became a fixture from then on in the Royal household. Gull was a specialist in paraplegia and diseases of the brain. As Dr. Gull's main specialty was in dealing with brain malfunctioning, it seems plausible that as personal physician to the Prince of Wales, Gull would also be the physician to his children. He may possibly have identified Prince Eddy's malady. There is also an early story of Dr. Gull treating Prince Eddy, curing the thirteen-year-old boy of typhoid in 1877. Even if this was Dr. Gull's first examination of Prince Eddy, as it was most likely not, he may have observed the symptoms of epilepsy while treating Prince Eddy for typhoid fever.

After recovering from typhoid, Prince Eddy and his younger brother, Prince George, along with their tutor, Dalton, boarded the naval cadet-training vessel, *The Brittania*. The Princes split studies and naval training over the next two years. After completing their two years, they moved on to another naval cadet-training vessel, H.M.S. *Bacchante*. Dalton always went along.

The initiation of new cadets was a time-honored naval tradition. The way British seamen had performed these initiations had drawn negative attention that resulted in the banning certain initiation practices in 1863. Life at sea was different, however, and the initiations of young cadets continued. One form of initiation was to strip off a cadet's pants and fill his rectum with tallow. The latent homosexuality within these rituals

may have started a young Prince Eddy down a road that would lead toward scandal. This second naval training voyage ended on August 31, 1882, when Prince Eddy was eighteen.

The following year Prince Eddy would enroll at Trinity College in Cambridge. This would be the first time that Eddy would be apart from his younger brother. Due to the separation of the Princes, a "companion" was chosen for Prince Eddy. This man picked by Eddy's father to help mold him and help him adjust to school was James Kenneth Stephen, five years Eddy's senior. This would be one of the most important relationships in the Prince's short life.

The year 1885 held a great deal of significance for Prince Eddy. On January 21, Eddy would enter the Freemasons, having been made a Bencher of the Middle Templar, at the request of his father, the Prince of Wales. According to the Royal Conspiracy Theory, Eddy would have his first child, a daughter, Alice Margaret Crook. Eddy left school in June of 1885 to become a lieutenant in the cavalry. James Stephen would remain behind at Cambridge, but the two had developed a deep bond, and they would continue to visit and communicate with each other. Eddy's cavalry career can best be described as efficient. He worked his way up to the rank of Major.

The Prince would remain in the cavalry for the rest of his life, yet as presumptive heir to the throne, there would be a sort of freedom from service not enjoyed by other military men. Simple requests for leaves of absence could not be denied. A leave of absence was requested and granted during the latter portion of 1886. This leave of absence coincided with a visit to Felixstowe to see James

Stephen, where an accident involving a windmill nearly took Stephen's life.

On October 31, 1889, Prince Eddy took a tour of India and other parts of the British realm. The tour lasted until the beginning portion of 1890. The tour in India came after a scandal that broke in June of 1889 involving a male brothel in Cleveland Street. The supervising police officer on this case was Inspector Abberline, who had run the ground investigation of the Jack the Ripper murders.

The investigation began as a young delivery boy named Swinscow was observed by the police to be spending more money than his wages should have allowed. During questioning, Swinscow revealed that he and another young boy, named Newlove, had participated in homosexual activities in a Cleveland Street brothel. Newlove told the police that a man called Veck, described as a pseudo-clergyman, was a key man involved in the male brothel and the recruitment of young male prostitutes. Newlove told police that Veck had offered to pay for his legal defense if any charges were brought in connection with his homosexual activities.

A trap was set to gather information on Veck's involvement. This information was obtained on July 9, 1889. The following day, furniture was removed from the brothel. Veck would not be arrested just yet. Veck's arrest took place on August 20. In the interim, two important men were allowed to flee the country. The first man was the proprietor of the brothel, Charles Hammond. Hammond escaped to France under the watchful eye of the police, who were keeping surveillance on the brothel. Hammond's escape from England assured that he could not be brought to trial or provide evidence against anyone involved.

The second man had direct ties to Prince Eddy through his father, the Prince of Wales. When the files on the Cleveland Street Scandal were released to the public in 1975, a letter contained within these papers showed that the Prince of Wales had known that the Prime Minister, Lord Salisbury, had allowed Lord Somerset, the Equerry and Superintendent to the Prince of Wales stables, to leave the country before he could be arrested. Of the men whom Somerset could have implicated, two come immediately to mind, the Prince of Wales and his son, Prince Eddy. The letter from the Prince of Wales to Lord Salisbury implies that Lord Somerset's arrest would have implicated one of them.

Additional papers in the Cleveland Street file name P. A. V. (Prince Albert Victor, or Prince Eddy) as an alleged patron of the male brothel. One enterprising journalist, named Ernest Parke, made the first public comment in August 1889, linking high-ranking members of society as patrons of the male brothel. This has been taken as indirectly implicating Prince Eddy. Parke edited the *North London Press* and named Lord Euston as a frequenter of the male brothel. Parke was not allowed to work his way up the ladder of nobility, however, as he would serve a twelve-month prison sentence for libel against Lord Euston, a charge that has been recently proved to have no basis.

Prince Eddy was given the titles of Duke of Clarence and Avondale, as well as Earl of Athlone. It was now time for Prince Eddy to choose a bride, and he chose a Catholic, Princess Helene d'Orleans of Paris, France. This would have caused severe turmoil in the political and religious climate of the time, so this choice was not sanctioned. Queen Victoria sent a warning to Prince Eddy of the problems that would be caused by this marriage. In December of 1891, Eddy was officially engaged to Princess May of Teck, who would go on to become Queen Mary after marrying Eddy's younger brother, George. Prince Eddy would never make it to the marriage ceremony. He died of pneumonia, which resulted from contracting influenza during the epidemic, on January 14, 1892.

Two later theories, the 1970 Dr. Stowell theory and the 1991 updated Royal Conspiracy Theory, both of which involve Prince Eddy claim that he did not die of pneumonia complications in 1892. The first theory explains that the pneumonia was a cover-up, a recurring theme in conspiracies involving Prince Eddy. This theory implies that Prince Eddy died later on, from a "softening of the brain," resulting from an advanced stage of syphilis. This terminology, "softening of the brain," comes directly from notes written by Dr. Gull. Dr. Gull was a specialist in diseases of the brain, so I believe that the proper terminology would have been utilized, even if in Gull's private notes only. One problem with this theory is that Dr. Gull died two years prior to Prince Eddy's recorded death of January 14, 1892.

The other theory goes way beyond merely stating that the Prince died sometime after his recorded date of January of 1892. This theory appeared in a 1991 book, *The Ripper and the Royals*, written by Melvyn Fairclough. In the updated version of the royal conspiracy, Joseph Gorman Sickert makes the claim that Prince Eddy did not die in 1892; instead, was kept imprisoned in Glamis Castle, Scotland. Gorman Sickert and Fairclough claim that Prince Eddy lived as a secret prisoner in this castle, *a la* Dumas's *The Man in the Iron Mask*, until he eventually died sometime in the 1930s.

There can be no way to prove or disprove this. However, the immediate question arises—if this information was in the possession of Joseph Gorman Sickert back in the 1970s, why did he hold it back from the BBC television program on which he appeared, and from Stephen Knight, who developed his theory to book length in 1976? Just as cover-ups were a recurring theme with Prince Eddy, the addition of information to fit in with current knowledge appears to be a theme with Joseph Gorman Sickert. Gorman Sickert had his original opportunity back in 1973, another in 1976, so when new information from the same source appears in the 1990s, it is even more suspect than his earlier theories, which have been shown to be untrue.

The first public mention of Prince Eddy as a purported suspect came in 1962. In a biography of King Edward VII, Phillippe Jullien stated that Prince Eddy and the Duke of Bedford were both rumored to be individually responsible for the murders. There was no real public uproar over this statement of rumor.

Eight years later in 1970, Dr. Thomas Stowell wrote an article for *The Criminologist*. In the piece, he outlined a new theory, naming his suspect "S." Despite Dr. Stowell's ambiguity toward the naming of his suspect, Stowell is known to have suspected Prince Eddy. This accusation shocked England and began a new public interest in the case that has lasted to this day. It also set the tone for Ripper research for the decade of the 1970s, when many of the theories centered on Prince Eddy, as either the murderer or a deeply involved conspirator.

Stowell's article claimed "S" had gone on a cruise at the age of sixteen among boys his own age, where he contracted syphilis in the West Indies. This caused him to cancel a public appointment, which Dr. Stowell relates to visible signs of a form of secondary syphilis. During the time of the murders, Dr. Stowell surmises that the thirty-nine-day gap between the double murder and the Miller's Court murder was due to the murderer being secretly confined in a private mental home to obtain treatment for his insanity. According to Stowell, the murderer escaped before the Miller's Court murder and was quickly captured again and treated.

Dr. Stowell's article claimed that "S," Prince Eddy, had suffered from syphilis of the brain. His source for this belief was in the form of personal notes written by Dr. William Gull, who had been the Royal Physician. Dr. Gull's daughter, Caroline Acland, was the wife of Theodore Dyke Acland. Theodore Acland was Dr. Stowell's former boss, who told him of the notes. Dr. Stowell was a regular visitor to the Acland house, and Caroline revealed a story from her father's notes which had made her believe that Dr. Gull had been the physician of Jack the Ripper.

The story of the psychic, Robert James Lees, comes full circle in Dr. Stowell's article. Stowell read about Lees in the company of an unnamed inspector identifying a West End physician thought to be Jack the Ripper. This is an obvious reference to the 1895 Chicago *Sunday Times-Herald* article. Interestingly, Dr. Stowell states that he was first told this tale in the 1930s. The 1895 article from the Chicago *Sunday Times-Herald* just happened to be reprinted in *The Daily Express* in 1931. Dr. Stowell saw the similarities between the Robert James Lees tale and the one told by Caroline Acland. As the story goes, one night a policeman, accompanied by a "medium," visited her mother's house, and began asking a number of questions about Lady Gull's husband. Dr. Gull would eventually come down from upstairs while the policeman and the medium were still asking Lady Gull questions. Dr. Gull supposedly stated that he had lapses in his memory since a stroke in 1887. Gull added that on one occasion he had discovered blood on his shirt. Dr. Stowell took this information as a connective link that Dr. Gull had medically examined Jack the Ripper after one of the murders.

Stowell does not provide a particular motive for the murders, other than insanity, yet the article makes a number of references to Prince Eddy's homosexuality. Eddy originally contracted syphilis, according to Dr. Stowell, at one of a number of "gay parties" that Prince Eddy took part in. Dr. Stowell made the leap that this syphilis may have caused his insanity, and that the murders resulted from this disease, Prince Eddy being in the tertiary stage at this point.

Some theorists have claimed that Dr. Stowell was not referring to Prince Eddy as a suspect. Crime historian Colin Wilson has basically obliterated these theories. Wilson harkens back to a meeting with Dr. Stowell in 1960, at which he says Stowell told him that his suspect was Prince Eddy. In an article in *Ripper Notes*, an American quarterly journal dedicated to research on the Jack the Ripper case, researcher and theorist Stewart P. Evans has found a connective link between Phillippe Jullien and Colin Wilson and has positively established Wilson's statement that Stowell deserved primacy for proposing Prince Eddy as a suspect.

The key to establishing the name of the suspect is in how Dr. Stowell examined his evidence. Stowell's preferred suspect was Prince Eddy, but the main source of his belief lies within the similarity of the story told him by Caroline Acland to the newspaper tale of Robert James Lees. Since the murderer could not have been Gull, Stowell concludes that from bloody cuffs that Gull's patient must have been Jack the Ripper. Stowell connects this information with notes by Dr. Gull concerning a patient who was dying from syphilis of the brain. Assuming that the murderer must have had some type of severe mental illness, Stowell deduced that Dr. Gull's patient must have been Prince Eddy.

There are some major problems with this theory. If Gull was medically examining his patient, why could he not remember how blood got on his shirt? If Gull were trying to protect Prince Eddy from incarceration, why would he inform a policeman about that event in the first place? Furthermore, why would the royal family allow Prince Eddy to travel around the world if it knew that he was Jack the Ripper, cured or not cured? According to Stowell, the murderer had escaped from custody between the double event and the Miller's Court murder. There was a real chance that he would go crazy again. If his family had known, as Dr. Stowell asserts, they would have wanted him under lock and key, with no chance for further possible embarrassment, not out in the open on a five-month cruise.

Another problem with Dr. Stowell's theory is that the story about Robert James Lees appears to have never taken place. Researcher Melvin Harris believes a group calling themselves the Whitechapel Club, with an axe to grind against the psychic community, made up the story. If this was the case, as nowhere in any files is Lees taken seriously or recorded as accompanying a policeman on an identification, then the story told to Dr. Stowell by Caroline Acland would be unrelated to this case. It appears this story is entirely made up, emanating from the reprinting of the 1895 Chicago newspaper article in 1931.

There is another serious problem with Dr. Stowell's theory. According to Stowell, among the papers of Dr. Gull was found a document that showed Prince Eddy did not die in the influenza epidemic of 1892. Stowell stated that Prince Eddy died in a mental home resulting from syphilis of the brain. The major problem here is that Dr. William Gull died in 1890. How could there be documents, amongst his personal papers, originating two years after his own death?

Despite Stephen Knight's Royal Conspiracy Theory clearly outlining what role Prince Eddy played in the Jack the Ripper murders, two years later Frank Speiring wrote *Prince Jack*. The 1978 book proposed that Prince Eddy committed the murders and told his lover, James Stephen, of his murderous activity. According to Speiring, James Stephen wrote the letters to the police that created the famous moniker Jack the Ripper. Speiring's book combines aspects Dr. Stowell's article and the biography of Prince Eddy written by Michael

Harrison, but it reads more like fiction than fact.

Fourteen years elapsed between Speiring's tale and a 1992 book written by Dr. David Abrahamsen. Dr. Abrahamsen concludes that Prince Eddy and James Stephen jointly committed the murders. While advancing the tale told by Frank Speiring, Dr. Abrahamsen's theory is marred by numerous historical errors.

These are the relevant theories that have named Prince Eddy as Jack the Ripper. The original reference to Prince Eddy as the murderer is based on assumptions taken from private notes that in no way indicate or implicate Prince Eddy. Once the first accusation was made, the floodgates opened and, due to his royal heritage, Prince Eddy remains one of the most popular suspects to this very day.

These theories have not stood the test of time. There has been no direct evidence to show that he could have committed the murders, although that can be said of about nearly all of the suspects over the years. After Frank Speiring made a direct challenge to the royal family, Prince Eddy's whereabouts at the time of the murders were released. These whereabouts were compiled from court circulars, diaries, journals and other various documents. From August 29 until September 7, 1888, Prince Eddy was staying at Yorkshire with Viscount Downe. From September 7 until the 10th, he was stationed at the Cavalry Barracks in York. From September 27 until the 30th, Prince Eddy was in Scotland, where Queen Victoria recorded that they lunched on the 30th. From November 2 until the 12th, he was at Sandringham.

These recorded events, taken at face value, should eliminate Prince Eddy as a suspect. It is not that far-fetched to suspect that the royal family might cover for one of their own, as was so plainly evidenced by the Cleveland Street Scandal, but until real evidence surfaces that disputes these reported dates, it must be concluded these records are valid and that Prince Eddy had alibis for all the dates of the Jack the Ripper murders.

Prince Albert Victor Christian Edward, affectionately known as Eddy, was by all means a simpleton. Whether or not his lack of academic knowledge resulted from childhood afflictions, his lack of common awareness seems to have continued through his adulthood. He had to be protected from himself a number of times, once sent from England to India, and had to be warned by his grandmother, the Queen, as to the potential result of marrying a Catholic. His activities can be directly linked to the friends Prince Eddy kept and the influence they had over him.

In Victorian times scandal occurred on a consistent basis, so the amount of scandalous activity that remained secret would likely be at least triple that which was released to the public. There were many rumors over the years that Prince Eddy was a homosexual, but so were many well-respected members of the nobility, who managed to keep up normal appearances for the public. One rumor about homosexuality can be ignored as mere conjecture, but numerous and repeated allegations of this behavior suggest that there was something to them. More likely, Prince Eddy was a bisexual brought up in a carefree royal environment. Prince Eddy wanted to quench his sexual appetites for all types of behaviors, whenever the whim or desire arose.

Abrahamsen, Dr. David. *Murder and Madness: The Secret Life of Jack the Ripper* (1992).

Aronson, Theo. *Prince Eddy and the Homosexual Underworld* (1994).

Begg, Paul, Martin Fido, and Keith Skinner. *The Jack the Ripper A–Z* (1996).

Clayman, Dr. Charles B. *The American Medical Association Encyclopedia of Medicine* (1989).

Evans, Stewart P. *Ripper Notes* (January 2003).

Fairclough, Melvyn. *The Ripper and the Royals* (1991).

Harris, Melvin. *The True Face of Jack the Ripper* (1994).

Harrison, Michael. *Clarence: Was He Really Jack the Ripper?* (1972).

Hyde, Montgomery H. *The Cleveland Street Scandal* (1976).

Jakubowski, Maxim, and Nathan Braund. *The Mammoth Book of Jack the Ripper* (1998).

Jullien, Phillippe. *Edward and the Edwardians* (1962).

Knight, Stephen. *Jack the Ripper: The Final Solution* (1976).

Speiring, Frank. *Prince Jack* (1978).

Stowell, Dr. Thomas. *The Criminologist* (November 1970).

ROBERT ANDERSON

In the 1976 Stephen Knight book on the Royal Conspiracy, Robert Anderson is originally suggested as the third man involved in a conspiracy to protect the Crown. Anderson is never accused of committing any murder, yet is rather named as a lookout on the night of the double murder. Knight comes to the conclusion that information provided to him by Joseph Gorman Sickert regarding Anderson as the third man, or lookout, is erroneous and perhaps offered to shield another suspect.

Born in Dublin, Ireland, in 1841, Anderson could easily be described as a devout or evangelical Christian. He penned over twenty books on theology. He was summoned to England on matters of politics and nationalism, due to the continuing threat of Irish terrorism. He arrived on December 19, 1867. Robert Anderson would never return to Ireland.

Anderson's father was a Crown Solicitor, and his brother Samuel worked as a Solicitor General. He would follow in the family footsteps, attending Trinity College in Dublin. In 1862 he graduated with a Bachelor of Arts and was called to the Irish Bar the following year. Through the connections of his older brother Samuel, Robert began working with the anti–Fenian movement in Ireland in an advisory and legal capacity. This early work against the Fenians in Ireland would lead him toward his future career and a place in history.

On December 13, 1867, a barrel of gunpowder was exploded against a wall of the Clerkenwell Prison, killing men, women and children. The bomb was set off by a group of Fenians and was believed to be the beginning of a terrorist campaign in England. The origins of the Criminal Investigative Department (CID) were born out of this bomb explosion. Anderson arrived in England six days later. Despite the CID closing in April 1868, he would remain at the Home Office as the political advisor on crime.

His main duties consisted of controlling and handling Thomas Miller Beach, an English spy deep within the Fenian movement in America under the pseudonym Major Henri Le Caron. Beach would only confer and deliver information to Anderson, of whom he left a glowing account in his 1892 memoirs. This loyalty would secure Anderson's job not only in 1868, but also in 1886, when Home Secretary Hugh Childers relieved Anderson of his political duties. Beach's insistence upon dealing only with Anderson secured his job again. As a result Anderson would be given the title of Secretary to the Prison Commissioners.

It was later revealed that in 1887 Anderson either wrote or contributed to articles in *The Times* smearing the name of the Irish political leader, Charles Stewart Parnell. Charges of condoning terrorism were investigated and these charges were brought before a commission that began just as the Jack the Ripper murders may have ended in late 1888. Parnell was cleared of all the charges, while Beach was brought out of the field to provide testimony that would effectively end his undercover career.

Robert Anderson was later appointed Assistant Commissioner of the Metropolitan Police Department on the morning after the murder of Mary Ann Nichols, September 1, 1888. This appointment came with the added control of running the CID. Just eight days later, on the morning after the murder of Annie Chapman, Anderson went to Switzerland on three months' prescribed sick leave for stress. After the night of the double murder, September 30, Anderson would be called back to London. He arrived on approximately October 6 and took over the case.

Anderson retired from the police force in 1901 and was knighted for his service. After his retirement he wrote extensively on the Jack the Ripper case, stating several times in print that he knew the identity of the murderer. He never placed a name on his suspect. His 1910 book of memoirs contains his most lurid revelations on the murders, as well as his involvement in the 1887 series on Parnell in *The Times*.

The 1991 book by Melvyn Fairclough that advances Stephen Knight's theory names Robert Anderson as a co-conspirator. Fairclough refers to Anderson as a lookout who had to have organized police patrols to favor the placement of the bodies in their intended locations.

The major weakness of this theory, other than the fact that Robert Anderson has never been accused of murdering any of the women attributed to Jack the Ripper, is that Anderson was away in Switzerland on sick leave during the time of the double murder, precisely when the theory claims he was a lookout, during the murder of Elizabeth Stride. Until information surfaces that places Anderson in London during the time of the murders, specifically the night of the double murder, he should be eliminated from consideration as the lookout involved in the Royal Conspiracy.

The great Evangelical Christian Robert Anderson, who wholeheartedly believed that the second coming of Christ was upon us, passed away in 1918 at the age of seventy-seven. His association with the Jack the Ripper murders lay dormant for close to sixty years until Stephen Knight revived it in 1976. Since then, Robert Anderson has become synonymous with the Jack the Ripper murders, as many researchers feel that his writing on the case will one day lead to the eventual solving of this mystery.

Anderson, Robert. *The Lighter Side of My Official Life* (1910).

Beach, Thomas Miller. *Twenty-Five Years in the Secret Service* (1892).
Begg, Paul. *Jack the Ripper: The Uncensored Facts* (1988).
_____, Martin Fido, and Keith Skinner. *The Jack the Ripper A–Z* (1996).
Fairclough, Melvyn. *The Ripper and the Royals* (1991).
Fido, Martin. *The Crimes, Detection and Death of Jack the Ripper* (1987).
Knight, Stephen. *Jack the Ripper: The Final Solution* (1976).

THOMAS BARNARDO

Thomas Barnardo was born in Dublin on July 4, 1845. He was converted to evangelical Christianity in 1862, preached in the slums of Dublin, and then moved to London to begin studying medicine. Barnardo developed a keen interest in anatomy, but always returned to his true love, religion. His goal was to become a medical missionary.

A small man in stature, measuring at most five feet two inches, Barnardo dedicated the latter part of his life to helping children, opening his first home for underprivileged boys on March 2, 1868. Barnardo would help underprivileged children for the rest of his life, helping over 8,000 of these children emigrate to Canada. He raised funds for shelters by taking "before" and "after" photographs of every child who entered the shelter, displaying the progress of his work. Due to the passionate work of Thomas Barnardo over fifty orphanages had been established in London by 1878.

Barnardo's preaching mainly dealt with saving children from a life on the streets. His preaching at lodging houses brought him to the attention of the police during the time of the murders. Gillian Wagner, Barnardo's biographer, has stated that Barnardo was preaching at 32 Flower and Dean Street on September 26. One of the women listening was Elizabeth Stride. Due to the preponderance of doctor theories, Barnardo came under the suspicion of the local authorities. In a letter written to *The Times* on October 6, Barnardo claimed to identify Stride from the mortuary, as one of the women he had preached to on September 26. Barnardo continued writing letters to various newspapers, mainly discussing the need to help destitute children. These letters continually mentioned his talk at 32 Flower and Dean Street, an illustration he used to demonstrate the horrors of life on the streets of the East End.

Originally mentioned as a possible suspect by Donald McCormick in 1970, Thomas Barnardo has recently been rediscovered as a viable suspect by Gary Rowlands, whose research is included in *The Mammoth Book of Jack the Ripper* by Maxim Jakubowski and Nathan Braund. Rowlands claims that, from early on, Barnardo was a loner and usually in trouble at school. Rowlands cites similarities between Barnardo's personal life and a number of the F.B.I. reports on serial killers. Other factors, such as struggles with other philanthropists over church idealisms, an intense hatred for prostitutes, and prior work as a journalist, all contribute to traits that Rowlands feels make Thomas Barnardo a strong candidate.

Despite the struggles and controversies that occurred in Dr. Barnardo's life, he still was able to help the citizens of Whitechapel, whether it was building shelters for underage children or delivering a small sense of hope in his preaching to prostitutes. For a man whose words were his actions, it seems unlikely that he would change his course of action so drastically to alert the women of the East End to the dangers of their community.

It has also been postulated by Rowlands that Barnardo was a friend of Robert Anderson and that through this friendship Barnardo was able to learn the secret tactics of the police in order to evade detection. While there may be a connection, or even a friendship, between Barnardo and Anderson, Barnardo was known to the police at the time of the murders. When Barnardo identified Stride in the mortuary, he had to be investigated. Thomas Barnardo's name was never brought up in connection with the case again, despite continuing to write letters to local papers on the dangers of life in the streets.

On the surface, Thomas Barnardo appears to have been a good man who attempted to help the community in which he resided. By the time of his death on September 19, 1905, Dr. Thomas John Barnardo had helped over 20,000 children of the East End to improve their lives. Nothing links him to Jack the Ripper, with the possible exception of preaching to one of the victims days before her murder. The fact that Barnardo mentioned this in a letter to *The Times* assured that his whereabouts would be investigated. A sought-after murderer generally does not call that kind of attention to himself.

Begg, Paul, Martin Fido, and Keith Skinner. *The Jack the Ripper A–Z* (1996).
Jakubowski, Maxim, and Nathan Braund. *The Mammoth Book of Jack the Ripper* (1998).
McCormick, Donald. *The Identity of Jack the Ripper* (1970).
Wagner, Gillian. *Barnardo* (1979).
http://intranet.qe.dorset.sch.uk/britishhistory/REbarnardo.html.

DANIEL BARNETT

The older brother of Joseph Barnett, the live-in lover of Mary Jane Kelly until a week before she was murdered, Daniel Barnett has recently come under suspicion. Born in 1851, seven years before Joseph, Daniel was one of five children, the second of four sons. His father passed away when he was only thirteen. His older brother Denis went to work, as did his mother Catherine, but it would not be long before Daniel had to help earn wages to support the family. This allowed his younger brothers, Joseph and John, to continue their studies in school. Daniel mainly earned his living as a market fish porter.

There are numerous theories as to why the murders were committed. There are also theorists who place the number of victims at higher than five or as low as three. In the scenario that involves Daniel Barnett as the murderer, the number of victims is drastically reduced to one.

Theorist Bruce Paley has put forth the suggestion that younger brother Joseph Barnett was the murderer. In 1982, Paley's work appeared in the magazine *True Crime*. Paley's full-length book on the murders did not arrive in print until 1995, yet in 1991 author and theorist Paul Harrison named Joseph Barnett as the murderer.

Research undertaken by Mark Madden and Neal Shelden, as well as by Paley, has shown that the Joseph Barnett proposed as the murderer by Paul Harrison was not the same Joseph Barnett who lived with Mary Jane Kelly until October 30, 1888, and therefore not the same man proposed as Jack the Ripper by Paley. During his research, Mark Madden came to the conclusion that both Joseph Barnett and Daniel Barnett should be considered as suspects. Daniel Barnett was in the area on the night of the Mary Jane Kelly murder. Or was he?

There are two sources responsible for placing Daniel Barnett with Mary Kelly the night before her murder. The first of these was a resident of Dorset Street named Maurice Lewis. Lewis was a tailor who stated that he had known Mary Kelly for about five years. On the night in question Lewis claimed to have seen Kelly, "Julia" who would have been Julia Van Turney, and "Danny." Some have concluded that "Danny" was Daniel Barnett. Some researchers have also suggested that Lewis might have been mistaken and wrongly identified Joseph Barnett as Daniel, due to facial similarities between the two brothers.

Maurice Lewis claimed to have known Mary Kelly for close to five years, meaning that he would have also known Joseph Barnett for at least ten months, as the couple were living in Miller's Court since the beginning of 1888. Having known both Mary Kelly and Joseph Barnett for this period of time, Lewis would not have referred to Joseph as "Danny" and most likely would have known the difference between the two brothers, as Daniel was almost eight years older than Joseph and approximately three inches shorter.

When discussing the suspect likeliness of Daniel Barnett, the above comments become somewhat moot. The second source placing Daniel with Kelly on the night before her murder is his own brother Joseph Barnett. In a statement given to *The Star* on November 10, Joseph Barnett declared that his brother had met Kelly on the night in question. Joseph does not offer an explanation of why Daniel was drinking with Kelly the night before her murder, but some have speculated that Daniel was sent by Joseph to convince Kelly to take him back.

But the reason behind Daniel's

meeting with Kelly becomes irrelevant pertaining to Daniel Barnett as a suspect. If Daniel Barnett were Jack the Ripper, then he would have murdered at least four women without any motive, then murdered Mary Jane Kelly, in the same vicious way, because she was leaving his younger brother Joseph. That theory fails because Joseph places Daniel at the scene of the crime when he does not need to. If the plot to murder Kelly was hatched after Joseph Barnett found out that Daniel was Jack the Ripper, he would not have placed him at the scene, for fear of implicating himself if Daniel's whereabouts were sought after and an alibi was not produced for the previous murders. Conversely, if Mary Jane Kelly was murdered by Daniel Barnett as a solitary copycat murder in a method similar to Jack the Ripper, there also would be no reason to place Daniel at the scene of the crime, whether Joseph was an accomplice or an accessory.

Madden's statement that Daniel Barnett should be viewed with suspicion directly correlates to the candidacy of Joseph Barnett. Either way, Joseph's statements to the police and the newspapers—that Daniel had spoke to Kelly on the night before the murder—should be enough to eliminate Daniel Barnett from further suspicion or consideration.

The rest of Daniel Barnett's life was spent in and around London. He continued working as a porter and general laborer. In at least once census poll, Daniel resided at the same address as his younger brother Joseph. He died on December 22, 1906, of heart disease. He was fifty-seven years old and resided at 18 New Gravel Lane, Shadwell. The informant on the death certificate was a J. Barnett of the same address. While the J. Barnett may have referred to the youngest of the brothers John, it could have easily been Joseph.

Begg, Paul, Martin Fido, and Keith Skinner. *The Jack the Ripper A–Z* (1996).
Harrison, Paul. *Jack the Ripper: The Mystery Solved* (1991).
Paley, Bruce. *Jack the Ripper: The Simple Truth* (1995).
_____. *True Crime* (1982).

JOSEPH BARNETT

Joseph Barnett was born in 1858, the fourth of five children, third of four boys. He remained in school until approximately the age of thirteen, thanks to his older brothers, Daniel and Denis, providing for the family after their father's death in 1864. Joseph worked at Billingsgate Market, primarily as a fish porter. A mandatory bylaw forced all market porters to be licensed on July 1, 1878. All four brothers are recorded as receiving their licenses on that specific date. As Joseph was already twenty years old, it was more than likely that he had been employed as a market porter for some time prior to July 1, 1878.

Barnett's life would take a dramatic turn when he met Mary Jane Kelly on

Good Friday, April 8, 1887. She was fair-haired, and Barnett took an immediate liking to her. They agreed to meet again the following day and decided to remain together thereafter. The couple lived at a number of different places before finally settling in a small room in Miller's Court, sometime close to the beginning of 1888. Joseph Barnett would remain with Kelly in this room until October 30, 1888.

Their existence together was a happy one, with Barnett described as taking very good care of her and giving her gifts within his means. Toward the end of their relationship, there were some fights that friends and neighbors described as violent. One fight led to the breaking of a windowpane. This broken windowpane was never fixed and became a convenient way for both Barnett and Kelly to re-enter the room, as the key to the door had been lost. It is not known exactly when the fighting started, but one suggestion has been made that their fighting steadily increased once Barnett lost his job at Billingsgate Market. He was fired and lost his license around July or August of 1888. The reason Barnett lost his job and his license has never been fully ascertained. Theorist Bruce Paley surmises that Barnett was caught stealing, resulting in the loss of his license. This is consistent with the fact that he enjoyed giving Kelly gifts, which mainly consisted of paying for their drinking, and he might have been stealing fish from work to eat, saving his wages to provide for Kelly's habits. After losing his job Barnett began selling oranges and carried on other various tasks.

Their final fight took place because Kelly allowed a prostitute friend, "Julia," assumed to be Julia Van Turney, to stay in their small room. Barnett thought that Van Turney was a bad influence on Kelly and protested allowing her to stay. In the end, Barnett decided to leave, taking up lodging at a boarding house in nearby Bishopsgate. While they were separated for that short period of time, Barnett frequently visited Kelly, often giving her whatever money he could afford. Barnett stated that he last visited Kelly on the night of her murder at approximately 7:45.

Caroline Maxwell, a fellow resident of Miller's Court, stated that she saw Kelly speaking to a man dressed similar to a market porter at approximately 9:30 A.M. outside the Brittania pub. This could have easily been Barnett, as Maxwell was far enough away not to get a great look at the man's face, yet Maxwell's evidence has been challenged by critics who state that she may have been wrong regarding the dates of her sightings.

According to John McCarthy, the landlord of Miller's Court, Kelly and Barnett were late in their rent. From what Kelly and Barnett owed, and what was basically charged for a room, their room perhaps smaller than others, I have surmised that they were approximately seven weeks overdue in their rent. As Barnett and Kelly's room was somewhat smaller than other rooms in Miller's Court, this may have increased the estimate to over two months late in their rent. A reasonable estimate of when their last rent payment was made is the beginning to middle of September. With Barnett not having full-time work, money was now becoming harder and harder to come by, ultimately leading Kelly back onto the streets, and toward the break up that occurred on October 30.

The bulk of what is known about Kelly's past comes directly from what she told Joseph Barnett, and what happened during the time of the murders comes from the same source. Corroboration of Barnett's statements to the police regarding the background of Mary Kelly came from a number of sources, including a Mrs. Carthy and a Mrs. Buki, two landladies that Kelly had formerly lived with. Barnett classified their houses as "bad," implying that they may have been brothels where Kelly had earned a wage as a prostitute.

On the afternoon after the murder, Barnett identified the body in Miller's Court. Due to the extreme facial mutilations, Barnett identified her by two characteristics. These characteristics have been stated as her ears and eyes, or possibly her hair and eyes. Different accounts hypothesize which two facial characteristics Barnett was forced to identify Kelly by. Explaining who he was, Barnett was taken to Commercial Street Police Station and questioned by Inspector Abberline for over four hours. Abberline's official report of this interview contains little information, especially after a four-hour interview session. The crux of the statement explained that Barnett had recently lost his job, had lived with Kelly for the past eighteen months, up until about a week ago, and that he visited Kelly on the night of her murder. Other information provided in Barnett's statement included background data on Kelly and possibly her family. Inspector Abberline felt that the information given by Barnett during the four-hour session was sufficient to allow Barnett to leave. The entire interview could not have been reduced to this single two-paragraph statement, so Barnett must have produced something of an alibi. It is known that Barnett stated he was at his new lodging house on the night of Kelly's murder, and he may have provided alibis for the other murders.

After the death of his beloved "Marie Jeanette" his nickname for Kelly, Barnett faded into obscurity. He moved in with his sister, and his brother Daniel gave this same address in 1891. Barnett's license as a fish porter was restored in 1906, the same year as Daniel's death. Joseph was listed as living with a Louisa Barnett up until her death. Despite no marriage certificate on file, Louisa was listed as his wife. Nothing is known about this woman other than that she died on November 26, 1926. It must be assumed that she was his common-law wife. Three weeks after Louisa's death, Joseph Barnett died at the age of sixty-eight.

In 1977, in *The Return of Jack the Ripper*, a novelist named Mark Andrews put forth the idea that the man who lived with Mary Kelly was Jack the Ripper. As this was a fictitious retelling of the murders, it cannot be viewed as the original source of the Barnett theory. In 1982, an article came out in *True Crime*, offering a new theory on the murders. Written by Bruce Paley, it firmly established Joseph Barnett as a suspect. It is important to note is that even before this article, and before the Andrews novel appeared, Paley had illustrated the basics of his theory to historian and researcher Donald Rumbelow. Paley's full theory and research into Joseph Barnett was not published until 1995. During the time between Paley's 1982 article and 1995 book, other researchers have delved into Barnett's background. One such researcher, Paul Harrison, re-examined the Paley's theory without furthering the case against Barnett, since he identified the wrong Joseph Barnett.

Barnett's presence as a suspect should be solely attributed to Bruce Paley. Paley's argument rests on three principles: that Barnett committed the murders to scare Mary Kelly off the streets and out of prostitution; that Barnett fits the eyewitness descriptions of Jack the Ripper; and that Barnett precisely corresponds to the FBI profile of Jack the Ripper, created in 1988.

When Barnett first met Kelly, he knew that she was a prostitute or that she had previously engaged in prostitution, whether on the streets or in various brothels. It might have been under those conditions that Barnett and Kelly originally got together. That having been said, Barnett truly believed that Kelly loved him, and she very well might have. When Kelly was living with him, she never went out on the streets, according to Barnett. Suddenly, Barnett had lost his job and money was needed. Does this necessarily mean that Kelly resorted to prostitution, or that Barnett began killing prostitutes in the area to scare her off the streets?

The murders attributed to Jack the Ripper may have started with the August 7 murder of Martha Tabram or the August 31 murder of Mary Ann Nichols. The second or third murder would have been Annie Chapman. If Barnett had been the murderer of these two or three women, he would obviously not have been with Kelly on those nights, as the murders were committed late at night. If Kelly were worried and fearful for her life, as Barnett claimed she was, and as the entire East End definitely was, Kelly would have known that Barnett was not with her on the nights of the murders. Couple this with

their fighting over money, and the fact that Barnett had lost his job, and an immediate red flag should have gone up in Kelly's head. Barnett states that he used to read the newspaper reports to her about the murders, but surely her neighbors and friends in the area constantly spoke about the man terrorizing the East End.

The night of the double murder has puzzled researchers. Did Jack the Ripper commit two murders, or were murders committed by two separate killers, within a half-mile radius, using cuts to the throat similar to the previous two murders? Obviously, there is no way to be certain, but it appears that the same man killed both Elizabeth Stride and Catherine Eddowes. So why kill two women in one night?

If the motive for the murders were to scare Kelly off the streets, wouldn't the murder of Elizabeth Stride have been enough? You could say that because Barnett was interrupted, he was not positive that Stride would die. That would be wrong. The anatomical knowledge shown by the murderer proves that he understood the cut to Stride's throat would have resulted in her death, as it did with both Chapman and Nichols.

Then there is the theory that, because the murderer was interrupted before he was able to mutilate the body, his blood thirst forced him to seek out another victim and take out his rage upon her. This deviates from Paley's theory of why Barnett committed the murders. Paley's theory is consistent: Barnett murdered prostitutes in order to scare Mary Kelly off the street, not because it thrilled him. Now all of a sudden, when it fits the known facts, Barnett's *modus operandi* changes. Barnett would have known that Stride was going to die, and he would have hurried home in order to not arouse more suspicion being out late on another night that Jack the Ripper had struck.

During the month of October, another murder might have really scared Kelly off the streets, yet there was none. As there was very little money coming in, the rent not having been paid as far back as early September, the need to scare her off the streets would have greatly increased. This month would have been the ideal month to murder another prostitute and, once and for all, scare Kelly off the streets. Yet, as is historically known, no murders were committed by Jack the Ripper during the month of October 1888.

The murder of Mary Kelly also does not fall into the theory of Barnett murdering prostitutes to scare her off the street. It is counter-productive, to say the least, to murder the person you are trying to save. Paley has used the murder of Mary Kelly to conclude that Barnett could take no more. Visiting Kelly on the night before her murder, and trying to convince her to reconcile, drove Barnett over the edge, according to Paley. The police however, questioned Barnett for four hours the very next afternoon. He never became rattled, or Abberline would not have allowed him to leave. There was also a young woman, most likely Lizzie Albrook, who saw Barnett talking to Kelly at approximately 7:45 P.M., less than twelve hours before her murder. Barnett was probably seen by others at that time, and had personally sent his brother Daniel to speak to Kelly later that evening. So if Barnett were Jack the Ripper, why wouldn't he have waited for a different morning to kill Kelly, on some night when he had not visited her and could easily be placed at the scene? Jack the Ripper had

already waited five weeks between murders, so he easily could have waited another day.

Barnett supposedly fit the eyewitness description of the murderer. This is an assertion that should be corrected. For the murder of Mary Ann Nichols, there was no eyewitness description of anyone. In the murder of Annie Chapman, the only eyewitness description that has lasted the test of time is that of Mrs. Long. Her description does not fit Joseph Barnett. Mrs. Long described an older man, approximately forty years of age, of foreign appearance, and only slightly taller than Chapman, who was five feet two inches tall at best. Mrs. Long only saw the man from behind, but that hardly constitutes a positive description of Barnett. In the case of Elizabeth Stride, many witnesses (PC William Smith, William Marshall, Matthew Packer, James Brown, Israel Schwartz, and J. Best and John Gardner) offered descriptions of a man seen with the victim. All the descriptions more or less matched (taking into account some minor variations) except for that offered by Israel Schwartz. Schwartz described the man as approximately five feet five inches tall, brown hair, broad shouldered and stoutly built. Schwartz's description is much closer to Barnett than that of Mrs. Long.

The specific positioning described by one witness, James Brown, suggests that the man Israel Schwartz saw attacking Elizabeth Stride was a different man. This is still a not completely accepted theory, yet the precise positioning description allows no other conclusion. This theory is backed up by the description by Israel Schwartz, who states that the attacker was between himself and Stride, walking toward her, while James Brown describes Stride as definitively closer to the street where she would be murdered than the man seen with her since 11:00 P.M.

Joseph Lawende furnished the only description of the man with Catherine Eddowes that has been used over the years. Different sources adjust the height of Lawende's man from five feet seven inches to five feet nine inches tall. The age remains the same, at about thirty years old, and the suspect has a small moustache throughout. The problem with Lawende's description, the description which Paley focuses on, is that neither Lawende, nor the other two Jewish witnesses, Joseph Hyam Levy or Harry Harris, got a good look at the man. By Lawende's own admission he would not have been able to recognize the man if he saw him again. This was stated at the Coroner's inquest into Eddowes' death, and also restated by Chief Inspector Swanson in his report to the Home Office on the Eddowes murder.

The final major description, from George Hutchinson, was of a man he saw go into Mary Kelly's room with her only eight hours before her body was discovered. Hutchinson stated that this was not Barnett. Hutchinson claimed to have known Kelly for years. Knowing Mary Kelly, Hutchinson would have certainly recognized if the man he saw was Barnett. Either way, Barnett also had an alibi for that time from his lodging house.

So the major eyewitness descriptions, Mrs. Long, Lawende, and Hutchinson, either fail relative to Joseph Barnett, or have definitive problems with their descriptions. The one description that basically conforms to Barnett is that of Israel Schwartz, but it is not a precise match. What Bruce Paley has done is match Barnett to what the police be-

lieved to be the basic description of the murderer. How the police arrived at this appears to be an amalgam of all descriptions, which does precisely match Barnett. A major problem with this amalgamated description is that it fits most of the known suspects, which is one of the primary reasons why these people are proposed as suspects.

In 1988, the centennial anniversary year of the murders, the Ripper Project was undertaken. This was an attempt to apply modern scientific techniques to ascertain the identity of Jack the Ripper. A number of well-respected people in the field of criminology took part and established a profile of the murderer. They came up with a list of traits or characteristics that the murderer should have possessed. Bruce Paley has taken these characteristics and determined that Joseph Barnett personifies each of these specific traits.

Even Paley does admit that Barnett does not fit into one of these characteristics. He explains it off by stating that a leading forensic expert, Robert K. Ressler, believes that "various attributes are not meant to be taken as absolute conditions, but rather are generally applicable to most serial killers." Joseph Barnett does precisely fit almost all of the F.B.I.'s listed characteristics as to who Jack the Ripper should have been. This is Bruce Paley's most convincing argument.

Researcher Alex Chisholm has recently presented a new theory regarding Jack the Ripper. This theory has specific and direct connections to Joseph Barnett. In reviewing Stewart Evans and Paul Gainey's book, *Jack the Ripper: First American Serial Killer*, Chisholm concluded that there remains the possibility that Jack the Ripper did not murder

Mary Kelly. In Evans and Gainey's book, the authors discount Elizabeth Stride as a victim, and Chisholm has taken this one step further. He claims that the assumptions of the police may have prevented them catching Jack the Ripper. The police were looking for the murderer of five or possibly six women. If a suspect could present an alibi for one of these murders, in the eyes of the police, he could not have committed the others.

This is by far the most innovative theory to come along in some time, but its flaws are apparent in regard to Joseph Barnett, the man that Chisholm proposes as the likely murderer of Mary Kelly. Discounting Elizabeth Stride as a victim still makes that suspect accountable for his whereabouts on the night of September 30. Discounting Stride and Kelly still leaves Nichols, Chapman and Eddowes, so a suspect would still be required to come up with an alibi for at least one of those dates. If all those women were murdered by the same person, and a suspect had an alibi for at least one of those dates, that suspect could not have been the murderer of any of those women, and therefore not Jack the Ripper.

How this applies to Joseph Barnett is that Barnett may have provided an alibi for any one of the four separate nights of the murders and then been released. In Alex Chisholm's theory, Barnett may have been responsible for the murder of Mary Kelly and Mary Kelly alone, so that his release from questioning may have occurred because he provided an alibi for any one of the three previous murder nights. If Barnett had murdered Kelly and Kelly only, he was therefore no Jack the Ripper. As Barnett was immediately questioned by the police, however, and had strong ties to the most recent murder victim, it seems illogical that his alibi was not fully checked out, especially in regards to this specific murder.

Researcher Dr. Frederick Walker views Joseph Barnett as the primary suspect in this case. Dr. Walker's essay on his theory appears in Stephen P. Ryder's *Casebook: Jack the Ripper*. One of the leading experts on the case, Stewart P. Evans, has rebuffed the major points of Dr. Walker's theory. Evans reminds Dr. Walker that the torn envelope found beside the body of Annie Chapman could not have come from Joseph Barnett. Dr. Walker theorized that the initials from the torn envelope refer to Barnett's address in Miller's Court, but a fellow resident of Crossingham's lodging house, William Stevens, saw Chapman pick up the torn piece of envelope from the kitchen floor to place some pills inside it five hours before she was murdered. Researcher Scott Morro has also contributed written rebuttals to Dr. Walker's theory regarding Joseph Barnett.

Joseph Barnett had lived in the Whitechapel area his entire life. His knowledge of the neighborhood would have rivaled anyone. In that respect he would have also been a familiar face to any unsuspecting woman working on the streets. His extreme love for Mary Kelly, which may have been known throughout the prostitute community, along with Mary Kelly's wicked temper, would have most likely precluded another prostitute from fornicating with Joseph Barnett, especially if that prostitute personally knew Kelly.

Paley describes Barnett as having a speech impediment called echolalia, in which a person repeats words or phrases spoken by another. Generally, people suffering from echolalia will repeat the last few words from questions asked of them. It has been suggested that echolalia has its roots within autism or schizophrenia, a possibility that Bruce Paley has taken to mean that echolalia surfaces in times of anxiety, pointing toward the Coroner's inquest, during which Paley considers Barnett's echolalia is clearly displayed under questioning.

Joseph Barnett was a simple man. He worked as a fish porter, until he was fired, likely thinking that he had to steal to keep his woman happy. He loved Mary Jane Kelly, affectionately calling her "Marie Jeanette." His press interviews show a simple man who did not have a fear of being caught.

Andrews, Mark. *The Return of Jack the Ripper* (1977).

Begg, Paul, Martin Fido, and Keith Skinner. *The Jack the Ripper A–Z* (1996).

Evans, Stewart, and Paul Gainey, *Jack the Ripper: First American Serial Killer* (1995).

Harrison, Paul. *Jack the Ripper: The Mystery Solved* (1991).

Paley, Bruce. *Jack the Ripper: The Simple Truth* (1995).

_____. *True Crime* (April 1982).

Reber, Arthur S. *The Penguin Dictionary of Psychology* (1985).

Ressler, Robert K. *Whoever Fights Monsters* (1993).

http://www.casebook.org.

EDWARD BUCHAN

On the exact date of Mary Jane Kelly's funeral, September 19, 1888, a twenty-nine year old shoemaker named Edward Buchan from Poplar, London, committed suicide by cutting his own throat on his birthday. Buchan had been described as acting strangely for some time, culminating in the taking of his own life. His obituary was written up in the November 23rd edition of *The East End News*.

In a 1990 article in *The Criminologist*, theorist Roger Barber proposed Edward Buchan as a suspect. Barber's argument rests on a number of theoretical points centering on Buchan's suicide on his own birthday and the day of the funeral of Mary Jane Kelly.

Born in 1859, Edward Buchan was twenty-eight years old at the time of the murders, close to the age of the suspect described by eyewitnesses. Another point that links Buchan to the murders, according to Barber, is the way people described him as "being strange in his manner for some time past." Another way of interpreting that statement is that Buchan could have been gone for undisclosed periods of time without anyone knowing where he was, which Barber acknowledges.

Barber's thesis centers on the November 19 suicide. Due to the lack of hard evidence for or against Montague John Druitt, other than the cessation of the murders coinciding with Druitt's body being found in the Thames, Barber has searched for similar suicides that happened directly after the murder of the last victim, Mary Jane Kelly. He found the suicide of Edward Buchan.

Barber's own theory regarding Druitt collapses when applied to his suspect, Edward Buchan. The lack of any evidence to connect Druitt to the murders prompted Barber to search for another suspect who died in a similar way to that of Druitt. On the surface Edward Buchan appears to have even less of a connection to the murders committed by Jack the Ripper than Montague John Druitt. Buchan had no ties with any of the victims, with the possible exception of Elizabeth Stride, whom he may have known while growing up as a child. He had no history of violence or maladaptive behavior, other than just prior to his death, having been described as "somewhat strange of late."

Less evidence links Jack the Ripper to Edward Buchan than to Montague John Druitt, adversely affecting Roger Barber's theory. Opposing one suspect due to lack of evidence and then promoting another on the same unsubstantiated grounds is a direct step backward. Rather than promoting Edward Buchan, Roger Barber should have focused on conducting research to clear Montague John Druitt. That might have allotted Barber the credibility to announce Edward Buchan as a possible suspect, without having to mention the obvious fact stated above, that Barber's suspect is no likelier than one of the prime historical suspects, Montague John Druitt. Since the 1990 announcing of Edward Buchan as a possible suspect, neither Roger Barber nor any other researcher has advanced the case for Edward Buchan as Jack the Ripper.

As with most suspects Edward Buchan's intimate knowledge of the East End and the surrounding areas would have allowed him to easily and freely maneuver away from the regular police beats after committing the murders. His November 19 suicide links him with the suspect named by Assistant Chief Constable Melville MacNaghten in his famous 1894 memorandum. MacNaghten stated that the murderer had committed suicide after the November 9 murder in Miller's Court. The main problem that arises is that MacNaghten was referring to Montague John Druitt. There is no evidence that MacNaghten ever heard of Edward Buchan. An additional problem is that recent scholarship has turned away from the memorandum written by MacNaghten, citing the numerous factual errors contained within.

Barber, Roger. *The Criminologist* (1990).
Begg, Paul, Martin Fido, and Keith Skinner. *The Jack the Ripper A–Z* (1996).
http://www.casebook.org.

WILLIAM HENRY BURY

On April 24, 1889, William Henry Bury was sentenced to hang for the murder of his wife Ellen. The sentence would be carried out a few days afterwards. Bury displayed no remorse for the murder of his wife. Just before his neck snapped Bury commented to the hangman on how "clever" he was for hanging him.

Bury was suggested as Jack the Ripper by *The New York Times* in 1889. That suggestion lay dormant for almost one hundred years until researcher Euan Macpherson called attention to it in 1986. Macpherson has never produced a full assessment of the viability of Bury as a suspect. Nine years later, William Beadle did just that, ardently stating that William Henry Bury could be none other than Jack the Ripper.

William Henry Bury was born in Stourbridge, Worcestershire, England on May 25, 1859. He worked as a horse butcher before moving to London in November 1887. While in the East End, Bury secured work as a sawdust collector. His early childhood is shrouded in mystery. Bury met Ellen Elliot, who was employed at a local bar as a prostitute, and the couple soon married. The couple lived off of Ellen's family inheritance after Bury was fired from his job for stealing. Bury's frequent visits to prostitutes led to his contracting syphilis, which he would pass on to Ellen. They remained in London until moving to Dundee, Scotland, on January 18, 1889.

On February 10, 1889, Bury walked into Dundee Police Station claiming that five days earlier he had found his wife lying dead on the floor. Bury also stated that there was a rope around her neck and that he had stabbed the corpse once with a knife and shoved it into a trunk. Bury's story was that his wife had committed suicide and that he was afraid to come forward earlier for fear that he would be thought of as Jack the Ripper. When the police went to his house they found two chalked messages alluding that Jack the Ripper had lived there. The police found Ellen Bury and discovered the extent of her injuries. William Henry Bury was charged with her murder.

The writing on the wall, it has been theorized, was Ellen Bury's. Beadle offers this as the reason for Ellen's murder. It is more likely that William Bury wrote the message in order to bolster his story about not coming forward earlier. If Ellen had found out something or had grave suspicions, she would not have remained with this man, as Bury had previously shown signs of rage toward her. Ellen Bury would have fled, as opposed to alerting her husband to her suspicions or, more importantly, alerting the community of Dundee.

The murder of Ellen Bury was quite dissimilar from the murders of the Jack the Ripper victims. From what can be gathered, Ellen was strangled with a rope, which was left hanging around her neck. The victims of Jack the Ripper showed distinct bruises about their necks and chests, indicating the marks of a thumb and fingers. These victims were strangled manually. Ligature marks from a rope were apparent in the case of Ellen Bury. She was then later stabbed and placed in a trunk. There was no attempt to conceal or hide the bodies left by Jack the Ripper.

Upon examining William Henry Bury, the prison doctor found several scratches on his arm and wrist, and a fingernail mark on his left hand. Unfortunately, this cannot be compared to Jack the Ripper, since he was never caught. On the surface, those marks are somewhat inconsistent with what would be expected in a Jack the Ripper murder.

Three days after this doctor examined Bury, Inspector Abberline was contacted. Abberline personally took statements of witnesses in the East End of London who knew Bury. Five witnesses made the trip to Scotland to give evidence at Bury's trial. Inspector Abberline's thoughts on an East End resident investigated at the time of the murders are of paramount importance. The picture from these witnesses painted Bury as a drunk who consistently fought with his wife. This convinced Abberline, who was the officer in charge of the ground investigation, that there was no real connection between Bury and Jack the Ripper.

William Beadle attempts to use psychological profiling, yet he selectively uses information that applies specifically to his suspect, while dismissing or attacking characteristics that do not. If a theorist chooses to include this as a part of his theory against a suspect, then there should be no selectivity. This is not the case in Beadle's theory regarding William Henry Bury.

Another main point of Beadle's theory was that murder was not his only goal. He was considered a thief and may have married his wife Ellen just to get her money. Bury not only murdered these prostitutes, according to Beadle, but he also robbed them. If part of the motive was robbery, then why choose prostitutes? The victims of Jack the Ripper were destitute, and other than Mary Kelly, showed outward signs of poverty. If robbery were a primary factor, Bury would not have chosen these specific women.

The major arguments against Bury as a viable suspect have been laid out above. They include such factors as Bury's motive, which included robbery,

modus operardi, and his clear dismissal as a suspect by Inspector Abberline, who interviewed witnesses that knew Bury in London.

If William Henry Bury was Jack the Ripper, he had committed at least five murders in the span of ten to fourteen weeks, without being suspected of committing these crimes. Bury had eluded the police and their efforts at every turn. Now Bury leaves England, murders his wife, and has five days to dispose of the corpse or flee from Scotland. Beadle interprets Bury leaving England as fleeing, so it must be assumed that Bury was adept at this type of behavior. So what does Bury do after murdering his wife Ellen? He turns himself in to the Dundee Police, concocting a story of suicide that he had read about in a local paper. Beadle's theory that Bury was Jack the Ripper suggests that Bury eluded Scotland Yard, the London Metropolitan Police Department and the City of London Police Department, yet turned himself in to a local Scottish police force for a murder that he could have easily hidden.

William Henry Bury did leave London, England, a short time after the murders are believed to have ceased. As a piece of evidence against Bury, this does not take into account that Bury left London nine weeks after the murder in Miller's Court, leaving him ample time to commit more murders. He did possess a geographic knowledge of the area, as he sold sawdust throughout the area from a horse-drawn cart. This allows Beadle to construct his most persuasive argument, that no murders took place during the month of October due to the dense fog. The fog would have hampered Bury's escapes. Beadle does not document the weather of each day between the double murder on September 30 and the murder on November 9. He only states that October 1888, was unusually foggy.

William Henry Bury hated his wife, in large part due to her former profession as a prostitute. The fact that Bury had contracted a venereal disease from a prostitute in May of 1888 did not help Ellen Bury. His hatred for her ultimately drove William Henry Bury over the edge, and it resulted in Ellen Bury's murder. Her murder displays few similarities with the murders committed by Jack the Ripper. Bury's behavior after the murder of his wife also varies from the behavior of Jack the Ripper.

Beadle, William. *Jack the Ripper: Anatomy of a Myth* (1995).
Begg, Paul, Martin Fido, and Keith Skinner. *The Jack the Ripper A–Z* (1996).

LEWIS CARROLL

Famous children's author Lewis Carroll was born Charles Lutwidge Dodgson on January 27, 1832, in Cheshire, a county just south of Liverpool. The first boy of eleven children born to Reverend Charles Dodgson and his wife Frances Jane Lutwidge, Carroll was eager to learn and explore as a child, performing magic, drawing and writing poetry. At twelve, Carroll was enrolled at Richmond School, where he excelled at mathematics. On his fourteenth birthday Carroll entered Rugby School.

Carroll would later reveal that he was more than likely sexually abused at Rugby School. Carroll described these encounters as an "annoyance, at night." Despite these problems at school causing the young Carroll stress and unhappiness, he continued to excel in his studies, focusing on mathematics. Carroll would leave Rugby School in 1849 and the following year enter Christ Church College at Oxford, his father's alma mater. A short time after his mother passed away, one day short of his nineteenth birthday, he would receive a fellowship in mathematics. In 1854 Carroll graduated with first class honors in mathematics and second class honors in classics.

After graduating Carroll became a librarian and mathematics lecturer at Christ Church. Soon after, a new Dean named Henry Liddell arrived and formed a close friendship with Carroll. Liddell had one son and three daughters, one of whom was named Alice. She would figure very largely in Carroll's later success. The following year Carroll bought his first camera after becoming interested in the art form the previous summer. Carroll took his first picture of young Alice Liddell in 1856.

In 1861 Carroll was ordained as a deacon of Christ Church. He would not pursue this work, due to a minor speech impediment. A stammer, or hesitation in his speech, led him to believe he would not prosper in this line of work. Some researchers and theorists have questioned this rationale, offering an alternative explanation of sexual shame over possibly engaging or wishing to engage in lewd and lascivious behavior with young girls or boys.

Carroll wrote throughout his life, publishing two textbooks on mathematics in 1860. Numerous books would follow over the next couple of years. In 1862, while on a boating trip along the Thames River, Carroll amused the Liddell children with stories of "Alice's Adventures Under Ground." The stories continued on later boating trips that Carroll took with the Liddell children. The first of the Alice stories would be published in 1865 with *Alice's Adventures in Wonderland*, perhaps the most well-known of the series. Three years later, Carroll's father would pass away.

In 1881 Carroll stopped lecturing in mathematics at Christ Church to focus entirely on writing. Throughout the 1870s he published numerous books, including more in the Alice series. He devoted his writing to nonsensical poems like "Jabberwocky," and to further stories in the Alice series. His love of mathematics continued, and he wrote books for children on mathematics, puzzles, games and logic. He attempted to make his writing more serious, yet the popularity of those books never achieved the status of the Alice stories. Charles Lutwidge Dodgson, also known as Lewis Carroll, would die on January 14, 1898, of pneumonia.

In 1990 author Richard Wallace wrote *The Agony of Lewis Carroll*. Wallace described a sexually tormented and aggressive Carroll who hid secret meaning within his writings. A lover of puzzles and word games, Carroll is seen by Wallace as revealing his entire psyche in his writing, from sexual abuses as a child at Rugby School, to a passionate long-

ing and possible marriage proposal to the young Alice Liddell. There is evidence that Carroll suffered some type of painful sexual relationship that weighed heavily on his mind. Wallace uses this and other conjecture to theorize that Carroll lived in a world of his own due to his traumatic past, a world where he could only relate to or be understood by children.

Wallace expanded his theory about Lewis Carroll in 1996 to suggest Carroll was responsible for the murders committed by Jack the Ripper. Wallace attributes the murders to Carroll and one of his Oxford colleagues, Thomas Vere Bayne. Bayne and Carroll were senior students at Oxford and became lifelong friends.

Wallace's assertions regarding Lewis Carroll hinge on word games and anagrams contained within Carroll's verse. Numerous critics and detractors of Wallace's theory have reorganized these anagrams to yield distinctly different sentences than Wallace's. A secret cryptic key book described by Wallace has never been found. To protect his name, Lewis Carroll's family has destroyed most of the secretive information contained in his diaries. What this information was the world may never know, but it is hard to believe that Carroll's family would destroy an entire cryptic key book revealing hidden meanings within his poetry.

Wallace attaches great significance to the number 42, which he says is contained as a code in at least two of Carroll's verses. Wallace points to the murders of Emma Elizabeth Smith, who was 45 years old, and Martha Tabram, who was stabbed 39 times, which averages out to 42 to suggest a pattern. The pattern includes Kelly, who was 24 years old (42 backwards), and Rose Mylett, who was murdered 42 days after Mary Kelly.

The "42" theory seems even more of a stretch than the anagrams. Minor additions, such as Carroll's closet homosexuality and his supposed inability to have normal adult relationships, have convinced Richard Wallace that Lewis Carroll was without a doubt Jack the Ripper.

There are numerous negatives to Wallace's theory, such as the anagrams having been reconstructed to reveal rather inconsequential alternatives. The "42" theory works and does not work within the known facts of the victims. The number does not perfectly apply to any one specific victim, and most researchers have devalued the combinations and permutations performed to arrive at 42. Despite Carroll never marrying, there is no relevant proof that he was a homosexual, and that, in and of itself, would not make someone a multiple murderer.

Karoline Leach has recently dissected Wallace's case. Leach's 1999 biography of Lewis Carroll hypothesizes that Carroll was attracted to Alice Liddell's mother, the wife of his friend Henry Liddell, rather than the young Alice. Leach theorizes that Carroll was not a pedophile at all, thus contradicting major elements of Wallace's theory regarding Carroll as Jack the Ripper.

Charles Dodgson, or Lewis Carroll, was a lifelong scholar in the field of mathematics. He also excelled at drawing, photography and, what he is most known for, storytelling. Both Charles Dodgson and Lewis Carroll had individual prosperous careers. The need to invent a pseudonym for his fictitious storytelling will no doubt one day be offered as convincing evidence of his guilt. Nowhere on the surface of Lewis Carroll's fiction does he display outward anger or violence toward women. While there may be angst or torment of times past contained deep within his verse, that is far from proof that Lewis Carroll needed to act out that torment against innocent women.

Leach, Karoline. *In the Shadow of the Dreamchild* (1999).
_____. *Ripper Notes* (January 2001).
Wallace, Richard. *The Agony of Lewis Carroll* (1990).
_____. *Jack the Ripper: Light Hearted Friend* (1996).
http://www.casebook.org.
http://www.members.aol.com/Marcin23/Lewis.html.

DR. FREDERICK R. CHAPMAN

Dr. Frederick Chapman was born in 1851, in Poona, India. His father was stationed in India as a commanding officer. In 1874, Chapman received his M.B. in Glasgow, Scotland. He was a medical officer for a smallpox hospital in Hull, England, while also acting as resident surgeon for the Hull and Sculcoates Dispensary. Research has tentatively identified (Dr. Frederick R.

Chapman) as the suspect Police Constable Robert Spicer called "Dr. Merchant."

The middle to late 1800s were a time for medical discoveries, and during his career Dr. Chapman wrote extensively on medical issues. Dr. Chapman came to London in 1886, leaving a provincial practice behind. His death on December 12, 1888, coincides with the cessation of the "canonical" murders, but it is how Dr. Chapman died that determines his status as a suspect. Dr. Chapman died of septicemia, commonly known as blood poisoning. Even today, septicemia is considered a life-threatening condition. This illness arises from an abscess that allows bacteria to escape from an infection located within the body. Researcher Nick Warren, in an article in *The Criminologist*, states that Dr. Chapman died as a result of psoas abscess tuberculosis. Psoas abscess is a rare disorder that develops due to a bone infection of the spine, and the advancing stage resulting from spinal tuberculosis. It appears highly unlikely that a man suffering from these conditions and diseases would have been able to commit these murders only months before the illness finally ended his life.

There does however remain the possibility that Dr. Frederick R. Chapman was not Spicer's suspect. Spicer claimed to have seen this man on a couple of occasions after the night of the double murder, but it seems unlikely that Dr. Chapman would have been able to roam the streets given his illness. Internal evidence regarding Spicer's account suggests the possibility that there was no suspect, and that the entire story was concocted to vindicate Spicer, who was discharged while drunk on duty the year after the murders.

On medical evidence alone, Dr. Frederick Chapman's status as Spicer's suspect has become questionable at best. That same medical evidence casts extreme doubt that a man in the condition that Dr. Frederick Chapman was in at the time could have committed these murders.

Begg, Paul, Martin Fido, and Keith Skinner. *The Jack the Ripper A–Z* (1996).
Clayman, Dr. Charles B. *The American Medical Association Encyclopedia of Medicine* (1989).
Warren, Nick. *The Criminologist* (Spring 1992).

FREDERICK NICHOLAS CHARRINGTON

In 1998 theorist M. J. Trow released *The Many Faces of Jack the Ripper*. This landmark book set two precedents: it presented a viable case against an entirely new suspect, Frederick Nicholas Charrington, and it then revealed that this very theory was created only to dissuade further attempts to name new suspects. M. J. Trow's cavalier attitude to the Jack the Ripper case at first glance appears appalling. Trow's naming a suspect he does not believe committed the murders suggests that everyone is a possible suspect until they can be conclusively exonerated. Frederick Nicholas Charrington is no different.

Born on February 4, 1850, Charrington was the heir to the wealthy Charrington Brewery Company. As a child he grew up directly across from the brewery owned by his family. His mother was an Anglican who helped the less fortunate. The work performed by his mother may have influenced Charrington's later path in life.

Charrington attended public boarding school at Marlborough and went on to Brighton College. In 1867 Charrington traveled in mainland Europe, visiting such countries as Italy, Switzerland and France. Popularly known as "The Grand Tour," this trip allowed a young man to indulge his vices before eventually settling down into a career and a family. On this tour of Europe, pubs and breweries were frequently visited perhaps providing Charrington with a chance to inspect the competition and the European market.

As a preamble to running the family business, Charrington returned to England and began work as an apprentice manager in a brewery that supplied to the Queen of Windsor. Before he could join his father's brewery, a singular event changed the course of Frederick Charrington's life. Charrington was out with a couple of friends and noticed a man and a woman fighting outside a pub. The man was extremely drunk and began to beat the woman, who was his wife. Charrington immediately stepped in and stopped the man. The police took

the man away, and Charrington had an epiphany. The drunkenness was the cause of the fight, and Charrington's family brewery was a major supplier of alcohol in the community that led to this incident.

After a discussion with his father over the ethics and morality of supplying alcohol to the community, which Charrington felt was solely responsible for the misery and turmoil he witnessed, he left the family business and his inheritance behind. Frederick Charrington would not follow in the footsteps of his father. He chose to walk the streets and preach the evils of alcohol, helping and instructing those less fortunate than himself. Frederick Charrington is considered one of the early leaders of the temperance movement. This movement would advance at a steady rate and is an early model for organizations like Alcoholics Anonymous.

Charrington chose to lead a life devoted to God. He practiced celibacy, had the most meager of possessions, and was instrumental in closing over 200 pubs. His street preaching regarding alcohol once drew a crowd of nearly 200,000 in Hyde Park. One of Charrington's main focuses was to "rescue prostitutes from their evil courses."

M. J. Trow combines psychological profiling and factual trends from recent serial killers to create suspicion surrounding Frederick Nicholas Charrington. Trow discusses Charrington's abnormal practice of chosen celibacy, freeing prostitutes from the evils of the street and his hatred for the abuse of alcohol to link him to Jack the Ripper. The use of alcohol in the cases of all the "canonical" victims of Jack the Ripper is one of the primary compelling factors for Trow's suspicion of Charrington.

After creating a solid case against Charrington, Trow revealed that this entire case was, in fact, aimed at persuading theorists to cease naming new suspects.

Trow's disdain for researchers and this case does not eliminate Frederick Charrington from consideration as a suspect. He lived and preached against the evils of prostitution and alcohol near where the murders took place. Charrington was described as ordinary and had a familiarity with the local women of the East End. This would not be the first time a religious zealot took his beliefs over the edge and committed murder to appease his God and save a soul.

Charrington had no history of violence other than standing up for battered women under attack by their drunken husbands. Charrington worked to better the lives of the unfortunate, at times sacrificing himself, and gave away his family inheritance. He was one of the pioneers of the anti-alcohol movement and joined the fight against child prostitution. Frederick Nicholas Charrington's main goal in life seemed to be helping and crusading for others who were unfortunate. He continued to be a leader in the temperance movement, as well as other movements, for the rest of his life. Since Trow's 1998 naming of Charrington as a suspect, no researcher has actively pursued a case against Charrington.

Jakubowski, Maxim, and Nathan Braund. *The Mammoth Book of Jack the Ripper* (1998).
Trow, M. J. *The Many Faces of Jack the Ripper* (1998).

GEORGE CHARLES SPENCER CHURCHILL

Lord Blandford, later the 8th Duke of Marlborough, George Churchill, was born on May 13, 1844, to John Winston Spencer Churchill, the 7th Duke of Marlborough, and Frances, the daughter of the Marques of Londonderry. Churchill married Albertha Hamilton, daughter of the Duke of Abercorn, on November 8, 1869. Their marriage would last fourteen years until 1883, the same year Churchill ascended to the dukedom.

George was notoriously wild and wicked and was expelled from Eton College. In 1876, an event occurred that would ensure his name would be remembered in the English peerage. While married to Albertha, Churchill secretly courted Lady Aylesford. Lord Aylesford was away in India, and word of the affair reached him. Lord Aylesford's friend, Prince of Wales Albert Edward, the future King of England, instructed Lord Aylesford to initiate divorce proceedings against Lady Aylesford. George's brother, Lord Randolph Churchill, blackmailed Prince Albert Edward to stop the divorce. (The Prince of Wales had written some compromising letters to Lady Aylesford, which were in the possession of Lord Randolph.) Prince

Albert Edward was infuriated and challenged Lord Randolph to a duel, which Lord Randolph had no choice but to decline. The "Lady Aylesford Affair" would forever link Prince Albert Edward and George Spencer Churchill.

After the 1883 divorce, George Churchill went to the United States in search of an American wife. He would succeed in July 1888, in marrying Lillian Price, daughter of Commodore Cicero Price of the United States Navy. While in America, Churchill visited Thomas Edison, and Edison was extremely impressed by Churchill's ingenuity and inventiveness. Churchill was known as an amateur scientist and is noted for having installed the first private telephone system in Blenheim Palace, the family manor.

George Churchill's name was not connected to the Jack the Ripper murders until Melvyn Fairclough's *The Rip-per and the Royals* was published in 1991. Fairclough listed George Churchill as a member of the Jack the Ripper group to protect the Crown. Fairclough does not reveal how deep George's involvement goes within the conspiracy, only that Walter Sickert told Joseph Gorman Sickert that George was in some way implicated in the murders.

As Fairclough involves twelve men in the Royal Conspiracy, George Spencer Churchill's actual part in the murders is never disclosed. His death on November 9, 1892, of sudden heart failure, seems to be enough for Fairclough to sense foul play. November 9 was the date of the final murder victim, Mary Jane Kelly, and is the birthday of Prince Albert Edward.

Fairclough, Melvyn. *The Ripper and the Royals* (1991).
www.blenheimpalace.com/timeline.htm
www.geocities.com/jesusib/EdwardVII.html

RANDOLPH HENRY SPENCER CHURCHILL

Lord Randolph Churchill is the second son of the 7th Duke of Marlborough and the brother of George Charles, the 8th Duke of Marlborough discussed above. Randolph was born on February 13, 1849, in Blenheim Palace, the family manor. He married an American, Jennie Jerome, in 1874, and the couple had two sons. One of them would become the legendary Prime Minister of England, Winston Churchill.

Randolph attended both Oxford and Cambridge, receiving an MA and an LLD. He entered the House of Commons in 1874 as the MP for Woodstock, a position he would hold until 1885. During this time he acted as private secretary to his father, the Viceroy of Ireland. In 1885 he was made Secretary of State for India, while also holding the position of MP for South Paddington. The following year, the thirty-seven year old Randolph would become Chancellor of the Exchequor and Leader of the House of Commons. Unfortunately, his meteoric political rise would end in 1886 when he resigned his office due to health reasons.

There has been some debate as to what exactly Randolph's ailment was. The ailment has been described as a tumor, yet all evidence leads toward Randolph dying of syphilis, of which he was in the tertiary stage. There have been stories written about how Randolph acquired the disease, the most famous coming from Frank Harris. In his 1925 book, *My Life and Loves*, Harris recounts that a prostitute was either snuck into Randolph's bed or that Randolph was too drunk to remember how the old prostitute had got there. This event took place shortly after the birth of Winston in 1874. Harris' accounts have been severely criticized as over-imaginative. A differing account arises from author Ted Morgan, a biographer of Winston Churchill, who states that Randolph contracted the disease from a Blenheim housemaid.

In 1881 Randolph suffered an attack that was manifested in partial paralysis, which severely affected his speech. By 1886 the syphilis had affected him enough to end his flourishing political career. Further corroborative evidence that the disease began to seriously affect Randolph is that Dr. William Gull, an expert in the treatment of syphilis, was one of the Churchill family physicians as far back as 1882. On January 24, 1895, Randolph succumbed to his affliction. By the end of his life he had lost the ability to speak, and his powers of thought had seriously deteriorated.

Similar to his brother, Randolph Churchill was first suggested as a suspect by Melvyn Fairclough in his 1991 book expanding on the Royal Conspiracy. Differing from his brother George, whose involvement has never been fully determined, Randolph is depicted as the overall leader of the conspiracy. Incorrectly labeled as the highest-ranking Freemason in the land, Randolph was supposedly responsible for organizing and gathering the group of conspirators whose goal was to protect the Crown at any cost. Never does Fairclough, or the source of his information, Joseph Gorman Sickert, state that Randolph personally murdered any prostitute, yet the entire blame of the murders is laid at Randolph's feet.

The simple organizing of the group that was responsible for the murders attributed to Jack the Ripper does not make Randolph Churchill Jack the Ripper. Under close scrutiny the Royal Conspiracy failed when it was originally proposed in the 1970s. The advancement of that theory has led to harsh criticism from the research community, who view the Royal Conspiracy as a disproved theory. Even Melvyn Fairclough has gone on record as stating he does not believe the statements provided to him by Joseph Gorman Sickert.

Randolph Churchill's illness had so adversely affected him in 1886 that he was forced to resign from a thriving political career. His speech had deteriorated. This would have made him stick out in the East End of London during the time that Jack the Ripper committed these murders. Randolph Churchill appears nowhere in any file relating to Jack the Ripper. That is explained away by the claim that Winston Churchill destroyed certain documents pertaining to his father's involvement in the murders when he became the Home Secretary in 1910.

Researcher Nick Warren claims that Randolph was considered a suspect before the historic 1970 article "Jack the Ripper—A Solution?" by Dr. Thomas Stowell. The article appeared in *The Criminologist* and proposed that a member of the Royal family was Jack the Ripper. Unfortunately, Warren provides no sources for his statements regarding Randolph Churchill. Warren is known for his steadfast research, and one hopes that the source is eventually retrieved so that more analysis of the case against Lord Randolph Churchill can be undertaken.

Begg, Paul, Martin Fido, and Keith Skinner. *The Jack the Ripper A–Z* (1996).
Fairclough, Melvyn. *The Ripper and the Royals* (1991).
Harris, Frank. *My Life and Loves* (1925).
Morgan, Ted. *Churchill: 1874–1915* (1983).
Stowell, Dr. Thomas. *The Criminologist* (October 1970).
Warren, Nick. *Ripperana* (October 1992).
www.geocities.com/Paris/Parc/9893/randolph.html

DAVID COHEN

Aaron Davis Cohen was arrested as a lunatic at large on December 7, 1888. He was taken to Whitechapel Workhouse Infirmary and placed there under the name David Cohen. His age was given as twenty-three; his address was stated as 86 Leman Street. Recent research has established that this is an incorrect statement, as 86 Leman Street was the address for a Protestant Boys' Club. Cohen was also said to have no relatives.

During Cohen's stay at the infirmary, he was reported as violent and difficult. He threatened other patients. Another report describes him as destructive and screaming loudly. He would be transferred to Colney Hatch Lunatic Asylum on December 21, 1888, under restraints. Colney Hatch listed Cohen's profession as "tailor." On December 28 Cohen was separated from the rest of the patients, as he was believed to be dangerous and destructive.

On the same day as the separation, Cohen was taken ill, but he would soon recover. Other than a continuing pattern of destruction and aggressive behavior, there is a gap in information regarding Cohen until the middle of October 1889. On October 15, Cohen was confined to bed. Five days later he would pass away. The listed reason was exhaustion of mania and pulmonary phthisis.

Theorist Martin Fido announced David Cohen as a suspect in 1987. Fido surmised that of all the lunatics incarcerated, the only one who matched Assistant Commissioner Robert Anderson's suspect was Cohen. Fido theorized that Cohen switched his name from Nathan Kaminsky. Fido found one existing record on Kaminsky that exactly matched the known characteristics of David Cohen.

In the same year as Fido's announcement, the emergence of the

Swanson Marginalia placed a major roadblock in front of this theory. The *Swanson Marginalia* is a set of handwritten notes on Chief Inspector Donald Swanson's personal copy of Robert Anderson's 1910 memoirs. Swanson identified Anderson's "Polish Jew" suspect as Kosminski. Fido persevered, believing that Anderson heard the name Kaminsky in reference to "Leather Apron" and might have made the leap to Kosminski. Leather Apron was an important aspect of Fido's theory regarding Cohen.

"Leather Apron" was mentioned in the local newspapers as early as September 6, 1888. On September 7, Inspector Joseph Helson filed a report to Scotland Yard. In his weekly report Inspector Helson announced that a search was being conducted for a "Jack" Pizer, also known as "Leather Apron." Pizer was arrested on September 10, but was able to sufficiently produce alibis for the August 31 murder of Mary Ann Nichols and the September 8 murder of Annie Chapman. Since "Jack," or John, Pizer was known locally as "Leather Apron," as Inspector Helson, Sergeant William Thick, and Pizer himself declared, there were no further inquiries into Leather Apron as a suspect. Fido however, believes that Kaminsky was the real Leather Apron, changing his name to David Cohen after his mention in the newspapers and the arrest of John Pizer.

There are logistical problems with this theory. If there were no further enquiries into the Leather Apron suspect, then whether or not Nathan Kaminsky, or David Cohen, was the real "Leather Apron" becomes a moot point when applied to Fido's theory. Swanson's statement that Anderson's suspect was Kosminski is deciphered by Fido to mean that Anderson heard the name Kaminsky in reference to Leather Apron and later misreported the name as Kosminski. Anderson would have had access to any Scotland Yard file on a possible suspect. Kaminsky, or even Kosminski, appears nowhere in any file as "Leather Apron." The only files relating to Leather Apron list his identity as John Pizer.

Inferential evidence may clear David Cohen's name. As far along as the murders of Alice McKenzie and Frances Coles, on July 17, 1889, and February 13, 1891, respectively, the police were investigating the possibility that Jack the Ripper was still at large. Commissioner James Monro, Anderson's immediate superior, believed that McKenzie was murdered by Jack the Ripper. This murder occurred while Cohen was safely locked away in Colney Hatch Lunatic Asylum.

Dr. Thomas Bond, Police Surgeon for Westminster, was called in to examine McKenzie. The request to have Dr. Bond examine the body was made by Anderson, who had asked Dr. Bond to write a report on the five murders the previous year. This solidified the notion that the police had not positively identified the murderer. If Anderson had positively identified Cohen as the murderer, if he thought Cohen to be the "Polish Jew" suspect, then it would have been unnecessary to have Dr. Bond examine the body of a victim murdered while Cohen was incarcerated.

In the scenario outlined by Fido, the evidentiary analysis does not support the conclusion. However, this does not necessarily preclude David Cohen as a suspect.

David Cohen was arrested at the beginning of December. He spoke either German or Yiddish, rambling incoherently. To what degree of fluency Cohen spoke English is a question that no researcher has answered. Cohen would not have been the kind of client a prostitute would take down a dark alley during the height of the murders or back to her own room.

Cohen's seriously aggressive tendencies, however, have been recorded in both Whitechapel Workhouse Infirmary and Colney Hatch Lunatic Asylum records. The scope of the murders lends credibility that an uncontrollable rage was possessed by Jack the Ripper, and Cohen fits that model. Cohen's rage was severe and possibly manifested itself in some deep-seated psychological ailment. He was familiar with the East End of London, and, with no relatives

to be accountable to, Cohen would have been free to roam the streets at all hours of the night.

David Cohen represents an entirely new suspect based on hard fundamental research. Research such as this has led to the discovery of many possible new suspects and has helped foster advancement of the case through the use of detailed research like that of Martin Fido.

Anderson, Robert. *The Lighter Side of My Official Life* (1910).
Beadle, William. *Jack the Ripper: Anatomy of a Myth* (1995).
Begg, Paul, Martin Fido, and Keith Skinner. *The Jack the Ripper A–Z* (1996).
Fido, Martin. *The Crimes, Detection and Death of Jack the Ripper* (1987).

CLAUDE CONDER

One of the more recent suspects, Claude Conder is remembered most for his work in the field of archaeology. Born in 1848, Conder is a direct descendant of the French sculptor Louis Francois Roubilac. His brother Charles studied art and became close friends with a group of young up-and-coming artists that included Oscar Wilde, Ernest Dowson, Walter Sickert, and William Butler Yeats, all of whom have been connected with the Jack the Ripper case as suspects, associates of suspects and or friends of suspects.

Claude Conder worked in the Middle East in the late 1860s. His duties included archaeology, cartography, surveying and the exploration of lands

considered to have their origins in Biblical history. Conder worked hard and became an Altaic scholar. In 1872, as a Lieutenant, Conder was placed in command of the survey of Western Palestine. Founded in 1871, the survey was designed to accurately map the entire land West of the Jordan River. Completed around 1878, the survey was an invaluable source of reference material for future researchers. One of the more famous discoveries made and mapped by Conder are the remains of a *bethso*, or latrine, where ritual cleansing took place. This landmark was previously undiscovered. Jewish historian Flavius Josephus has traced its written origins back to the middle of the first century A.D.

While conducting Biblical exploration in the Middle East, Claude Conder developed a close working relationship and friendship with Charles Warren. In 1857 Warren was appointed to the Royal Engineers. Ten years later, as a Captain, Warren explored Palestine and contributed to our basic knowledge of the topography of ancient Jerusalem. Warren is considered key to the discovery of tunnels and shafts underneath Jerusalem between 1865 and 1870.

Warren eventually would move on to become the Commissioner of the Metropolitan Police Department from 1886 until November 8, 1888, a period encompassing the Jack the Ripper murders. It is this close friendship with Warren that has led theorists Tom Slemen and Keith Andrews to recently propose Claude Conder as a suspect.

Warren was a devout Freemason, founding and taking an active role in numerous lodges, including the Quator Coronati, which was devoted to Masonic research and history. Slemen and Andrews believe that Warren was covering up for Conder by erasing the Goulston Street Graffito. This idea has its origins in the Royal Conspiracy Theory of the 1970s. Supposedly, this mysterious message in Goulston Street was a message from Conder to Warren, admitting the former's identity as Jack the Ripper. But, if they were such close friends, why would Conder need to post a secret note in a public place? (Slemen argues that the word, "Juwes," which appeared in the grafitti, is a Manchoo word for "too's," a code word that would have been understood by Warren and Conder.) There are, of course, alternative explanations.

There are other facets to Slemen and Andrews' theory regarding Claude Conder: Conder was a practicing Satanist; the murders were committed because Annie Chapman stole relics such as coins and artifacts brought back from Conder's explorations in the Middle East; and Mary Kelly knew the identity of Jack the Ripper due to the breath sweeteners found in Elizabeth Stride's hand when her body was discovered. These and other allegations have never been proven. If they are ever proven, this still is not enough evidence to hang Conder for these murders.

Claude Conder was more than likely a Freemason. His brother Charles was a Freemason and wrote on the subject. Claude's close personal friendship with Charles Warren more than likely would have granted him membership in the Freemasons. He was also a well-respected scholar, archaeologist, explorer cartographer and royal engineer. Conder's professional life would not have warranted exclusion from a society such as the Freemasons, yet rather garner his admittance. There appears to be an element of Freemasonry connected with the Jack the Ripper murders, yet that specific connection has yet to be fully deciphered.

Confusion has arisen as to exactly where Claude Conder lived during 1888. During the time of the murders, Conder worked for Ordinance Survey in Southampton. However, documentation has not surfaced yet to place Conder out of the East End of London on the specific dates of the murders.

Conder continued to write throughout his lifetime, focusing his work on aspects dealing with his prior work in Palestine. One volume on Palestine was published in 1889. He was fluent in numerous languages such as Altaic, Hittite and Arabic, on which he wrote extensively. Conder remained an active figure in the Palestine Exploration Fund until his death in 1910. Academia and the world have been great beneficiaries of his ardent research and exploration of what is considered by many to be the Holy Land.

http://www.casebook.org
http://www.mara.org.uk/reignier_conder.htm
http://www.pef.org.uk/Pages/Conder.html

JOHN COURTENAY

John Courtenay is only mentioned in one book pertaining to Jack the Ripper, implicated as one of the twelve-member gang of Melvyn Fairclough's updated Royal Conspiracy. Even Fairclough admits within his 1991 text that the information regarding Courtenay is sparse at best.

From what Joseph Gorman Sickert described, John Courtenay was a "man-servant" for the leader of the conspirators. Courtenay may have been a Lieutenant Commander in the Royal Navy. Alternatively, he may have worked in the diplomatic corps as a Naval Attaché. Joseph Gorman Sickert could not be entirely certain as to which. Gorman Sickert added that Courtenay was run over by a tram in 1936. He supposedly got his foot caught in the railroad line. Fairclough never found Courtenay's death in any recorded listing.

The family history of the name Courtenay belongs to the Earls of Devon, who resided in Powderham Castle. Over 600 years old, Powderham Castle lies along the River Exe, in Exeter, England. The castle is currently opened to the public. Joseph could not be sure that John Courtenay was related to this familial line, yet when the subject was brought to him by Fairclough, Gorman Sickert added that Courtenay's family had been somewhat embarrassed by Courtenay's unconventional lifestyle. As an older man, Courtenay was around both a young Gorman Sickert and his mother, Alice Margaret Crook. He may have felt a need to watch over the young boy and his mother out of remorse. Gorman Sickert stated that they felt both uneasy and comfortable when he was around and relieved when he ultimately passed away.

The nature of Courtenay's involvement in the Jack the Ripper murders remains a mystery to this day. Fairclough could not unearth valuable information regarding Courtenay, despite the possibility that he may have been related to the Earls of Devon. When Fairclough revealed this information to Gorman Sickert, the latter immediately remembered further information to corroborate Fairclough's findings. Gorman-Sickert never documented this additional information. There remains the possibility that Courtenay had nothing to do with the Jack the Ripper murders or even that the John Courtenay accused of conspiracy by Gorman Sickert and Fairclough never existed.

Fairclough, Melvyn. *The Ripper and the Royals* (1991).

DR. THOMAS NEILL CREAM

Dr. Thomas Neill Cream was arrested and convicted in Lambeth, a borough of London, for the poisoning of four prostitutes between 1891 and 1892. This is not where Dr. Cream's criminal history begins, however. He was incarcerated in Joliet Prison in the United States for the murder of Daniel Stott in 1881. Dr. Cream had been having an affair with Stott's wife. She eventually testified against Dr. Cream, claiming he had murdered Daniel Stott with a lethal dose of strychnine. This managed to save Mrs. Stott, but Dr. Cream was not so lucky, as he was incarcerated in November of 1881.

In 1974 theorist Donald Bell proposed Dr. Cream as a suspect based on the accounts of the hangman at the gallows where Dr. Cream was executed. Just before his neck snapped, the hangman allegedly overheard Dr. Cream say, "I am Jack...." Dr. Cream would have gotten away with his most recent murders, if it were not for his habit of writing letters to the police, intending to incriminate others. These letters led to his downfall in 1891, ultimately to his death by hanging, but not before Dr. Cream had murdered at least eight different people, seven of them having been female prostitutes or patients. According to Bell, these letters to the authorities are an additional link, stating that Dr. Cream's handwriting is similar to that within the Jack the Ripper letters.

The main problem with Dr. Cream as a viable suspect is that he was incarcerated in Joliet Prison from November 1881, for a ten-year period encompassing the murders. It is an unquestioned fact that he was in prison at the times of the murders. Inspector Abberline, in his 1903 interview with *The Pall Mall Gazette*, dismisses any notion that Dr. Cream could have been the murderer and states that he was not in the country at the time. That alone should warrant his exclusion as a suspect, yet Bell states that Dr. Cream may have bribed his way out of Joliet early enough to have committed the murders. What is additionally wrong with this statement is that Dr. Cream was a serial poisoner. That was his *modus operandi*. He poisoned women from Canada to the United States before his arrest in Illinois, and returned to poisoning women in London after he was released.

There appears the possibility that the tale from the hangman Billington may be simply that, a tale. Dr. Cream is alleged to have voiced the words, "I am Jack," just as his neck snapped. The sole witness to this apparent confession was Billington. Henry Smith, Acting Commissioner of the City Police during the night of the double murder, was in attendance at Dr. Cream's hanging. Smith never mentions Dr. Cream's partial confession in his memoirs, published in 1910. Smith was known for storytelling and had a particular interest in the Jack the Ripper case, as he claimed that there was no man living who knew more about the murders than he did. If the confession did take place, Smith would have documented it in his memoirs, unless it was investigated and discovered that Dr. Cream was incarcerated at the time of the murders. Smith may not have actually heard the "confession," but Dr. Cream was still incarcerated in an American jail at the time of the murders.

If by some small chance Donald Bell were right, that Dr. Cream was able to bribe his way out of Joliet prison early, it seems highly unlikely that he would have resorted to the mutilations associated with Jack the Ripper. In addition, Dr. Cream was not very fortunate when it came to evading the authorities. It would seem that he had a habit of being caught. It seems unlikely that he would roam around the streets of London for over three years without getting caught, then be caught for murders outside the realm of Jack the Ripper. Dr. Thomas Neill Cream was in prison at the time of the murders and must therefore be eliminated from consideration as a suspect.

Begg, Paul, Martin Fido, and Keith Skinner. *The Jack the Ripper A–Z* (1996)
Bell, Donald. *The Criminologist* (Summer 1974).
McLaren, Angus. *A Prescription for Murder* (1993).
Rumbelow, Donald. *The Complete Jack the Ripper* (1987).
www.crimelibrary.com/serial_killers/history/cream/index_1.html?sect=3

THOMAS HAYNE CUTBUSH

Thomas Hayne Cutbush, the nephew of former Executive Superintendent of Scotland Yard Charles Cutbush, was suggested as Jack the Ripper in a series of articles featured in *The Sun*, beginning on February 13, 1894. Born in 1865, Cutbush contracted syphilis from a prostitute in 1888. Soon after, he began experiencing delusional behavior. He left his job once the paranoid behavior took over. He would often roam the streets at night mumbling incoherently.

Cutbush had been incarcerated for almost three years when the newspaper made its suggestion regarding Jack the Ripper. It has never been determined why these allegations were made against Cutbush, but they led to one of the most historically significant documents written on the case, the MacNaghten Memorandum.

On March 5, 1891, Cutbush was detained as a wandering lunatic, but escaped only hours later. He was arrested four days later, but not before he had stabbed one woman and attempted to stab another. After his trial, Cutbush was incarcerated for the rest of his life in Broadmoor Criminal Lunatic Asylum, eventually dying in 1903.

Written in response to the allegations made by *The Sun*, Assistant Chief Constable Melville MacNaghten prepared his now famous memorandum. Three versions are said to exist, all of which contain numerous discrepancies and errors. The memorandum runs seven pages long and names three suspects which, MacNaghten believed, were far more likely candidates than Cutbush. The first four pages of the document deal specifically with the case of Thomas Cutbush. After naming and briefly describing his three suspects, MacNaghten returns to the case against Cutbush. It is this beginning and ending section, dealing primarily with Thomas Cutbush that shall be examined.

MacNaghten provides the details of Cutbush's arrest, escape, and arrest four days later before examining the case against him. According to MacNaghten, a man named Colicott stabbed six women from behind, but due to a faulty identification he was subsequently released. This occurred approximately one month prior to Cutbush's attacks. MacNaghten states that there was a marked difference between the cuts of the two men, and that *The Sun*, which was stating that Cutbush had stabbed six women, simply confused the case of Cutbush with that of Colicott.

Three police officers were placed in charge of investigating the past history of Cutbush and discovered, among other things, that Cutbush most likely contracted syphilis in 1888. After that point Cutbush basically did nothing. The syphilis affected Cutbush's brain and he believed someone was poisoning him. The knife that was found in his possession was purchased only one week prior to his original detainment and, according to MacNaghten, purchased "*2 years*

& 3 months after the Whitechapel murders ceased." Policemen never fully ascertained Cutbush's whereabouts on the nights of the murders.

MacNaghten points out another inaccuracy from the article in *The Sun*, with regards to drawings found in Cutbush's room. The article stated that drawings of mutilated women were found in his room, while, in fact, two drawings of women in indecent positions were found torn to pieces. There are other minor erroneous statements in the article dealt with by MacNaghten, yet he seems to have missed the most telling factor about Cutbush.

Cutbush's attack on these two women occurred only after he was detained as a wandering lunatic. Cutbush was then picked up four days later after one of these attacks. Jack the Ripper murdered at least five women over the course of ten weeks and the police never came close to arresting him. Before Cutbush's detainment in March of 1891, Thomas Cutbush had never showed a history of violence, only a degree of paranoia. In his state, after being detained for the first time in his life, Cutbush lashed out against two women in a way unlike the murders during autumn of 1888. The linking of the knife to Cutbush is another factor that distinguishes Cutbush from Jack the Ripper.

In 1993 theorist A. P. Wolf attempted to advance the case for Cutbush as Jack the Ripper. Wolf's central thesis is an examination of Cutbush's mental behavior, history of violence, including undocumented attempted murders of his own mother, aunt, and a maid. Wolf also postulates that Catherine Eddowes had discovered the secret identity of Jack the Ripper and was about to expose or blackmail Cutbush when she was arrested for drunk and disorderly outside the apartment where Cutbush lived, only hours before her death.

Wolf makes a number of valid points, yet these aspects apply to suspects other than Thomas Cutbush. It has never been fully ascertained that Cutbush's syphilis drove him insane, or even fanatical enough to commit these horrific acts of savagery. No murders occurred in London during 1890, while Cutbush freely roamed the streets. This in itself contradicts the theory put forth by Wolf.

MacNaghten quickly and summarily dismissed Thomas Cutbush as a suspect in 1894. The heavy reliance on MacNaghten in the 1960s when research into Jack the Ripper blossomed and expanded, virtually eliminated Cutbush from consideration. The trend today has moved away from a reliance on MacNaghten, whose factual errors within his memorandum have been researched and revealed. Perhaps it is time to begin further research on the main suspect MacNaghten dismissed. A. P. Wolf, however, has not presented a strong enough argument for Thomas Cutbush as Jack the Ripper.

Begg, Paul, Martin Fido, and Keith Skinner. *The Jack the Ripper A–Z* (1996).
Jakubowski, Maxim, and Nathan Braund. *The Mammoth Book of Jack the Ripper* (1998).
Wolf, A. P. *Jack the Myth* (1993).

DR. MORGAN DAVIES

Born in Whitechapel in 1854, Morgan Davies earned his M.B. in 1879 and went on to achieve his M.D. in 1884. Dr. Davies was the house physician and surgeon for London Hospital during the time of the murders. He died in 1920 after a medical career that did not garner much attention. Dr. Davies is mostly remembered as a suspect in the Jack the Ripper murders.

Dr. Davies is not the classical suspect. He is the suspect of another suspect, the writer and occultist Robert Donston Stephenson. Stephenson became convinced of Dr. Davies' guilt during the time of the murders. While a patient in London Hospital, Stephenson claimed that Dr. Davies came into his semi-private hospital room and reenacted the murder of Mary Jane Kelly. Upon hearing from W. T. Stead, editor of *The Pall Mall Gazette*, that the final "canonical" victim, Mary Jane Kelly, was sodomized, Stephenson was further persuaded of Dr. Davies' guilt.

Once released from London Hospital, Stephenson and his associate, George Marsh, an unemployed Ironmongery Assistant, began to investigate Dr. Davies. Their partnership quickly turned sour. The two eventually informed Scotland Yard of their contempt for each other. Marsh informed the authorities that Stephenson was a habitual drinker and should be looked into as a suspect. A report was written on

Stephenson, but no further investigation of Dr. Davies commenced.

According to the surviving reports regarding the murder of Mary Jane Kelly, she was not sodomized. Stephenson's claim that W. T. Stead passed this information along to him has never been proven. The authorities made no further effort to scrutinize Dr. Davies as a suspect, as Stephenson apparently stopped investigating him after his split with George Marsh. Some inquiry must have been made regarding Dr. Davies, yet it seems that it proved fruitless, as Dr. Morgan Davies was never mentioned in any police files regarding the case.

Begg, Paul, Martin Fido, and Keith Skinner. *The Jack the Ripper A–Z* (1996).

FREDERICK BAILEY DEEMING

In 1892, a dead woman was found buried underneath a fireplace in Australia, and the search for Frederick Bailey Deeming, who had recently disappeared, commenced. The story becomes almost fantastic after that. While searching for Deeming, who had changed his name to at least three known aliases, five more bodies were found, murdered and buried in cement under a fireplace in England. These murders were all linked to Deeming. His connection to Jack the Ripper comes as a result of the murders of his two wives and four children.

Frederick Bailey Deeming was born in Leicestershire in 1853. As a teenager he left home for a life at sea. The murder of his wife in Australia eventually led to the discovery of the murders of a woman and four children in England. Further research led the police to the knowledge that Deeming had married a woman named Marie James in 1881 and had four children with her. The couple had moved around, settling in Australia, where the first two of their four children were born. They had also spent some time in South Africa in the mid–1880s. A third child was born while at sea. Deeming's two brothers identified the bodies of Marie James and the four children. They explained that Deeming had brought his family back from Australia only a few months before. It was eventually learned that Deeming had returned in 1890 to England, where his fourth child was born. The family stayed with the two brothers but then left without leaving word of where they were going.

The account from Deeming's two brothers might mean he was not in London during the time of the murders. Inferentially, it can be determined that they believed Deeming's return with his family to London in 1890 was his initial return to the land of his birth. Reports alternatively have Deeming in London at the time of the murders as well as abroad, possibly in South Africa, where he had been implicated in certain crimes during 1888 that involved fraud and confidence trickery. What is known for sure about Deeming's whereabouts is that there happens to be an eighteen-month stretch, encompassing the "canonical" murders, during which Deeming cannot be sufficiently accounted for.

Rumors arose that Deeming had confessed to committing the last two Jack the Ripper murders. Which murders were considered to be the last two with regards to this statement has never been ascertained. It is generally accepted that the five victims of the "canon" were the only women murdered by Jack the Ripper. In this instance, the last two victims would have been Mary Kelly and Catherine Eddowes, yet the "last two" murders of Jack the Ripper to which Deeming allegedly confessed are never named. Deeming's lawyer denied this confession had ever taken place. Without the names of these "last two" victims and a confirmation of this confession, this second-hand hearsay should be viewed with extreme caution.

These confession rumors might have been circulated by the press. The press can be thanked for originally connecting Deeming to the Jack the Ripper case. His English background and what was discovered to be his murderous past allowed the press to paint Deeming as Jack the Ripper. In the press, Deeming was assumed to be in London at the times of the murder, under a false name and seen by a woman with Catherine Eddowes. Deeming's penchant for aliases made this an attractive suggestion. With the murders still fresh in the memory of the police, they examined samples of Deeming's handwriting.

Deeming is known to have used a number of aliases. One of these aliases, "Druin," is where Deeming's most recent connection to the case comes from. After the press first linked Deeming to Jack the Ripper in 1892, he remained stagnant as a suspect until ninety-four years later. In 1987, researchers and authors Keith Skinner and Martin Howells concluded that the Australian document by Dr. Lionel Druitt that originally implicated Montague John Druitt may have been connected to the alleged Deeming confession. There are still many doubts regarding this and other Australian documents that have not been made public, yet the parallels to Deeming, his Australian arrest in 1892, his use of the alias "Druin," and his obvious murderous activities, are apparent. Howells and Skinner made an important breakthrough in this document's traveled history. What does this document amount to? Even if this document was the "alleged" confession of Deeming, that does not necessarily mean that Deeming was Jack the Ripper. All logic points in the other direction. Deeming went to his grave without even confessing to the five murders that were directly connected to him. Why admit to the 1888 murders attributed to Jack the Ripper but not the murders of his two wives and four children? Even if the document were Deeming's confession and that could be proven, why should anyone trust it as the truth?

The 1987 re-announcement of Deeming's involvement with the case did little to improve his status as a viable suspect, similar to the original, 1892 press announcement that Deeming could have been Jack the Ripper. Back then, Deeming may have been investigated by the police but was never seriously taken as a suspect. There is a police file relating to Deeming, with Robert Anderson merely making note of receiving a letter from someone who believed Deeming was Jack the Ripper. It is, however, a rather small file, which does not include the police's investigations regarding Deeming. From the size of the police file on Deeming, the police did not regard him as a serious suspect, and his name was not viably connected with the case as a suspect until the 1987 Howells and Skinner research into Deeming's possible confession. While the Australian documentation is interesting, it cannot be taken seriously, as Deeming appears to be an untrustworthy source of information.

Deeming's known method of killing was dissimilar to that of "Jack the Ripper," including his method of the disposal of the victims' bodies. His marriage to these women, considered to be his *modus operandi*, implies an intimacy that Jack the Ripper lacked. While the argument of changing your mode of killing has been discussed at length within the research community, this is such a drastic change from the murders in London in 1888 that it does not seem at all likely that there could be a connection.

No theorist to date has seriously advocated Frederick Bailey Deeming as a suspect. While that is not enough evidence to dismiss Deeming as a suspect, it does send a strong message. Even at a time when new suspects were being thrust into the spotlight, Howells and Skinner's research connecting Deeming to the Australian document seen by Daniel Farson as early as 1959, he was never advanced or expanded upon as a truly viable suspect. This may be due to the simple fact that Deeming's presence in London at the time of the murders has never been established, and that his method of killing so differed from that of Jack the Ripper.

Begg, Paul, Martin Fido, and Keith Skinner. *The Jack the Ripper A–Z* (1996).
Howells, Martin, and Keith Skinner. *The Ripper Legacy* (1987).
Sugden, Philip. *The Complete History of Jack the Ripper* (2001).
http://www.casebook.org
http://www.frostburg.edu/dept/psyc/mbradley/psyography/gall.html
http://www.leicesteroverseas.com/Whos_Who1.htm

ERNEST DOWSON

Theorist Martin Fido has recently identified Ernest Dowson as the pseudonymous suspect named "Mr. Moring," advanced in 1935 by writer R. Thurston Hopkins. Ernest Dowson was born on August 2, 1867, in Kent, England. He traveled throughout Europe as a youngster, due to his parents suffering from consumption, commonly referred to today as tuberculosis. They sought a more suitable climate to aid their illness, which allowed Dowson to see and experience numerous cultures and societies. Quite possibly as an inherited trait, Dowson was practically an invalid.

In 1886 Dowson entered Queen's College at Oxford. He would only remain there for two years before leaving without obtaining his degree. Leaving school was a direct result of the failing status of his father's business. Dowson began to help his father, and he lived over the actual building that housed his family's business in 1888, during the time of the murders.

At around this time Dowson joined a society of poets called the Rhymer's Club. Their basic philosophy was that art in any form should be produced merely for the sake of artistic value. This faction, known also as the Aesthetic Movement, was born as a reaction to Victorian art. One famous Londoner among the members of the club was William Butler Yeats. Yeats would become a close friend, describing Dowson as, "timid, silent and a little melancholy."

Dowson's poetry would be influenced by his infatuation with a twelve-year old girl named Adelaide Foltinowicz. Dowson proposed marriage, but she refused and eventually married a waiter who had worked for her father. A poem inspired by her contained the famous line "gone with the wind," which is considered the inspiration for the title of Margaret Mitchell's Civil War novel of the same name. Dowson also coined the witticism, "Absinthe makes the tart grow fonder."

During this time a number of events changed the course of Ernest Dowson's life. In 1891 he converted to Catholicism. The worst year of his short life, by far, was 1895. His father died of consumption, his mother committed suicide a short time after the death of his father, and he learned that he was suffering from tuberculosis as well. Dowson wandered around Europe until his love of alcohol took his life in 1900, at the age of 33.

In 1935 writer R. Thurston Hopkins advanced a suspect who fit the description provided by George Hutchinson on the night of the Miller's Court murder. Hopkins used the pseudonym "Mr. Moring" for this suspect. Theorist Martin Fido identified Dowson as this suspect, citing numerous parallels between Hopkins' description of "Mr. Moring" and Dowson. There are differences as well. Hopkins described the father as a well-to-do tradesman. Dowson's father was not well off. His business was failing, prompting Ernest to leave college in 1888. Dowson was also never known to be addicted to any drug other than alcohol, which would not characterize him as the "drug-addicted poet" described by Hopkins. The truth of the matter is that the public may never know who exactly "Mr. Moring" was, and there has been doubt cast upon the validity of Hutchinson's description.

Ernest Dowson did reside in the immediate vicinity of Whitechapel during the time of the murders. He was known for walking the streets late at night and the alcoholism that took his life is that of legend. Dowson had no history of violence against women, and the verse of his poetry does not depict him as a violent misogynist. Those who knew him well describe him as frail and timid.

Dowson died in relative obscurity. After the deaths of his parents, he continued writing and has only recently become known as one of the top lower-tier poets of his day. His pure belief in art is admired in current times, but he is mainly connected with the way he destroyed his life through abusing alcohol. If he had taken better care of himself and lived longer, he might have achieved the status of major poet, akin to his friend Yeats, who believed in the same principles as Ernest Dowson.

Hopkins, R. Thurston. *Life and Death at the Old Bailey* (1935).
http://www.fortunecity.com/tinpan/quick step/1103/dowson_ernest.htm

http://www.photoaspects.com/chesil/dow son/

MONTAGUE JOHN DRUITT

Extremely little was known about Montague John Druitt when he was originally named as a suspect in the Jack the Ripper case. Incorrectly identified as a doctor by Melville MacNaghten, Druitt has long been considered the prime suspect in this investigation. There are more books and theories dedicated to Druitt than any other single suspect. More research has been conducted on Druitt than almost any two other suspects. Due to the diligent work of numerous researchers, a complete chronology of Montague John Druitt may be offered.

Montague John Druitt was born in 1857, in Wimborne, Dorset, in Southern England. Formally educated at Winchester and New College, Oxford, Druitt received a Bachelor of Arts in Literature and Humanities. After graduating in 1880 he was employed as a schoolmaster at Mr. Valentine's School for Boys in Blackheath. Druitt would remain at Mr. Valentine's until approximately November 30, 1888, when he was mysteriously dismissed from his duties. All that is known about Druitt's dismissal is that he was "in serious trouble at the school."

While performing his duties as schoolmaster at Mr. Valentine's, Druitt began studying for the bar examination to begin his career as an attorney. Three years later, in 1885, he was called to the bar and attached to the Western Circuit, while still employed by Mr. Valentine in Blackheath. In 1887 Druitt became a Special Pleader for the Western Circuit. A Special Pleader mainly handled civil disputes, performed administrative duties, such as preparing briefs, or acted as arbitrator before cases went to court. Special Pleaders did not have the authority to address judges or juries. His status apparently rose during the time of the murders, as there were a number of cases where Druitt actively participated in court, most notably arguing and winning an insanity defense in September of 1888. When research revealed that Druitt was not a doctor, as Melville MacNaghten had intimated in his 1894 memorandum, Druitt was initially perceived as a failed barrister, yet further study of Druitt's legal career proved otherwise.

While at school Druitt excelled at sports, including cricket and fives, a game somewhat similar to handball. His amateur cricketing career continued after school when he joined the Morden Cricket Club in the summer of 1881, later becoming the Club's Secretary in 1884. One year later he would achieve the position of Honorable Secretary and

Treasurer of the Blackheath Cricket and Lawn Tennis Company. This allowed him to be closer to his job at Mr. Valentine's. Druitt would remain in this post at the Blackheath Cricket club until December 21, 1888, when during a meeting it was announced that Druitt would be effectively removed from his post. Only one month prior to that, on November 19, Druitt actively participated in the club's monthly meeting. It was during this one-month span that something occurred to facilitate his removal from the post and from the club. As this was a local club of Blackheath, it may be inferentially determined that the club was reacting to Druitt's untimely dismissal from Mr. Valentine's School for Boys.

According to Neil Rhind, a local historian and authority on Druitt and his connection to Blackheath, Mr. Valentine was either a member or a patron of the local sporting clubs. It seems therefore likely that Mr. Valentine leaked the reason why Druitt was dismissed from the school to one of the members of the cricket club, prompting Druitt's removal from his post and the cricket club. Rhind has asserted that secrecy regarding this 1888 dismissal still exists among the historians in the town of Blackheath.

Druitt's family has been another point of controversy. At the inquest into Montague's death, his older brother William reportedly stated that he and his mother were Montague's only living relatives. This was untrue. At the time of the inquest into Druitt's death, both William and his mother Ann were alive, but there was also Druitt's first cousin, Lionel, three sisters who were alive in 1885, one of whom later committed suicide, and two brothers, also alive in 1885. Death certificates on these five

other siblings, one of whom is known to have lived well after the death of Montague, have not been traced, so it must be assumed that Druitt's brothers and sisters were still alive only three years after the death of their father William Sr. So why did William lie? A theory proposed by researcher Andrew Holloway on this question will be discussed shortly.

When Montague's father died in middle to late 1885, his mother's health soon began to deteriorate, taking the form of paranoid delusions. There was a history of both insanity and suicide in Druitt's family. When Ann's health got worse in the summer of 1888, she attempted suicide. Ann was hospitalized at Brooke Asylum, Clapton, in July 1888, where she was certified insane. During September 1888, she was transferred to an asylum in Brighton. Ann would remain in Brighton until May 1890, when she was transferred to Chiswick. Six months later, Ann Druitt would die in a Chiswick mental asylum.

During the time of the murders, Druitt held down two jobs, working at both Mr. Valentine's School and Arthur Jeff's Chambers, where he had practiced law for three years. He continued to actively play cricket during this time. A chronology of what is known of Druitt's movements until his death is as follows. On the 3rd, 4th, 10th, and 11th of August, he played cricket at Bournemouth. On the 1st of September, the morning after Mary Ann Nichols was found, he was playing at Dorset. On the 8th of September, only hours after the murder of Annie Chapman, he was playing cricket at Blackheath, his local club. Sometime during September, Druitt made a successful insanity defense for a client in court, indicating that he had moved up the ranks from Special Pleader. On the 1st of October, one day after the double murder, Druitt appeared in court for local conservatives during voter registration hearings. He would return on the 6th of October in connection with this case. On November 19, Druitt actively participated in the monthly meeting of the Blackheath Cricket and Lawn Tennis Company, still to this date acting as their Secretary and Treasurer. Three days later, Druitt would make a successful appeal on behalf of the local conservatives in their voter registration case. On November 30 Druitt was dismissed from his position at Mr. Valentine's School for "unspecified reasons." It is likely that Montague John Druitt committed suicide, unbeknownst to the cricket club members, on December 1, although a date of December 3 or 4 is generally accepted, dates derived from testimony provided by William Druitt.

On the final day of 1888 waterman Henry Winslade discovered Druitt's body floating in the Thames River. Winslade summoned policeman George Moulson, who reported the finding of the body. Stones were found in the pockets of Druitt's overcoat. One can only presume this was done to weigh him down, which is awkwardly inconsistent with a suicide attempt. Committing suicide by drowning is relatively simple—just do not come up for air. The Coroner's inquest was held on January 2, 1889. Begun and ended on the same day, the overall conclusion of the inquest was "suicide whilst of unsound mind."

After the Coroner's inquest Montague John Druitt's name lay in public obscurity for seventy-six years. The first public mentioning of Montague John Druitt as Jack the Ripper was in Tom Cullen's 1965 book, *Autumn of Terror*. It should be noted that six years earlier, researcher Dan Farson revealed the initials M. J. D. on his television program, *Farson's Guide to the British*. Farson and Cullen had received the suspect's name from the same source, yet the real story begins at a much earlier date.

On February 13, 1894, *The Sun* began running a series of articles postulating that Thomas Cutbush was Jack the Ripper. Ten days later, a report marked "confidential" was filed at Scotland Yard, authored by Assistant Chief Constable Melville MacNaghten. This report, known as the MacNaghten Memorandum, was written to refute the claims made about Thomas Cutbush. What this memorandum has done is provide the names of three suspects thought much more likely than Cutbush to be Jack the Ripper.

In MacNaghten's report, of which there are two known versions, and another version alluded to, it is clear that MacNaghten leans toward Montague John Druitt as his preferred suspect. There is definitive language difference between the two known existing copies of the MacNaghten Memorandum. The document filed at Scotland Yard reflects a polished version of MacNaghten's report, while the Lady Aberconway version resembles what one would find in an early draft. Lady Christabel Aberconway was MacNaghten's youngest daughter. The language within this document has made Montague John Druitt the major suspect. The language differences between the two known versions reveal MacNaghten's personal preference for Druitt as the prime suspect.

The segment where Druitt is named also displays noteworthy variances. MacNaghten's personal copy, transcribed by his daughter Lady Aberconway, reads,

(1) A Mr. M J Druitt, said to be a doctor & of good family, who disappeared at the time of the Miller's Court murder, whose body (which was said to have been upwards of a month in the water) was found in the Thames on 31st Dec.—or about 7 weeks after that murder. He was sexually insane and from private info I have little doubt that but that his own family believed him to have been the murderer.

The Scotland Yard version of the MacNaghten Memorandum reads,

No. 1. Mr. M. J. Druitt a doctor of about 41 years of age & of fairly good family, who disappeared at the time of the Miller's Court murder, and whose body was found floating in the Thames on 31st Dec: i.e. 7 weeks after the said murder. The body was said to have been in the water a month, or more—on it was found a season ticket between Blackheath and London. From private information I have little doubt but that his own family suspected this man of being the Whitechapel murderer; it was alleged that he was sexually insane.

This is the pivotal section where MacNaghten lays the foundations of his beliefs against Druitt. The major biographical errors are worth reexamining. In both reports, the official and the draft, Druitt is described as a doctor. Druitt worked two jobs, one as a barrister and the other as an assistant master at a boys' school. He was never a doctor. In the draft report, his age is stated as 41. Druitt was only 31. Both versions have Druitt disappearing at the time of the Miller's Court murder. Again, both versions are wrong. During November, after the Miller's Court murder, Druitt made a successful appeal in court, contributed to his cricket club's monthly meeting, and stayed on at Mr. Valen-

tine's until dismissed at the end of the month. Druitt continued on with his normal daily life after the November 9 murder.

Examining the two separate versions, the end statements regarding Druitt are strikingly similar. One version is more readable than another, but the internal meanings coincide. There are three major items within this segment. Druitt was either "sexually insane," or alleged to be so. This knowledge appears to have come from MacNaghten's "private information." An internal examination of MacNaghten's private information makes that statement a leap of faith. What it could refer to one can only speculate. It may refer to Druitt's dismissal from Mr. Valentine's school for taking liberties with a student or students. It could also be a supposition on the part of MacNaghten due to his beliefs about the murderer.

The next two items co-exist perhaps as one: MacNaghten's private information and the fact that Druitt's own family believed that he was the murderer. Where did this private information come from? Many researchers and theorists have arrived at numerous possibilities. One such possibility is the Private Secretary to three consecutive Police Commissioners, Walter Boutlbee. Boutlbee married Ellen Baker, the niece of Alfred Mayo, who was a distant relative of Thomas Druitt. As Boutlbee was in Scotland Yard when MacNaghten appears to have obtained his private information, most feel the information came from Boutlbee. The immediate problem is this: How would Thomas Druitt have known that Montague was "sexually insane"? And what was their specific relation to one another?

There is a more distant link between the two families. In 1855 Mac-Naghten's father appointed Druitt's aunt's brother to the board of the East India Company. This possible connection has never led anywhere.

Researcher Stephen P. Ryder has theorized a third possible familial connection in a recently rediscovered letter sent to Robert Anderson by the 26th Earl of Crawford, James Lindsay. Lindsay was considered a close friend of antiquarian book dealer Bernard Quaritch. Quaritch was the editor of a number of books collaborated on by Emily Druitt, Montague's cousin. From the letter, Lindsay states that the woman, whom he did not know by name, was afraid that suspicion would be placed upon her and her family. Lindsay also states that the woman was "supposed to be nearly related" to this man. Despite the lack of a date on this letter, it would appear that the unnamed woman made her fears known during the time of the murders. This would imply that a cousin of Montague believed that he was Jack the Ripper while he was calmly carrying out his day-to-day duties. No suspicion was ever cast on Montague Druitt during the time of the murders, so far as is known. It would have been investigated by Anderson, or there would have been some mention of Emily Druitt's suspicion in the files. There is none. Therefore, it appears that the possibility that this letter was sent after the murders stopped is a strong one. This could explain why the woman was fearful of having suspicion cast upon her family, yet was not afraid of being violently murdered by one of her own "near" relatives. Assuming this to be the case, the question arises that if this information came from Emily Druitt, whom did she get it from? This may directly correlate to MacNaghten's

statement that Druitt's own family believed him to be the murderer. Recently, Ryder has discovered that the Emily Druitt whom he hypothesizes was the woman discussed in James Lindsay's letter to Anderson is a different Emily Druitt than the one related to Montague. As a result, Ryder's theory becomes null and void regarding Mac-Naghten's private information.

These are just a couple of the possible explanations of where MacNaghten might have received his private information. Future research will provide us with more possibilities.

There have been other suggestions as to where MacNaghten picked up his private information. Donald McCormick has suggested that it came from painter and suspect, Walter Sickert. According to McCormick, this information regarding Druitt was passed on at a dinner at the Garricks Club. McCormick claims that he was told this by an unnamed London doctor whose father had been at Oxford with Druitt. The man knew Sickert and told Sickert about Druitt, which in turn Sickert repeated to MacNaghten, convincing MacNaghten of Druitt's guilt.

This statement has serious temporal and internal issues. The doctor's father was at Oxford with Druitt, which would make them about the same age. If this unnamed father of the London doctor had his son as early as the time he was attending Oxford, the son would have been approximately ten when his father realized these suspicions. If the London doctor then told McCormick, then this could not have taken place until well past 1911, which is the year Donald McCormick was born. A reasonable date for this conversation would be some time in the 1930s, when Mc-

Cormick states his research into Jack the Ripper began. This would mean that a fifty-year-old doctor was telling a forty-year-old story that he had heard when he was approximately ten, but more likely younger, to a researcher who then waited forty years to reveal it.

McCormick had viewed the list of suspects from the MacNaghten Memorandum, working closely with Dan Farson in 1959, the same year McCormick came out with a book proposing his own suspect. In this first edition McCormick mentions nothing about the story involving the London doctor, Sickert, and MacNaghten. McCormick must surely have heard the story by 1959, if he had heard it at all. So why would McCormick wait eleven years, and two editions, to print it in 1970? The answer may lie in two books by Osbert Sitwell. Sitwell stated that Walter Sickert told him about an elderly couple that rented him a room some years after the murders stopped. Researcher Roy Hidson has identified this room as No. 6 Mornington Crescent. The couple supposedly told Sickert that their previous lodger was Jack the Ripper. Sitwell stated that Sickert's conversations continually revolved around Jack the Ripper, due in part to his knowledge of the identity of the murderer. How this relates to Druitt is simple. McCormick published the first naming of Sickert's unnamed veterinary student in 1970, as "Drewen," "Drewitt," or "Hewitt." Using Walter Sickert as a possible source for MacNaghten's private information might have helped diffuse scrutiny surrounding McCormick's own untraced research, as Sickert was known to have a deep interest in this case. All the elements of McCormick's tale are of a historical nature, with the exception of the source that supplied this information.

Researcher Paul Feldman has taken McCormick's tale and theorized that MacNaghten's private information might have come from poet and suspect James Kenneth Stephen rather than Walter Sickert, and that only the initials M and J were given to MacNaghten. Feldman is obviously pushing his own suspect, James Maybrick, claiming that MacNaghten misinterpreted what was intended. These possibilities will also continue to arise as long as the identity of Jack the Ripper remains a mystery.

Two later public references to Druitt occurred in 1898 and 1902. The first one came from Arthur Griffiths, a crime historian and the Inspector of Prisons. In his 1898 *Mysteries of Police and Crime* he published the direct opinions of MacNaghten. These opinions were taken from MacNaghten's personal draft copy of the memorandum. Griffiths did not mention the names of MacNaghten's three suspects, probably part of an agreement with MacNaghten. No new information was added to any of the three suspects, so it can also be assumed that MacNaghten considered the case closed.

Journalist George R. Sims was a regular writer for *The Referee*. Under the pseudonym "Dagonet," he continually referred to the Jack the Ripper case. In 1902, writing under his pseudonym, Sims stated that while an intense suspect investigation was going on, the real Jack the Ripper had thrown himself into the Thames. This was an obvious reference to Druitt. Sims continued by stating that the police were actively searching for Druitt when he was found dead. This has never been established, and the fact that Druitt continued his daily life as if nothing were different should indicate that he was not sought after, before his death. No police files outline a December 1888 search for any suspect matching Druitt. The Scotland Yard version of the MacNaghten Memorandum is neatly filed with the additional police records on Jack the Ripper. If a search was conducted for Druitt during December 1888, why is the documentation on this investigation nowhere to be found?

One year later Sims was at it again. He reiterated his statements that the police suspected Druitt at the time they found him in the Thames. In this article Sims states that he is not betraying a confidence in revealing this information and further mentions that Griffiths had been given access to a Home Office Report containing the same information. It was Sims's article to which Inspector Abberline made the statement, *"I know all about that story. But what does this amount to? Simply this. Soon after the last murder the body of a young doctor was found in the Thames, but there is absolutely nothing beyond the fact that he was found at that time to incriminate him."* Abberline's statement cements the fact that there was no investigation or search for Druitt in December of 1888. If Abberline did not know about the search for Druitt, then it did not take place.

MacNaghten discussed the case publicly on two separate occasions. In 1913, he gave an interview to *The Daily Mail*. In this interview MacNaghten explained that he had destroyed all of his notes regarding the information that led him toward Druitt as a suspect. A year later, his own book was published, titled *Days of My Years*. He confidently asserts the murderer's brain had given way and that he had killed himself soon thereafter. This echoes both versions of the memorandum and is still incorrect.

This brings us back to Dan Farson in 1959. While compiling information for his television program, Farson appealed to the public for any information concerning Jack the Ripper. This appeal produced the notes shown to him by Lady Aberconway. It also produced another document that has become one of legend over the years.

Farson received a letter from Australia from a man named A. Knowles. Knowles claimed to have read a document, titled *The East End Murderer—I Knew Him*, written by a Lionel Druitt, Drewitt, or Drewery. Knowles was relying on his memory, so he could not be positive of the author's last name. The document was never found, and a great deal of research into it has been undertaken. What the Australian link seems to amount to is that this document may be an article in an 1890 newspaper, the *St. Arnaud Mercury*, in which Montague John Druitt is never mentioned or implied. The entire Australian connection turned up nothing with regards to Druitt.

While Farson only revealed Druitt's initials in 1959, six years later Tom Cullen revealed his full name, along with the portion of the MacNaghten Memorandum related to the suspects, directly from the notes in the possession of Lady Aberconway. The following year, Scotland Yard released their version of the memorandum. The relevant section of this document displayed the differences in the two versions. Robin Odell, in his 1966 book, *Jack the Ripper in Fact and Fiction*, published the relevant section.

In 1970 Donald McCormick printed the updated version of his 1959 book, *The Identity of Jack the Ripper*. McCormick continued to push the case for his suspect, Vassily Konovalov, despite not adding on his information that Mikhael Ostrog was an alias used by Konovalov. Instead McCormick told a story, outlined earlier, about a possible link to MacNaghten's private information. As McCormick never has pushed for Druitt as a suspect, the question arises of why McCormick related this tale regarding Druitt? As the Scotland Yard version of the memorandum had been recently published in 1966, the memorandum's lesser reliance on Druitt as the murderer afforded McCormick an opportunity. McCormick had already connected Ostrog to Konovalov, and was apparently trying to sabotage Druitt as a suspect.

In 1972 Dan Farson came out with his own book on the subject. His further research into Druitt revealed that he had found a Dr. Lionel Druitt, Montague's cousin, listed in the medical directories for Australia. Farson also found that Lionel had maintained a general practice in the East End during 1879. Farson assumed that this was where Montague not only picked up his medical knowledge, but also his knowledge of the East End. This was an unnecessary last link, that Druitt became familiar with the East End from his cousin, as Montague's office was in the East End, at 9 King's Bench Walk. Farson also remembered receiving the letter from A. Knowles in 1959 regarding a document in Australia written by Lionel Druitt. Despite this document never having been traced, Farson believed it existed and viewed it as a substantial piece of evidence against Montague John Druitt.

The following year an article was published in *The Cricketer* which, on face value, could have eliminated Druitt as a suspect forever. The author, Irving Ro-

senwater, traced the amateur cricketing career of Druitt. He found that Druitt was playing cricket on the day that Mary Ann Nichols was found dead, and only hours after the murder of Annie Chapman took place. Research has established that trains ran to Blackheath starting at 5:10 A.M., so Druitt could have caught one after the murder of Chapman, returned home to Mr. Valentine's, cleaned up, got some sleep and then went to the Cricket field at the Blackheath Cricket Club.

Only one new theory regarding Druitt was offered over the next couple of years. During 1975, in the *International Journal of Psychiatry*, Seymour Shuster argued that Druitt might have witnessed some type of surgery that produced a trauma. This trauma manifested itself and was expressed in the murders of these women. This is an inarguable point, because there is no tangible point. Druitt's state of mind has always been a cornerstone of controversy. If Druitt were the murderer, then it would be obvious that there was something wrong with his mind. The fact that there were doctors in his family could have caused this, prevented it, or had no lasting effect whatsoever.

Martin Howells and Keith Skinner next examined Druitt in 1987. Their book, *The Ripper Legacy*, added a number of new theories on the subject. One such theory was that Druitt was one of a group of upper-class Oxford homosexuals. They found out that he was Jack the Ripper, lured him to Chiswick and murdered him to protect their own names. This point must be briefly examined. If Montague was the murderer and was caught, why would this have placed these men in jeopardy? This brings us to Howells and Skinner's second theory.

Howells and Skinner believed that one member of this alleged group of homosexuals was Prince Albert Victor, the Duke of Clarence. While there is external support for Prince Albert Victor engaging in homosexual activities, claiming that he was involved in a secret group of upper-class homosexuals is something that can never be disproved or, unfortunately, proved. If Prince Albert Victor were a member of this group, due to his social standing he would be protected at all costs, as evidenced by the Cleveland Street Scandal. Any ravings from an insane sexual serial killer linking Prince Albert Victor to this group would be chalked up as simply that, insane ravings.

The duo also attempted to provide a direct link between Druitt and the Prince. They tried to establish that Druitt might have been a personal friend of the Prince. Druitt was invited to a function attended by the Prince during the middle of December, but so were many others, and not all could be considered friends of the Prince. Druitt was also supposed to be a look-alike of the Prince, and this is intertwined with the above theories as to why Druitt was murdered.

Druitt's suicide has been a debated question over the years. Howells and Skinner state that it might have been his brother William who helped with the staged suicide, possibly taking an active part. There is strong evidence that Druitt did not commit suicide, but in this specific scenario, these upper-class homosexuals would have to have confided in William as to why Montague needed to be killed. Then William would have been privy to the story, and he, not a homosexual, would know a secret that could bring shame to the Crown. Con-

sidering the lengths to which the Royal Family will go to protect itself from public scandal, it is doubtful it would have recruited Montague's own brother to assist in his execution.

These are some of the major theories Howells and Skinner put forward in trying to establish Druitt as Jack the Ripper. They establish some important conclusions, such as Druitt's resemblance to Prince Albert Victor and that Druitt's suicide possessed a number of strange elements. Perhaps their most important contribution to this field was their research into the Australian connection, begun with the letter sent to Daniel Farson. While there still has been no Australian document to surface, Howells and Skinner's research into this possibility led them to the conclusion that if a document existed, it pertained to Frederick Bailey Deeming, and not Montague John Druitt.

Another article in *The Cricketer* was written in 1990 concerning Druitt. The author, Andrew Holloway, suggested that Montague's older brother, William, in a plot to gain control of the family fortune, murdered him. Holloway further postulates that it was William who planted the story to the police that Montague was Jack the Ripper. This was done to shift suspicion away from any investigation into Montague's suicide. Holloway goes on to state that Montague was drugged and subsequently dumped in the Thames.

A number of problems arise with this theory. After Montague's father died, William was given the bulk of the estate, inheriting the family farm in order to take care of his mother. Montague had been given a sizeable amount of money, but it was relatively small in comparison to that received by his brother and three sisters. Montague had already borrowed against that money to begin studying for the bar. Montague's wages were ample enough to support himself, but as far as the family fortune was concerned, it would make no sense for William to murder him for money.

The planting of the idea that Montague was Jack the Ripper was also suggested as a source for MacNaghten's private information regarding Montague. This theory is erroneous in its basis, because if William murdered Montague, then decided to frame him as Jack the Ripper, a full-scale investigation into Montague's life would have taken place. This may have led them back to the mysterious happenings surrounding his suicide. Because William lied at the coroner's inquest, stating that Montague only had two living relatives, this could have led the police directly back to him. The inquest was opened and closed on the same day. There was no detailed investigation or search into Montague's habits and practices during the time of murders, indicating that it was not William who provided this information. When Montague was found in the Thames River, MacNaghten was not even a member of the police force. Why would William plant this information at least six months after his brother's suicide case had been closed?

The idea that Montague was drugged has been medically challenged. Coroner Thomas Diplock presided over the inquest into the death of Montague Druitt. During this inquest it was declared that the autopsy showed no signs of poison. This is not to conclude that Montague was not murdered and that William was the not the man who committed this murder. In Holloway's theory, however, his ideas and postulations do not add up to the known evidence.

The rest of the 1990s saw a couple of eclectic theories regarding Druitt thrust upon this field. Christopher Smith wrote in a three-part article series that Druitt was still considered the prime suspect, while listing reasons for suspecting Dr. William Wynn Westcott. William Henry argued that astrological evidence proved Druitt to be Jack the Ripper. Through the use of anagrams in the Goulston Street Graffito, John Wilding combined Druitt with James Kenneth Stephen as co-murderers. The murders were supposedly committed to protect both Prince Albert Victor and the Prince of Wales. Furthering this, Andy and Sue Parlour's research led them to a similar conclusion of co-murderers, including Dr. William Gull as the man who sought out and recruited Stephen and Druitt.

Discussed above are the relevant theories that researchers and theorists have put forth over the years regarding Montague John Druitt's viability as a suspect. At the heart of all these theories lies MacNaghten's belief that Druitt was the murderer, but the evidence known today shows that MacNaghten's beliefs were almost totally wrong concerning Druitt.

Montague John Druitt was an educated man holding down two jobs and excelling at various sports. As the murders were committed at night, the question of where the murderer lodged comes to the forefront. Much has been made of the possibility that the murderer lodged at one of the many doss houses that did not require anything other than payment for a room. Druitt had an office in the East End, so it has been suggested that he lodged there.

This is inconsistent with the pattern of movement on the night of the double murder, as Druitt inevitably had to return to where he lived at Mr. Valentine's School in Blackheath. This brings up an important question. What exactly were his duties at the school?

Druitt was a lawyer by day, so he must have worked at the school during the night. He was an Assistant Master and may have been employed there to watch over the school at night. These duties would have included watching over the children in case of any emergencies. If Druitt committed these murders, he would have had to leave the school unattended at night on at least four separate occasions. Some might attempt to describe this as the "serious trouble" that prompted his dismissal. That does not seem to be the case. It is highly doubtful that this "serious trouble" could be attributed to the Jack the Ripper murders. This is evident, as Mr. Valentine never informed the authorities of such a connection. If Mr. Valentine had known Druitt to be a murderer and it was later revealed that he had known, the school he helped create would most likely have been shut down.

Another problem is that there were no trains after 12:25 A.M. or before 5:10 A.M. in order to get Druitt back to Blackheath. This would mean that on the night of Mary Ann Nichols' murder, Druitt would have waited at least an hour for a train to get back home. On the night of the double murder, increase that time to at least two and a half hours. On the night of the Mary Ann Nichols investigation, the railway lines were checked soon after the discovery of the body, and nothing was found to be suspicious. Druitt had to get back to Blackheath before the morning and the arrival of the schoolmaster in charge of the boys during the day. On the night of the double murder, there were two separate police force investigations, and the time Druitt needed to wait to get home had almost tripled from the night of Mary Ann Nichols's murder.

Druitt was dismissed on November 30 from his job at Mr. Valentine's. His brother William describes this dismissal as "serious trouble." The lack of public communication regarding this "trouble" indicates it was most likely sexual in nature. That would make Druitt either a pedophile or an ephebophile, which is the correct psychological term for an adult engaging in sexual activity with adolescents after puberty but before adulthood. This was probably discovered toward the end of the school term, when the young students were getting ready to go home. Perhaps one of them alerted a parent, who in turn contacted Mr. Valentine. An accusation like this, if Druitt did not strenuously challenge it, could have forced Mr. Valentine to dismiss him. This might account for two checks found on his possession if Mr. Valentine felt bad for dismissing his longtime friend but knew it to be the right move. If there had been any direct evidence against Druitt, as opposed to mere conjecture, there would have been grounds for non-payment of services, as well as grounds for Druitt's arrest. This suggest the possibility that his dismissal was based on speculation or, perhaps, an outright accusation from a student or a parent.

Researchers have suggested that this "serious trouble" was in reference to a mental breakdown. As he committed suicide on the following day, this is something that must be discussed, not only in regards to his dismissal, but also regarding the possibility that he could have been Jack the Ripper. From Mac-Naghten, it was thought early on that the murder in Miller's Court weighed heavily on Druitt and that he killed himself immediately thereafter. That misstatement has been thoroughly discussed and discredited. That said, what exactly was Druitt's state of mind during this time?

During September and October, Druitt was successfully arguing cases in court, while also playing numerous cricket matches. The murders obviously did not affect him during the first two months. After the Miller's Court murder, Druitt carried on with his normal daily patterns, practicing law during the day and watching over the children at night. Druitt also attended his monthly cricket club meeting on November 19, where he actively participated. His participation during this meeting implies that, on November 19, there was no suspicion outwardly displayed toward Montague. MacNaghten could not have been more wrong. There is still the suicide to contend with and the note found by his brother William.

Suicide had run in the Druitt family, along with diabetes. His mother Ann had attempted suicide in June 1888, and was committed to an asylum the following month. She would be transferred to a number of different asylums before finally passing away. She suffered from diabetes and believed she was being electrocuted. Ann displayed paranoid delusions, such as the sensation of being electrocuted, severe depression encompassing melancholia, and suicidal urges. There are different forms of diabetes, but it is safe to assume that she suffered from the most common form, diabetes mellitus.

Diabetes is a disorder where the pancreas produces little or no insulin. Insulin is the hormone responsible for the absorption of glucose into cells for energy, and into the liver for fat storage. A body's inability to store glucose results in fatigue. Montague John Druitt did not suffer from fatigue. Diabetes is acquired through a predisposition of heredity. One point to mention is that the suicides occurring in the Druitt family were specific to females. His mother, his younger sister, his aunt, and his grandmother all committed suicide or attempted suicide.

It is possible that this hereditary trait of diabetes, culminating in depressions and suicide were specific to the women of the Druitt family. There is a disease known as diabetic pregnancy, in which a woman can acquire diabetes mellitus during pregnancy. As diabetes is hereditary, one would imagine that the predisposition for diabetic pregnancy would exist within that hereditary scheme. This would eliminate Montague Druitt from carrying that gene for diabetes, negating the predisposition for side effects that go along with diabetes and calling his suicide into question.

The date of Druitt's dismissal is known from evidence given at the inquest by William Druitt. William gave the date as December 30, but, due to Druitt's earlier death, this date has been interpreted as November 30. As there was no formal investigation into Druitt, this vital date was never checked. Oral tradition regarding this matter has been relatively quiet, according to local historian Neil Rhind. The dismissal took place on a date between his monthly cricket club meeting on November 19 and the following month's meeting on December 21. Examining what was found on Druitt's body when it was pulled from the Thames River offers a more plausible date of death as December 1. Based on that evidence, it is safe to say that the dismissal occurred between November 19 and December 1. November 30 is so readily accepted because it perfectly lines up with Druitt's dismissal. Druitt's suicide, however, has recently been challenged by a number of previously mentioned researchers and theorists.

There appears to be no hereditary predisposition toward diabetes or suicide in the males of the Druitt family. The items found on Druitt when he was pulled from the Thames and, more importantly, what William Druitt found when Montague's residence was searched must also be re-examined. When Montague was pulled from the Thames, his body was already decomposed, but there were no signs of injury indicative of a suicide. There were, however, four large stones found in his jacket pockets, more indicative of a murder than a suicide. The two checks found on his body have been discussed above as possibly coming from Mr. Valentine, as his dismissal was prompted by allegations that were never publicly proven. There were also a couple of rail tickets, one a first class season ticket from Blackheath to London, and an unused return-trip ticket from Hammersmith to Charing Cross. Why would he purchase this return ticket if Druitt was intending to commit suicide?

What William Druitt found among his brother's things is of equal relevance. In William's inquest testimony, where it is known he lied about Montague's living relatives, William produced a letter he claimed was addressed to him from Montague. The letter read, "Since Friday I felt I was going to be like mother,

and the best thing for me to do was die." As suggested by the evidence found on Druitt, most notably his unused return ticket, his death took place on December 1, a Saturday. As a result of William's inquest testimony, it has been accepted that all of a sudden, and after only one day thinking he was going to become insane, Montague Druitt committed suicide. Generally, a man considering suicide thinks about it for more than just one day. Druitt's dismissal may have caused him to commit suicide. Why, then, would the note mention Montague's fear of his mother's insanity? The note may have been manufactured. The likeliest candidate would be William, who discovered the note and produced it as evidence during the inquest.

William Druitt lied about the number of living relatives Montague had. He is also responsible for the inaccurate dating of Montague's death made by researchers in the twentieth century. William said that he was told on December 11 that Montague had not been seen in chambers for more than a week. Researchers and theorists trying to correctly place Druitt's death have estimated, from William's statement that death occurred on either December 3 or December 4. A correction was prompted by the evidence of the unused return-trip train ticket found on his body. This ticket was dated December 1. If William had written the suicide note, he slipped up and has gotten away with it for all these years. Even the dismissal of Montague from Valentine's comes from William and might be incorrect. Who is to say that the dismissal might not have occurred days prior to November 30? Certainly, not anyone connected with Mr. Valentine's School, or Blackheath, as there is still silence in Blackheath regarding Montague John Druitt's dismissal.

It is possible that Montague contacted William to let him know what had happened at Mr. Valentine's. William might then have arranged to meet him at Chiswick, an out-of-the-way place where William would eventually place their mother Ann in an asylum. William then produced the suicide note, but not until after the body was found. If William had found the note earlier, then why did he not contact the authorities to search for his brother?

Montague John Druitt was an able barrister and a sporting man, yet also most likely a sexually disturbed pedophile. Attacks on women are not consistent with pedophiles, who prey on younger children, as opposed to people their own age. Time constraints, however, negatively affect the case against Druitt. The original case against Druitt, made by Melville MacNaghten, was built upon an improper foundation. Subsequent research into proving Druitt's guilt has come up short at every turn. Further research has indicated that Montague John Druitt may have been murdered.

It must be reiterated, however, that Druitt worked in close proximity to the murder sites and had an intimate knowledge of the East End, going as far back as 1879, when his cousin Lionel worked as an Assistant House Surgeon in the immediate area. Research shall continue into the background of this legendary suspect. As more information surfaces, theorists and historians shall continue to interpret evidence on both sides of the issue, making Montague John Druitt not only a suspect, but also an important investigative tool.

Beadle, William. *Jack the Ripper: Anatomy of a Myth* (1995).

Begg, Paul. *Jack the Ripper: The Uncensored Facts* (1988).

_____, Martin Fido, and Keith Skinner. *The Jack the Ripper A–Z* (1996).

Clayman, Dr. Charles B. *The American Medical Association Encyclopedia of Medicine* (1989).

Cullen, Tom. *Autumn of Terror* (1965).

Farson, Dan. *Jack the Ripper* (1972).

Feldman, Paul. *Jack the Ripper: The Final Chapter* (1997).

Griffiths, Arthur. *Mysteries of Police and Crime* (1898).

Henry, William. *The Criminologist* (Spring 1993).

Holloway, Andrew. *The Cricketer* (December 1990).

Howells, Martin, and Keith Skinner. *The Ripper Legacy* (1987).

MacNaghten, Melville. *Days of My Years* (1914).

McCormick, Donald. *The Identity of Jack the Ripper* (1970).

Odell, Robin. *In Fact and Fiction* (1966).

Parlour, Andy, and Sue Parlour. *The Jack the Ripper Whitechapel Murders* (1997).

Reber, Arthur S. *The Penguin Dictionary of Psychology* (1985).

Rosenwater, Irving. *The Cricketer* (January 1973).

Rumbelow, Donald. *The Complete Jack the Ripper* (1987).

Ryder, Stephen P. *Ripperologist* (March 2003).

Shuster, Seymour. *International Journal of Psychiatry* (1975).

Sims, George R. *The Referee* (1902–1903).

Sitwell, Osbert. *A Free House* (1947).

_____. *Noble Essences* (1950).

Smith, Christopher. *The Criminologist* (Winter 1992–Autumn 1993).

Sugden, Philip. *The Complete History of Jack the Ripper* (2002).

Wilding, John. *Jack the Ripper Revealed* (1993).

http://www.casebook.org

FRANK EDWARDS

In 1959, George Edwards informed two newspapers that he believed his cousin Frank was Jack the Ripper. After the double murder of Elizabeth Stride and Catherine Eddowes, Frank had visited his cousin George. Among Frank's possessions, according to George, were a razor and a shirt with a bloodstained collar. After reading about the Leon Goldstein sighting, both George and another cousin came to the conclusion that Frank was the murderer.

Leon Goldstein had walked into Leman Street Police Station on October 1, the day after the double murder. Goldstein had been walking home just prior to the murder of Elizabeth Stride and had been seen by Mrs. Fanny Mortimer. Goldstein was carrying a small black bag that he claimed was filled with empty cigarette boxes. It is from this description that the rumor that Jack the Ripper had carried a black bag around with him first gained prominence.

Here is an another instance of someone suspected of committing these horrific murders but not accused for upwards of 70 years, well after the suspect has died. In this particular instance, George Edwards suspected his cousin Frank after the double murder, yet said

nothing. He also remained silent after the November 9 murder in Miller's Court.

Jack the Ripper's weapon was a knife, not a razor. The matter of the bloodstained collar could have resulted from anything, including cutting himself shaving with the razor. The black bag incident that pertained to Leon Goldstein is nothing more than that, pertaining to Leon Goldstein. Frank Edwards, in this story, carried an attaché case, not a small black bag. All of these facts together should set Frank Edwards aside.

It is noteworthy that George Edwards' story about his cousin was finally revealed in 1959, the same year that Daniel Farson produced his Jack the Ripper episode for the BBC. Daniel Farson had appealed for any information regarding Jack the Ripper, and it appears that the story revealed by George Edwards may have arisen out of Daniel Farson's appeal. Frank Edwards remains a minor suspect at best.

Begg, Paul, Martin Fido, and Keith Skinner. *The Jack the Ripper A–Z* (1996).
Sugden, Philip. *The Complete History of Jack the Ripper* (2002).

HENRY JAMES FITZROY, EARL OF EUSTON

Known alternatively as Lord Euston, Henry James Fitzroy is most remembered today as having been involved in the Cleveland Street Scandal. Born in London on November 28, 1848, Euston was the eldest son of Augustus Charles Lennox Fitzroy, the 7th Duke of Grafton, and Anna Balfour. In 1873 Euston married Kate Walsh.

In the summer of 1889 the police set up a sting in Cleveland Street when it was learned that post office telegram boys were paid for immoral sexual acts at a male brothel run by Charles Hammond. Journalist Ernest Parke, who edited a radical newspaper called *The North London Press*, began writing a series of articles on the closed brothel, implicating a number of upper-class members of society, including the Earl of Euston. Lord Euston immediately sued Parke for criminal libel. Parke was tried and, when he refused to reveal his confidential sources, he was sentenced to twelve months imprisonment. Euston's name was cleared. Papers released in 1975 revealed the involvement of Euston, as well as other members of the nobility.

Theorist Stephen Knight briefly wrote about Euston in his 1976 royal conspiracy theory. Knight never intimates that Euston was involved in the Jack the Ripper murders, yet he recognizes that Euston was a Mason. For his part in silencing Ernest Parke Lord Euston was reportedly made the Grand Master of the Mark Masons.

In 1991 Melvyn Fairclough's updated royal conspiracy theory included Euston among its twelve-member group. Fairclough garners his information directly from Joseph Gorman Sickert and a set of diaries that Gorman Sickert states were written by Inspector Abberline. Euston's involvement is not clearly defined in the diaries, yet Walter Sickert told Joseph that both Euston and Lord Arthur Somerset were in the East End of London on the nights of each of the murders. They were supposedly look-out men.

There has been no documentation that places Euston in the East End of London on the specific nights of the murders. But then nothing has surfaced that places Euston out of the country on these specific nights. Having been born in London, Euston would have been quite familiar with the surrounding areas. The diaries, however, do not reveal his true involvement in the Jack the Ripper murders. If anything, Euston may have been no more than a lookout, and that alone does not indicate Euston as a true suspect.

Henry James Fitzroy, the Earl of Euston, led a privileged life. He got whatever he wanted and was able to do whatever he pleased. When a journalist challenged Euston, Euston fought back and used his power to railroad the journalist into a twelve-month prison sentence. Lord Euston passed away on the 10th of May 1912.

Fairclough, Melvyn. *The Ripper and the Royals* (1991).

Hyde, Montgomery H. *The Cleveland Street Scandal* (1976).

Knight, Stephen. *Jack the Ripper: The Final Solution* (1976).

http://genealogy.milin.net/genealog/d322.html

JOSEPH FLEMING

Researcher Mark King recently discovered the case of a lunatic at Claybury Mental Hospital who died in August of 1920. This man's name was given as "Joseph Fleming otherwise James Evans." In the hospital records, Henrietta Fleming was listed as the person to contact.

According to Joseph Barnett, Mary Kelly lived with a Mrs. Carthy for some time during 1886. She then moved in with a man named Joe, who was a mason or plasterer. Mrs. Carthy corroborated this fact. After the murder at Miller's Court, Mrs. Carthy told the press that Kelly left her house, which Barnett called "a bad house," late in 1886 to move in with someone connected to the building trade. This man is presumed to be Joseph Fleming. After Kelly and Fleming split up, sometime in early 1887, Kelly met Barnett and remained with him until one week prior to her death. A friend of Kelly's, Julia Van Turney, stated that another man named Joe had recently visited Kelly and may have given her some money. This man is also presumed to be Joseph Fleming.

There is no basis for the argument that the man Mary Kelly lived with for a short period of time, no longer than five months, was the same man who died as a lunatic in 1920. Fleming was not exactly an uncommon name at the time, and Joseph could have been one of the most popular. If by some chance these men were one and the same, the mere fact that Fleming wound up in a mental hospital does not in any way connect him with the atrocities committed by Jack the Ripper.

It cannot be positively stated that Joseph Fleming was the man who Kelly lived with prior to Barnett, although it seems plausible. Furthermore, it cannot be definitely stated that the "Joe" referred to by Kelly's friends as visiting her prior to her death was Fleming. Basically, there isn't much that is known about Joseph Fleming. Joseph Barnett circulated his name at the time of the murders as an individual formerly living with one of the mutilated victims. Despite no mention of an investigation into Joseph Fleming in any police files, it seems highly unlikely that the police did not look into him as a possible suspect.

Logic decrees that a jealous former lover does not visit his ex-lover a number of times to give her money then murder her after her most recent lover has left. There are also the murders of at least four women, Nichols, Chapman, Stride, and Eddowes, to account for, as well as the problem of such a stealthy murderer as Jack the Ripper being seen a number of times in public visiting the final victim. Joseph Fleming, a plasterer or mason born in 1859, whether or not he was the lunatic discovered by Mark King, seems unlikely to have committed all the murders attributed to Jack the Ripper.

Begg, Paul, Martin Fido, and Keith Skinner. *The Jack the Ripper A–Z* (1996).

Jakubowski, Maxim, and Nathan Braund. *The Mammoth Book of Jack the Ripper* (1998).

Paley, Bruce. *Jack the Ripper: The Simple Truth* (1995).

http://www.casebook.org

FOGELMA, THE NORWEGIAN SAILOR

An article from *Empire News* on October 28, 1923, stated that a Norwegian sailor named Fogelma was the man responsible for the murders during the autumn of 1888 in London. An unnamed student of criminology, who claimed to have known Fogelma while he was incarcerated in Morris Plains Lunatic Asylum in America, authored the article. Fogelma had been sent from Jersey City, New Jersey, to the asylum where his sister Helen, along with another woman, named Olga, visited him. These two women told the criminology student of Fogelma's various press cuttings of the Jack the Ripper murders, and that he had done some terrible things in London that had forced him to leave for the United States.

The article was written in response to William Le Queux's 1923 book *Things I Know About Kings, Celebrities and Crooks*. In his book, Le Queux stated that the identity of Jack the Ripper was known and that he was a Russian criminal named Dr. Alexander Pedachenko. The unnamed criminology student wrote this article in order to refute Le Queux's theory. So why did the criminology student wait so long? Even in the United States the Jack the Ripper murders had attained legendary status. It is possible that the student did not have a particular interest in Jack the Ripper, or serial murder, yet that would negate him attempting to set the record straight after the Le Queux book. One would assume that a student in criminology would have an interest in Jack the Ripper and that he would not have been quiet on the subject for twenty-one years.

The Norwegian sailor Fogelma died in 1902. There had been numerous books and articles in the press since then that claimed to provide the identity of Jack the Ripper. Only a year after the death of Fogelma, an accusation was made against serial poisoner George Chapman (Severin Klosowski), but this student never mentioned anything at the time about his knowledge of Fogelma and the information supplied by the suspect's sister. The 1903 case of serial poisoner George Chapman was far more publicly recognized than the 1923 book by Le Queux. Still, the question remains, why did this story lie dormant for twenty-one years?

It would have been interesting if the author of the article had spent those twenty-one years researching Fogelma and learning more about this mysterious man, but that was not the case. It would appear that since forming the theory that Fogelma was actually Jack the Ripper, this student had just sat on the theory for twenty-one years. That does not lend credibility to his story.

Fogelma did not leave London immediately after the murders. From the article, it can be determined that he came to America some time around 1898, ten years after the murders took place. What happened during those ten years in London? There is no documentation on Fogelma outside of the *Empire News* article. Upon arriving in the United States, Fogelma was described as clothed in rags, appearing extremely weak, almost skeletal. Based on his appearance, he could not have been employed recently in London, so what was he doing?

It is a real shame that the criminology student who actually knew Fogelma did not take the time to learn more about this man and did not announce his beliefs sooner than 1923. No further evidence has surfaced about Fogelma, and owning press clippings of the murders does not necessarily connect him with the actual murderer. The author of the article may have attempted to do the requisite research into the history of his suspect and come up with nothing tangible. Why the author waited for twenty-one years is one of the primary issues here, along with Fogelma remaining in London for close to ten years after the murders attributed to Jack the Ripper took place. As a sailor, Fogelma would have had many opportunities to leave London, yet he did not do so.

Begg, Paul, Martin Fido, and Keith Skinner. *The Jack the Ripper A–Z* (1996).
Le Queux, William. *Things I Know About Kings, Celebrities and Crooks* (1923).
http://www.casebook.org

JOHN GEORGE GIBSON

John George Gibson was born in Edinburgh, Scotland, on August 14, 1859. He would move to London and attend Spurgeon's College, studying divinity. He became a pastor, working at St. Andrews Church in Scotland from 1881 to 1887, whereupon Gibson resigned. The following year Gibson's whereabouts are unaccounted for. It is documented that Gibson left England for America in December 1888. He would eventually end up in San Francisco, where he would deliver his first sermon as pastor of the Emmanuel Baptist Church on November 11, 1894. Less than a year later there would be two deaths connected to Pastor Gibson's church.

The first mention of "Jack" Gibson in association with this case came in 1999, when author Robert Graysmith named Gibson as a suspect in his book, *The Bell Tower*. Graysmith theorized that Pastor Jack Gibson was responsible for the murder of two women in a San Francisco Church in 1895. While reexamining this one hundred and four year old case, Graysmith also attributes the murders committed by Jack the Ripper to Gibson. Gibson was in London at the time of the murders and suddenly left London in December of 1888, when the murders are alleged to have ceased.

Throughout Graysmith's book, he hypothesizes that the man who was accused and imprisoned for the crimes of murder against Minnie Williams and Blanche Lamont, Theo Durrant, was innocent. Durrant was one of two men who had access to the place where the bodies of these women were found. The other man was Jack Gibson. An exciting tale is told regarding the history of the church where the bodies were found, as three prior pastors had been involved in murderous scandals. Graysmith cites this as "evidence" that the fourth pastor, Jack Gibson, fell into their category. While describing anecdotes and stories about the 1895 murders in San Francisco, Graysmith briefly and very vaguely intertwines certain facts, theories, newspaper clippings, and accounts of the Jack the Ripper murders, proposing that Gibson was responsible for both series of murders.

In regards to the San Francisco murders, Graysmith fails to conclusively prove that Theo Durrant was not the murderer of Minnie Williams and Blanche Lamont, or that Jack Gibson was. Graysmith relies on an alleged deathbed confession of Gibson, to Charlie Floyd, who simply wrote it down in his journal. The first known account of this confession appears twenty years later by a fiction mystery writer. This supposed confession never mentioned anything about the Jack the Ripper murders, only those of the two women in San Francisco. Graysmith himself admits that Charlie Floyd is a mixture of three separate characters. Charlie Floyd never existed, and the alleged confession made to him by Jack Gibson was never reported, only alluded to by a writer of fiction twenty years after the fact.

Graysmith states that a second confession links Gibson to Jack the Ripper. In 1931 crime writer Guy Logan briefly discussed the Bell Tower murders in San Francisco. Logan claimed that another deathbed confession indicated that the confessor was responsible for the Bell Tower murders and also the murder of a young Indian woman. Graysmith postulates that the confessor alluded to by Guy Logan may have been Jack Gibson, who recovered from his earlier illness after providing the first "deathbed confession."

This second confession, never connected to Jack Gibson until recently by Graysmith, in some ways suggests that the first confessor was not the same person as the second. If they had been the same person, he would have had to confess on his "deathbed," then recover to live approximately twenty more years, then confess the same material to a different person. This is what Graysmith wishes the reader to believe.

Even in this second confession, nowhere is the name Jack the Ripper or the murders in London in 1888 mentioned. For a man so guilt ridden that he had to make two deathbed confessions, he apparently was not so guilty that he needed to clear his conscience about the murders and mutilations of a number of women in London. Graysmith has used a template of the Jack the Ripper criminal profile and posted into it a suspect he believed committed two or more murders in America. He attempts to neatly fit Gibson into these crimes, yet the foundations for his arguments are extremely weak and he uses a character that does not exist to bolster his argument. Despite Graysmith's attempts, doubt still exists as to whether Jack Gibson was the Bell Tower murderer. Of the two different murder cases, Graysmith provides even less of a compelling case for Gibson having been Jack the Ripper.

Graysmith, Robert. *The Bell Tower* (1999).
Logan, Guy. *Great Murder Mysteries* (1931).

GEORGE ROBERT GISSING

One of five children, George Robert Gissing was born in Yorkshire on November 22, 1857. His father was a chemist who died when George was only 13. Gissing was awarded a full scholarship to Owen's College in 1873, where he excelled in his various studies. Among his academic pursuits were history and literature, which would pave the way for his later career as a novelist.

His academic career in England was halted on May 31, 1876, when Gissing was caught stealing money to give to a prostitute named Nell Harrison. Gissing spent one month in jail for his crimes. He was then sent to America, where he began writing short stories for *The Chicago Tribune*. His return to London in late 1877 led to his first marriage, to prostitute Nell Harrison.

Gissing's marriage was a failed one. Nell Harrison returned to a life of prostitution and would die in the early part of 1888, most likely from a venereal disease. Gissing identified her body. His second marriage was in February 1891, to Edith Underwood. Edith may also have been working the streets to earn her keep. This second marriage, which resulted in two sons, would also fail when Edith's mental instability landed her in an asylum.

Gissing would leave his family in 1897 due to Edith's violent and unstable condition. A third marriage to a young French woman named Gabrielle Fleury can also be deemed a failure. He moved to Paris, but grew homesick for London, all the while nursing emphysema that would make him an invalid before taking his life on December 28, 1903.

George Robert Gissing combined elements of fiction with episodes from his troubled everyday life to weave novels about very real people struggling with the monotony and misery of middle- to lower-class existence. He slowly developed a following and began to mix within the literary circles of the times. His novels are looked upon today as depicting his own battles with despair over personal failures. Seen as a genius and a visionary, a cult following has emerged to pay homage to an author who harnessed his own difficulties to create works of literary art.

In 1961 author and noted Jack the Ripper historian Colin Wilson co-wrote *An Encyclopedia of Murder*. Wilson's co-author was Patricia Pitman. Pitman expressed her opinion to Wilson that she believed Gissing was Jack the Ripper. Wilson is on record as stating that Pitman's belief is on "no discernable grounds." Her beliefs had become known by 1970, as they appear in the updated version of Donald McCormick's *The Identity of Jack the Ripper*. McCormick states that Pitman "even mentioned the idea" that Gissing was the murderer. In 1975 Richard Whittington-Egan briefly mentions Gissing as one of a number of unlikely suspects. Whittington-Egan cannot positively remember where Gissing is first proposed as Jack the Ripper. Since within the same sentence Whittington-Egan includes painter Walter Sickert in the list of suspects, it can be assumed that he obtained this reference from McCormick, who also makes the first public allegation that Walter Sickert was Jack the Ripper in his 1970 book.

There is no particular theory regarding the proposal of George Robert Gissing as Jack the Ripper. Pitman has never developed her beliefs regarding Gissing in print, and no researcher to this date has taken up the case for advancing Gissing as a viable suspect. Gissing may have had an affinity for prostitutes, marrying at least one and possibly three, but that alone is not a practical link to murdering and mutilating women of the same stature in London.

After the death of his wife, Nell, on February 29, 1888, Gissing began work on his novel *The Nether World*. Upon its completion, Gissing left London for Italy, on September 16, 1888. One biographer does not mark his return until March 1889. Another source states that Gissing's trip to Italy was five months long. If Gissing had been in Italy for the entire five-month period then he can be cleared of suspicion. Until documentation arises that shows George Robert Gissing had returned to London prior to the night of September 29, 1888, the possibility that Gissing was Jack the Ripper must be considered unfeasible.

Begg, Paul, Martin Fido, and Keith Skinner. *The Jack the Ripper A–Z* (1996).

McCormick, Donald. *The Identity of Jack the Ripper* (1970).

Whittington-Egan, Richard. *A Casebook on Jack the Ripper* (1975).

Wilson, Colin, and Patricia Pitman. *An Encyclopedia of Murder* (1961).

http://www.casebook.org

http://ehlt.flinders.edu.au/english/Gissing/Biog.htm

WILLIAM GRANT GRAINGER

Grainger was arrested in February of 1895 for stabbing a woman in Spitalfields. Almost immediately, rumors began to surface that Grainger was Jack the Ripper. These rumors were mentioned in *The Pall Mall Gazette* on May 7, 1895. This article has been the primary source for Grainger's connection to the Jack the Ripper case. No researcher to this date has seriously lobbied for Grainger's inclusion as a suspect, but he has not been seriously dismissed, to my knowledge. Grainger's existence as a suspect has, unfortunately, supported the push for new suspects.

Grainger was born in Cork, England, in 1858. He left for sea at the young age of fifteen. Ten years later Grainger would join the Cork City Artillery. He was dismissed in 1889 due to problems with his character. These character problems have never been elaborated, yet Grainger consistently spent time in Cork Workhouse between 1887 and 1890, indicating that there may have been legal troubles as well. Two later imprisonments for drunkenness in the East End display a pattern for troubles with the law.

Similar to James Thomas Sadler, the man accused and acquitted of the Frances Coles murder, William Grant Grainger was a ship's fireman. There is another similarity that has caused much controversy over the years: Both Sadler and Grainger were identified by witnesses who have never been named, and there is no police corroboration of these apparent identifications. Sadler was accused of the murder of Frances Coles,

which happened February 13, 1891, and is considered by some to be the work of Jack the Ripper. He was brought before a witness for identification. This witness has remained unnamed over the years and, other than Assistant Police Commissioner Robert Anderson and Chief Inspector Donald Swanson no policeman saw this identification. Grainger's identification in some respects differs from that of Sadler's. The source for one is an important dissimilarity.

The original source for Grainger's status as suspect is an article in *The Pall Mall Gazette*, May 7, 1895. In this article, it is stated that only one person had ever seen the Whitechapel murderer and that that person had now unhesitatingly identified Grainger. As such a long time had elapsed since the Whitechapel murders took place, close to seven years, this identification could not be considered reliable. The article also states that the person who saw the murderer only had "so cursory a glance." No policeman, including Chief Inspector Donald Swanson and Assistant Commissioner Robert Anderson, has verified this witness identification of Grainger. The only known reference to the identification occurs within this particular article. It seems questionable whether any such identification took place.

Grainger was arrested for the near-fatal wounding of Alice Graham. His knife had caused a cut in her stomach approximately two inches deep, which was considered serious but not life-threatening. Graham was allegedly left in the street bleeding while Grainger fled the scene. This is not inconsistent with stories regarding Grainger. It was stated within the article that prostitutes frequently robbed him and took his clothing while Grainger was in Ireland. One story describes a prostitute who may have robbed him of his clothing while he was in Whitechapel. It would appear that Grainger's known prior dealings with prostitutes ended up with him on the losing end, until this most recent one with Alice Graham.

His whereabouts during the period of the Whitechapel murders were listed in the article. Unfortunately, there has been no discovery of where Grainger was on the precise dates of the murders attributed to Jack the Ripper. Grainger's presence in London on these dates has also not been documented. He regularly traveled out of London as a ship's fireman and also attended the annual artillery trainings in Cork.

This attack on Graham displays marked differences from the murders committed by Jack the Ripper, including length of the knife used and failure to complete the murderous act. According to Graham, she and Grainger went searching for a room in a number of public houses before Grainger snapped and stabbed her. This is another important distinguishing factor. If Grainger were Jack the Ripper, he likely would not have secured a public house room where the deputy of the lodging house could easily identify him.

The primary source linking Grainger as a suspect addresses the extreme differences between Grainger and Jack the Ripper. Inferentially, it would appear that the author of the article seriously doubted Grainger's value as a true suspect. No researcher has attempted to further develop a case against Grainger. While Grainger was in prison, his lawyer, Mr. Kebbel, made the claim that he was Jack the Ripper. This statement garnered little attention until crime historian L. Forbes Winslow refuted this suggestion in 1910, but Winslow may have refuted Mr. Kebbel's claim based solely on his belief that G. Wentworth Bell Smith was Jack the Ripper.

The article, and Grainger for that matter, has since been used to push the witness identification most closely connected to Robert Anderson. While Anderson is not mentioned in this article, it is important to establish the chronology of how early Chief Inspector Donald Swanson's beliefs regarding Jack the Ripper had developed. Since there was no police refutation of this article, one would think that the police accepted the article's reported findings.

Begg, Paul, Martin Fido, and Keith Skinner. *The Jack the Ripper A–Z* (1996).

Fido, Martin. *The Crimes, Detection and Death of Jack the Ripper* (1987).

Jakubowski, Maxim, and Nathan Braund. *The Mammoth Book of Jack the Ripper* (1998).

DR. WILLIAM GULL

Dr. William Gull was born in Colchester on December 31, 1816. He was the youngest of eight children. His father, John Gull, died of cholera when

William was ten. His mother moved the family to Thorpe-le-Soken, which was owned by the authorities running Guy's Hospital in London. This would change the course of Gull's life. In 1837 he was accepted as a medical pupil at Guy's Hospital. Gull would continue his medical studies and earn his M.D. in 1846. He would serve on the Senate for the University of London from 1856 to 1889.

Gull lectured and taught at Guy's Hospital. He would rise to the post of Resident Physician. In 1871 Gull's life would again change. The Prince of Wales came down with typhoid fever, the same illness that had taken the life of the Prince's father. At this time the Royal Physician was Dr. William Jenner, but Princess Alexandra brought Gull in to cure her husband. Queen Victoria wanted Jenner, but Princess Alix insisted on Gull. Gull cured the Prince of Wales, and the following year Gull was made a baronet. Later titles to follow would be Physician Extraordinary, then Physician in Ordinary to the Queen.

During this time he kept teaching and lecturing at Guy's Hospital. In the autumn of 1887 he suffered a stroke that rendered him partially paralyzed. Gull was 71, and this stroke forced him to retire from medical practice. He would suffer three more strokes, labeled as epileptiform attacks, the final one occurring on January 29, 1890. Gull had the attack, fell into a coma, and eventually passed away.

Much has been made of the 1887 stroke that forced Gull to retire from his medical practice. In an 1892 book discussing the history of Guy's Hospital, Gull's first stroke in 1887 is described as "slight paralysis on the right side and aphasia." Aphasia is a disruption of language skills caused by a dysfunction within the cerebral cortex. It generally affects the ability to speak, write, comprehend, and read. As Gull continued to serve on the Senate for the University of London until 1889, it should be concluded that the aphasia was not severe. The 1892 book states that Gull rapidly recovered from these attacks, which included the 1887 episode. Stephen Knight cites this fact to support the claim that Gull did in fact possess the strength necessary to commit the murders outlined in the Royal Conspiracy. Most other researchers in the field are of the opposite opinion, that Gull's stroke would have prohibited him from involvement in the murders committed by Jack the Ripper.

Stephen Knight and the supporters of the Royal Conspiracy have also challenged the date of Dr. Gull's death. Their major basis for debate over Gull's date of death results from two stories appearing in separate newspapers, thirty-six years apart.

In 1895 an article in the Chicago *Sunday Times Herald* stated that a famous London doctor was responsible for the Jack the Ripper murders. This doctor, who remained unnamed in the article, had been certified insane by a round table of fellow eminent doctors, and a fake death was staged. The article goes on to state that the psychic Robert James Lees had positively identified the doctor and was asked to leave the country by Queen Victoria as a result of this identification. Lees agreed, and the doctor was put quietly away in an insane asylum, with the country never knowing the real truth. Judging from inferential data within the article, this doctor is William Gull. He was said to be still alive at the time of this writing, incarcerated under a false name. Researcher Melvin Harris claims that an American group calling itself the Whitechapel Club created this article.

In 1931 *The Daily Express* published a condensed version of the Chicago *Sunday Times Herald* article. The newspaper stated that the article was actually a document left by Robert James Lees to be opened after his death. The newspaper also prefaced its condensed article by stating that it did not fully believe the authenticity of the content within the document left by Lees. Theorist and researcher Melvin Harris believes that the claim that Lees left the document to be opened after his death was deliberately invented.

The first time William Gull's actual name was associated with the Jack the Ripper case was in a 1970 article by Dr. Thomas Stowell. In this legendary article in *The Criminologist*, Stowell refers to one of Gull's patients, who supposedly showed up on one of the nights of the murders with bloodstains on his clothing. Without mentioning his suspect by name, Stowell seemed to be referring to Prince Albert Victor. Stephen Knight has suggested that Stowell, among others, was really hinting at William Gull, not the Prince. The first time Gull was actually mentioned as Jack the Ripper was in 1973, when Joseph Gorman Sickert revealed the early story of the Royal Conspiracy.

In 1973 Joseph Gorman Sickert was interviewed on television. This brief interview laid the foundation for the Royal Conspiracy Theory. In 1976 Stephen Knight published his full-length theory on the Royal Conspiracy. Dr. William Gull's involvement in this conspiracy is as follows: Knight states that Dr. Gull was the man responsible for operating on Annie Elizabeth Crook, the alleged wife of Prince Albert Victor, and mother of their child, Alice Margaret. This operation was performed to destroy her memory and turn her into a raving lunatic who could not be trusted to give proper evidence. The murders attributed to Jack the Ripper were supposedly committed to quash a blackmail plot by Mary Jane Kelly and three of her friends, Mary Ann Nichols, Annie Chapman and Elizabeth Stride. Gull was the man chosen to silence these women and protect the Crown.

John Netley, who acted as a secret driver for Prince Albert Victor when he would sneak out of the palace to Cleveland Street, chauffeured Gull around the East End. Under the scope of Knight's theory, the victims were lured into the carriage, and Gull would commit the murders, and subsequent Masonic mutilations, while still in the carriage. John Netley was the man responsible for placing the bodies at their final spot. According to medical evidence from the doctors on the scene during the murders, all the victims were killed at the spot where they were discovered. This piece of medical evidence destroys the Royal Conspiracy Theory outlined by Stephen Knight.

In 1991 Melvyn Fairclough updated the Royal Conspiracy Theory by adding a number of new conspirators and suspects. Unfortunately, Fairclough did not address the medical evidence that disproves the victims having been murdered inside a carriage and then later placed where they were discovered. In Fairclough's updated theory, Gull is still the murderer within the carriage, protecting the Crown. Fairclough does not provide any further evidence to support the theory of Gull's carriage murders.

Andy and Sue Parlour theorize that Dr. Gull was the man responsible for choosing the two assassins to commit the murders attributed to Jack the Ripper. To protect the name of Prince Albert Victor's father, Prince Albert Edward, the Prince of Wales, Dr. Gull chose James Kenneth Stephen and Montague John Druitt to commit these murders. Stephen and Druitt were named as co-murderers only four years previously in John Wilding's 1993 book, *Jack the Ripper Revealed*. The Parlours cite an oral tradition from Gull's hometown of Thorpe le-Soken that claims Gull did not die in 1890 and played some part in the murders attributed to Jack the Ripper.

Dr. William Gull worked hard all his life to achieve positive gains in the field of medicine. He mastered physiology and anatomy, was one of the foremost experts in diseases of the brain, as well as the kidney, working alongside the leading renal authority in England, Dr. Henry Sutton. As a seventy-two year old man who had just suffered a slight stroke it would seem impossible for Gull to have walked the streets, to have committed these murders and then to have quickly escaped detection. Dr. Thomas Stowell stated that it was rumored that Gull was seen in Whitechapel on more than one occasion on the nights of the murders. This speculation regarding Gull has never been documented, yet is used by Stowell to further his own suspect.

Gull's standing within the Freemasons, a secret organization that went back to the early 1700s, provided the requisite impetus for a scandal and conspiracy. The Freemasonic excerpts of Knight's theory seemed attractive and made his 1976 effort an international bestseller. There is still secrecy regarding Freemason practices and rituals, so that anything that is known may only scratch the surface or, conversely, make what is known to look like conspiracy.

There are still the 1895 and 1931 newspaper articles that, without a doubt, implicate Gull as involved in the Jack the Ripper murders. Melvin Harris claims these newspaper articles were deliberate hoaxes, but this does not eliminate Dr. William Gull from suspicion. It should be noted that Dr. Thomas Stowell claims to have received the information regarding his suspect from Caroline Acland, Gull's daughter, some time in the early 1930s. Perhaps there was a reason why Acland needed to attempt to vindicate her father's name, using notes that have never been released.

Acland, Theodore Dyke. *William Withey Gull: A Biographical Sketch* (1896).

Begg, Paul, Martin Fido, and Keith Skinner. *The Jack the Ripper A–Z* (1996).

Clayman, Dr. Charles B. *The American Medical Association Encyclopedia of Medicine* (1989).

Fairclough, Melvyn. *The Ripper and the Royals* (1991).

Harris, Melvin. *The True Face of Jack the Ripper* (1994).

Knight, Stephen. *Jack the Ripper: The Final Solution* (1976).

Parlour, Andy, and Sue Parlour. *The Jack the Ripper Whitechapel Murders* (1997).

Stowell, Dr. Thomas. *The Criminologist* (November, 1970).

Wilding, John. *Jack the Ripper Revealed* (1993).

Wilks, S., and G. T. Bettany, *Biographical History of Guy's Hospital* (1892).

DR. JOHN HEWITT

According to Walter Sickert, the famous Victorian painter, he rented a room from an elderly couple at No. 6 Mornington Crescent a few years after the murders took place. Sickert stated that the couple positively asserted that the prior occupant was Jack the Ripper. The couple eventually provided further details regarding this lodger to Sickert. The main elements to Sickert's story were that the lodger was a young veterinary student, had burned his clothing on the nights of the murders, and that the student's widowed mother took him back to Bournemouth, England, where he died three months after the murders.

In 1985, while researching this story, Steward Hicks discovered Dr. John Hewitt. Hicks proposed Dr. Hewitt as Sickert's unnamed veterinary student. Born in 1850, Hewitt had practiced some form of medicine—whether he was an M.D. or a veterinarian has never been made fully clear—in Manchester, England, just prior to his confinement in Coton Hill Asylum in 1888. Dr. Hewitt married a nurse from Coton Hill Asylum, and moved to Bournemouth, eventually dying in 1892 of general paralysis of the insane. Hicks noted the similarity of Dr. Hewitt moving to Bournemouth and eventually passing away there, yet the main compelling factor was that Dr. Hewitt's name resembled the name of a suspect, although a name given by Walter Sickert.

In 1970, theorist Donald McCormick claimed that the name of this student was something like Drewen, Druitt,

or Hewitt. McCormick connects these three names to a tale told by Walter Sickert to a "London doctor who knew Sickert and whose father had been at Oxford with Montague John Druitt." McCormick states that his doctor had said that the student's name was something similar to Druitt. So where do these three names, Drewen, Druitt, and Hewitt come from?

In 1959 researcher Daniel Farson was collecting any and all material relating to Jack the Ripper for the BBC program, *Farson's Guide to the British*. McCormick appeared on this program, most likely to promote his book, *The Identity of Jack the Ripper*. McCormick had access to all of Farson's material relating to Jack the Ripper, including Melville MacNaghten's personal copy of his 1894 memorandum, shown to Farson by MacNaghten's daughter, Lady Christabel Aberconway. The MacNaghten Memorandum contained the name Montague John Druitt, which is of little consequence, since Druitt's full name would be revealed in 1965 by researcher Tom Cullen. It was from another document, sent to Farson in 1959, that McCormick lifted the three names.

A document, titled *The East End Murderer—I Knew Him*, was allegedly seen by a Mr. A. Knowles in Australia. According to Knowles, a Lionel Druitt, Drewett, or Drewery wrote this document. Research conducted by Martin Howells and Keith Skinner has connected this document to multiple murderer Frederick Bailey Deeming. Deeming used the alias "Drewen" in Australia.

There is no connection to Montague John Druitt. This is important because Walter Sickert never proposed a name for the young veterinary student. The closest Sickert ever came to divulging the student's name was telling author and close friend Osbert Sitwell that he had written the name down in the margin of a copy of *Casanova's Memoirs*, which Sickert had given to Albert Rutherston. This book was lost during the bombings of World War II, but Rutherston has stated that he could not decipher Sickert's writing. Dr. Hewitt's similarity in name is due to a misinterpretation by Donald McCormick.

There is still the similarity of Dr. John Hewitt moving to Bournemouth with a nurse from Coton Hill Asylum and passing away three years (though not three *months*) later. Dr. Hewitt was confined to Coton Hill Asylum during 1888 but was released a number of times throughout the year. With this information, Dr. Hewitt might seem like a highly likely candidate. But documentation was released in 1988 from Coton Hill showing that Dr. Hewitt was confined inside the asylum during the nights of the murders. This evidence clears Dr. John Hewitt as a suspect.

Begg, Paul, Martin Fido, and Keith Skinner. *The Jack the Ripper A–Z* (1996).
Jakubowski, Maxim, and Nathan Braund. *The Mammoth Book of Jack the Ripper* (1998).
McCormick, Donald. *The Identity of Jack the Ripper* (1970).

GEORGE HUTCHINSON

The first mention of George Hutchinson as a suspect may not refer to the Hutchinson who provided a statement to Inspector Abberline. He was first named as a suspect in January of 1889. *The Pall Mall Gazette* reported that *The Panama Star and Herald* had described an escaped criminal lunatic from America with the name "George Hutchinson." This man had escaped from two separate lunatic asylums in Elgin and Kankakee, Illinois, around 1880 or 1881. At the time of the murders, he was reportedly at large. The murder of a woman in Chicago has been attributed to Hutchinson. The woman was mutilated in a way similar to the victims of Jack the Ripper. There are two earlier press reports, occurring on November 16, 1888, in *The Evening Star*, out of Washington, D.C, and *The Ottawa Journal*, which mention the same facts. This American Hutchinson shall be discussed first.

The police might not have been aware of the American and Canadian reports of the lunatic from America, but when the story surfaced in an influential London paper, the police, in particular Inspector Abberline, would have known of the report's existence. Inspector Abberline is the officer who personally took the statement of a man named George Hutchinson on November 12, 1888, hours after the inquest into the death of Mary Jane Kelly had closed. There is no mention in any police files of Abberline ever re-interviewing Hutchinson, despite this newspaper account. It is known that Abberline accepted Hutchinson's statement and a description of the man Hutchinson had seen with Mary Kelly on the night of her murder. The Hutchinson arrested in America is assumed to have been an American. If this were the case, Abberline would have distinguished the American Hutchinson from the Hutchinson whose statement he took. If by some chance this Hutchinson was not American, but English, there was no mention of this fact in the *PallMall Gazette* article, which may have misled Inspector Abberline into believing that in no way could this escaped lunatic be the Hutchinson he had interviewed.

If the escaped criminal lunatic Hutchinson was English rather than American, then Abberline missed a major suspect. If these were the same man, then Hutchinson had been arrested three times previously in America, at least once for the mutilation of a woman, had escaped all three times, had then murdered at least four women in the East End of London before waiting outside the apartment of Mary Jane Kelly, where he was spotted, and eventually murdering her. He then shows up at Commercial Street Police Station to provide a statement? The Hutchinson described in the newspapers was a habitual criminal who would not go to a police station, especially after mutilating a woman that he may have been seen with on prior occasions. He would not have taken that chance.

It is hard to positively state whether or not these two Hutchinsons were the same man. What can be inferred from that single report in three separate newspapers is that the American Hutchinson would not have gone anywhere near a police station after committing the grisly murder in Miller's Court. If the American Hutchinson and the British Hutchinson were not the same person, it's inconceivable that the man the latter saw in the East End was actually the American Hutchinson. It has also never been proven that the American George Hutchinson was in London during the times of the murders.

It took over 100 years for the English George Hutchinson, to be named as a suspect in print. Hutchinson had been discussed for some time since the murders took place. In 1996 theorist Brian Marriner became the first to advance him as a suspect. Since then, theorists like Bob Hinton, Stephen Wright and Garry Wroe have written on Hutchinson as a possible suspect. In 2002 John Eddleston published *Jack the Ripper: An Encyclopaedia*. In this reference work, Eddleston comes to the conclusion that Hutchinson is the primary suspect and, in his words, "...the only one I can accept."

The basic premise behind Hutchinson as a suspect lies in his statement to Inspector Abberline. Hutchinson's statement to Abberline occurred at 6:00 P.M. on November 12. As the inquest into the death of Mary Jane Kelly had closed earlier that day, the evidence and description provided by Hutchinson could not be admitted into record. Hutchinson's description of the man he saw with Kelly was very detailed. Some say it was too detailed and suggest Hutchinson created this man to cover himself.

By his own admission, Hutchinson followed Kelly and the man she met on the corner of Commercial and Fashion streets, to the entrance to Miller's Court.

Kelly and the man went into Miller's Court together and disappeared from sight, presumably going directly into Kelly's small room. Hutchinson stated that he went to the court and stood there for about forty-five minutes waiting for them to come out. When they did not appear, Hutchinson claims he left. Sarah Lewis testified that she saw a man standing on the opposite side of Dorset Street who appeared to be waiting for someone to come out of Miller's Court. It has been suggested this was Hutchinson.

Why did Hutchinson wait so long? If he suspected this man with Kelly, why didn't he check it out further? Why did he not immediately come forward with his information? These are the questions that cast doubt upon Hutchinson as a credible witness and also suggest him as a possible suspect.

It has been suggested that Hutchinson was a former client of Kelly's. Hutchinson said that Kelly occasionally asked him for money and addressed him by name, indicating a sense of familiarity. They may have known each other prior to Kelly living with Joseph Barnett. Possibly, they conducted business while Kelly worked at one of her various brothels. Admitting this to Inspector Abberline would have been taking a big chance if Hutchinson had been the murderer, even if this information were provided after the end of the inquest. This would have placed Hutchinson at or around the scene of the crime at approximately the time when police surgeon Dr. Thomas Bond estimates the murder took place. A murderer with something to hide would not have done this.

One reason Hutchinson may have come forward is that he read the published statement by Sarah Lewis. By Lewis's own admission, she could not describe the man she had seen. If Hutchinson had been the man seen by Sarah Lewis, he could have thrown the police off his trail by providing a detailed description of someone else.

There is controversy surrounding not only the description Hutchinson furnished, but also the timeframe in which he delivered it. It is a risky proposition for the murderer (to come forward days after the murder). From Inspector Abberline's November 12 report, it is known that Hutchinson's story was believed to be true and that he intimated details about himself that would have made him a suspect, most notably that he was out of work for several weeks. Hutchinson also made himself available to the police, identifying Kelly's body the following day in the mortuary.

If by some chance there was only one George Hutchinson, he would not have made himself readily available to the police. This suggests the conclusion that the American Hutchinson and the English Hutchinson were not the same man. For a George Hutchinson from England to provide a detailed description of another George Hutchinson from America seems too much of a coincidence.

A rather undetailed description of a man standing outside Miller's Court would not have brought the murderer into a police station to identify himself as that person, yet George Hutchinson did just that. Also, indicating to Abberline that he was on familiar terms with Kelly would have placed him in a position to be investigated.

Begg, Paul, Martin Fido, and Keith Skinner. *The Jack the Ripper A–Z* (1996).

Eddleston, John. *Jack the Ripper: An Ency-clopaedia* (2002).

Evans, Stewart P., and Keith Skinner. *The Ultimate Jack the Ripper Companion* (2000).

Hinton, Bob. *From Hell ... The Jack the Ripper Mystery* (1998).

Marriner, Brian. *Murder Most Foul* (1996).

Wright, Stephen. *Jack the Ripper: An American View* (1999).

http://www.casebook.org

"JILL THE RIPPER"

Every single solitary piece of evidence known about the murderer, including all the eyewitness testimony, points to the conclusion that Jack the Ripper was not a woman. There is not a shred of evidence, circumstantial or otherwise, that lends to the theory that Jack the Ripper was a woman.

The first proposal that Jack the Ripper was a woman occurred during the times of the murders. The Reverend Lord Sydney Osborne wrote a letter to *The Times* suggesting that fellow street-walkers, carrying out threats against one another, committed the murders. William Stewart originally proposed the term Jill the Ripper in 1939. Mystery writer Sir Arthur Conan Doyle proposed that a midwife could escape suspicion from the police if bloodstains were found on her clothes. Conan Doyle added that it might have been a man dressed as a woman, again to escape suspicion. In 1939 theorist William Stewart advanced Conan Doyle's theory, inventing the name "Jill the Ripper" and claiming that she was an illegal abortionist.

First and foremost, "Jill the Ripper" does not exist. It is an invented, fabricated name. Stewart never proposed any real woman's name as the murderer. To declare her as the murderer is the factual equivalent of stating the murderer was Jack the Ripper. Articles in *The Sun*, written by former Chief Superintendent Arthur Butler in 1972, added to Stewart's 1939 theory using oral traditions as a source. Butler also failed to provide any real woman's name.

Begg, Paul, Martin Fido, and Keith Skinner. *The Jack the Ripper A–Z* (1996).

Stewart, William. *Jack the Ripper: A New Theory* (1939).

NATHAN KAMINSKY

There is only one documented piece of evidence as to the existence of Nathan Kaminsky. On March 24, 1888, Kaminsky was treated for syphilis in Ward BB of the Whitechapel Workhouse Infirmary. Six weeks later he was released, having been cured. This documentation was unearthed by the diligent research of Martin Fido. It is Martin Fido who has suggested that Kaminsky may have been Jack the Ripper.

The basic premise of Fido's theory is that Nathan Kaminsky was the real "Leather Apron." Once rumors began to circulate in the newspapers that the murderer was known as "Leather Apron," and once John Pizer was arrested and released after providing an alibi, Nathan Kaminsky supposedly changed his name to David Cohen, a sort of Jewish "John Doe." Fido surmised that the vital statistics of what is known regarding Nathan Kaminsky clearly matched what was known of David Cohen. Both men were twenty-three years old, had no known relatives and were of foreign Jewish origin.

Another major point of Fido's theory revolves around the identification mentioned by Assistant Commissioner Robert Anderson. Anderson revealed in his 1910 memoirs that Jack the Ripper was a "low-class Polish Jew." Anderson declines to mention the name of the suspect. In 1987 the Swanson marginalia named Anderson's suspect as Kosminski. This has been assumed to be Aaron Kosminski. Fido again dissented.

Fido declared that Anderson was wrong in tagging Aaron Kosminski as the suspect. This error may have arisen from Anderson remembering an early search for Nathan Kaminsky, whom Fido believes was the real Leather Apron. Once David Cohen was incarcerated, after changing his name from Nathan Kaminsky, Anderson let slip the information that a Kosminski was identified, erroneously misremembering Nathan Kaminsky as Kosminski. The evidence of the Swanson marginalia does not perfectly fit Aaron Kosminski, yet rather fits combined aspects of both Kosminski and David Cohen. Out of these errors, Fido has declared that David Cohen, the Jewish "John Doe" who was formerly Nathan Kaminsky, was Jack the Ripper.

Unfortunately, records have been lost over the years. There is no way to confirm that Nathan Kaminsky changed his name to David Cohen. The fact that Aaron Kosminski's physical characteristics, such as age and ethnicity, matched those of David Cohen leaves room for three possible suspects, Kosminski, Cohen and Kaminsky.

Under Fido's theory, Nathan Kaminsky does not exist outside of David Cohen. There is no proof of this, and it is almost impossible to disprove Fido's theory. There still remains no real tangible evidence to link Kaminsky to David Cohen. There are multiple parallels that make Fido's theory an interesting possibility, but interesting possibilities alone cannot prove a real connection between Kaminsky and Cohen.

Anderson, Robert. *The Lighter Side of My Official Life* (1910).

Begg, Paul, Martin Fido, and Keith Skinner. *The Jack the Ripper A–Z* (1996).

Fido, Martin. *The Crimes, Detection and Death of Jack the Ripper* (1987).

JAMES KELLY

James Kelly was sentenced to death for the murder of his wife, Sarah Ann, in 1883, but his sentence was reduced to life imprisonment in Broadmoor Criminal Lunatic Asylum. He remained in Broadmoor until escaping in January of 1888. Kelly traveled to both France and the United States and returned to England every so often over the following years, voluntarily returning to Broadmoor in 1927.

Two theorists have positively determined James Kelly to be Jack the Ripper. John Morrison, who claimed to have all the requisite evidence to prove this claim, originally proposed Kelly in 1986. Morrison has never provided the information he claimed to have in his possession. The second theorist to advance James Kelly as a suspect was James Tully. Tully developed the case against Kelly to book length, calling on nearly twenty-five years of research, which Tully believes fully shows that James Kelly was Jack the Ripper.

The central thesis behind John Morrison's theory is that James Kelly was having an adulterous affair with Mary Jane Kelly during 1883. This affair caused a rift between Kelly and his wife, Sarah Ann, that resulted in James Kelly murdering Sarah Ann. When he escaped almost five years later in 1888, he attempted to reconcile with Mary Kelly. When he found out that she had become a prostitute and had also aborted a baby from their earlier affair, he murdered her. In turn, he murdered all the prostitutes whom he had approached regarding Mary Kelly's whereabouts.

According to Joseph Barnett, Mary Kelly did not arrive in London until sometime in 1884, well after James Kelly had been incarcerated for the murder of his wife. While this information comes directly from information given to Joseph Barnett by her, she would not have had any reason to lie about the time when she came to London. By the time she met Barnett in 1887, James Kelly had been locked away for almost four years. Even if she had been linked to James Kelly and his wife, Mary Kelly never needed to cover her tracks, as there would have been no one to challenge her.

This is where Morrison's theory contradicts itself, yet it is possible that Mary Kelly did arrive in London prior to when she told Barnett. This, however, does not make her the woman who came between James Kelly and Sarah Ann. If John Morrison were right, and the affair had caused Sarah Ann's murder and James Kelly's incarceration, why would James Kelly murder the other women? Morrison states that it was because he had asked them about Mary Kelly. He murdered them to cover his tracks. There are numerous problems with this.

According to Morrison's theory, Martha Tabram was the first victim. In theory, James Kelly would have approached Tabram to ask her where he could find Mary Kelly. James Kelly would then have murdered Tabram to cover his tracks. If Martha Tabram did not know Mary Kelly or where she was, then there would have been no reason to murder her. If Tabram did know where she was, why did it take three months for James Kelly to find her? Furthermore, why would Kelly have killed Tabram? He had not found Mary Kelly yet, so he obviously had not learned that she was a prostitute, or that she had aborted his baby. Based on this theory, there would be no reason to murder Tabram. The same conclusion applies to Mary Ann Nichols, if she was the actual first victim of Jack the Ripper. Morrison's theory is speculative, with no foundations in logical deduction.

A little over ten years after Morrison's work, James Tully advanced the case against James Kelly. Tully built upon Morrison's weak foundation and centered his case on a theoretical police cover-up involving James Monro and Home Secretary Henry Matthews. Tully's main concern arises from a September 22 memo from Matthews to his private secretary, Evelyn Ruggles-Brise, in which Monro intimates some secret knowledge. Tully believes this memo relates to a search for James Kelly. It is the easiest thing to take this memo and twist it to fit a researcher's theory. What cannot be manipulated is this: During September, Monro was actively working within the parameters of the Special Branch, which dealt specifically with the Fenian terrorist movement in London. To claim that eight days before the double murder, both Matthews and Monro knew the identity of Jack the Ripper, an insane escapee from Broadmoor Criminal Lunatic Asylum, is a claim that has no foundation.

It is known that immediately following James Kelly's escape from Broadmoor, Scotland Yard was alerted. Monro, Assistant Commissioner at the time, investigated the escape and conducted a search for a friend of James Kelly's who might have helped him. Scotland Yard requested James Kelly's picture, which they received, and circulars providing a description of Kelly were distributed. This search for Kelly began almost immediately after his escape, yet there was not much concern over it. He was almost caught soon after, but he eluded a constable. So James Kelly knew that the authorities were actively seeking him out in London. But Morrison and Tully want us to believe that Kelly remained in London during 1888, where he was actively sought after, at the same time committing at least five grisly murders.

James Kelly was born on April 20, 1860, to an illiterate teenager named Sarah. Kelly's father, a clerk named John Miller, left Sarah upon finding out that she was pregnant. His grandmother, Teresa, raised young James, as his mother Sarah left to make a new life. Sarah married a Master Mariner in 1870, but liver disease claimed her life on July 29, 1874, a little over a month after her husband's death. Kelly's inheritance from his mother's will allowed him to return to school to learn clerical skills. Mental instability, which may have run in his family, surfaced in the early 1880s, affecting his work.

Kelly traveled to all areas of the East End of London, frequenting pubs and hiring prostitutes on a regular basis. He would meet Sarah Ann Brider some time before December 1881, eventually moving into her family home as a lodger. Their romance was slow paced, but Kelly continued to see prostitutes, one of whom gave Kelly a venereal disease. The disease affected his libido, and a growing mental instability affected his brain, but James Kelly and Sarah Ann Brider were wed on July 4, 1883.

Kelly's mental problems continued, and a lack of work weighed heavily on the family, which included Sarah Ann's mother. These issues culminated on June 21, 1883, when during a heated argument Kelly stabbed Sarah Ann in the throat with a penknife. She was taken to the hospital but died on June 24. James Kelly would remain at Broadmoor until his escape in January 1888.

No one has ever been able to positively establish James Kelly's whereabouts during 1888. As smart as James Kelly must have been to make a key in order to escape Broadmoor, he would not have remained in the country where he was wanted. Even though it is known that the search for James Kelly was not conducted with the utmost zeal, Kelly, who was constantly described as "paranoid," would have thought that his capture was the main interest of the authorities. Kelly would have wanted to be as far away from London as possible.

In 1896, James Kelly submitted himself to the British Consulate in New Orleans, Louisiana, asking to return to England under pardon. When Scotland Yard was contacted, the consulate found that Scotland Yard really did not care

about Kelly. If Scotland Yard knew Kelly was Jack the Ripper, as suggested by James Tully, they would have desperately wanted him back in England to pay for his crimes. If James Kelly were Jack the Ripper, he would not have wanted to return to England, because he would have been immediately arrested if the authorities knew. His desire to return and be granted a pardon in England had to be in reference to his escape from Broadmoor. Anyone who had murdered and mutilated a number of women in the country's most notorious murder case would have understood that there would be no pardon for those crimes. Kelly returned to England and was met by no one in law enforcement, despite the authorities having the name of the ship he was traveling on.

James Kelly would travel the world, returning to London every so often. He eventually returned to the gates of Broadmoor Criminal Lunatic Asylum in early 1927, where he was readmitted and remained until he died in 1929.

It would be intriguing to know where Kelly was during 1888, yet all logic points to James Kelly having been as far away from London as possible. There is no correlation between the murder of his wife Sarah Ann, whom he attacked with a penknife, and the murders committed by Jack the Ripper. The foundation of this case against James Kelly is extremely weak. The conclusions based on the general knowledge associated with the Jack the Ripper case appear not to apply to this suspect.

Begg, Paul, Martin Fido, and Keith Skinner. *The Jack the Ripper A–Z* (1996).
Morrison, John. *Jimmy Kelly's Year of the Ripper Murders* (1986).
Tully, James. *Prisoner 1167: The Madman Who Was Jack the Ripper* (1998).

SEVERIN KLOSOWSKI

In his 1959 book, theorist Donald McCormick relied on three volumes of crime written by the historian Dr. Thomas Dutton. McCormick used these crime volumes from the 1930s to weave Severin Klosowski into his personal theory on Jack the Ripper. According to McCormick, Dr. Dutton believed that Jack the Ripper was a Russian named Pedachenko, an alias used by Vassily Konovalov. Dutton also stated that Klosowski and Pedachenko were look-alikes and that they might have switched identities on certain occasions. Dr. Dutton went so far as to say that Klosowski worked as a barber under the White Hart pub during the time of the murders and that he had come under the suspicion of the police, possibly as a result of having been mistaken for Dr. Pedachenko.

Severin Klosowski trained as an Apprentice Surgeon in Poland from 1880 until 1885. He graduated to the position of a qualified junior surgeon in 1887 and moved from Warsaw to England. He first gained employment in London as an assistant hairdresser, which is what he would make his living as for the rest of his life. Klosowski was running his own barbershop on Cable Street during 1887. His first job has been said to only last about five months, which would have taken him into the beginning of 1888. If Klosowski was not employed in the Cable Street barbershop during the time of the murders, then his whereabouts are unknown during the autumn of 1888.

He was still living on Cable Street when he married Lucy Baderski, in October of 1889. In 1890, not in 1888, Klosowski met Wolff Levisohn while working in the basement below the White Hart pub. Thirteen years later, at Klosowski's murder trial, Levisohn provided testimony against Klosowski, claiming that Klosowski was calling himself Ludwig Zagowski. Lucy gave birth to a son during September of 1890, and by that time Klosowski had begun to run the barber's shop below the White Hart.

This son died of pneumonia on March 3, 1891, and, soon after, Klosowski took Lucy to America. He began working at a barber's shop in New Jersey, but soon after their arrival the couple began fighting. Lucy returned to London in February 1892, by herself. They may have fought over Klosowski's habit of chasing after women. A few months after her return to London she gave birth to their second child, a girl, and Klosowski would return to London shortly after the birth. At the 1903 trial, Lucy described a fight during which he threatened her with a knife. According to Lucy there was a knife under the pillow of the bed. She saw the handle, but he never took it out to use on her. Whether Klosowski was going to use the knife as a weapon is something no one can answer, but the mere suggestion that she was threatened, when, actually, she only *felt* threatened, may have evoked memories of Jack the Ripper.

Klosowski was a womanizer, and his reunion with Lucy would be short-lived. In 1893 he met Annie Chapman (no relation to the murder victim) and began living with her. They lived together for over a year until a pregnant Annie walked out on him when Klosowski brought another woman home to share their bed. In early 1895 Annie returned to Klosowski to ask for his help, but he refused. At about this time, he began calling himself George Chapman, the name that he would eventually be hung under.

Toward the middle of 1895, Klosowski, now known as George Chapman, began having a secret affair with Mary Spink at their lodging house. This began a streak of three successive false marriages for Klosowski and the poisoning of his fake wives. He remained with Spink until her death on Christmas Day in 1897. Klosowski slowly poisoned her with tartar-emeric, which contained a metal called antimony. This would become his downfall.

While with Mary Spink, Klosowski had a large sum of money transferred over to him, enabling him to take over the lease of a barber's shop, and later a pub, where his poisoning ways would continue. He hired a barmaid named Bessie Taylor, and another false marriage was arranged. During their time together, Klosowski and Bessie fought continually, with one such event involving a revolver. Three years after they first met, Bessie Taylor began showing signs of the same illness that had befallen Mary Spink. Taylor would die at the new pub leased by Klosowski on February 13, 1901.

Six months after the death of his second false wife, he hired Maud Marsh, falsely married her, and they lived together as man and wife. She would have the same fate as Mary Spink and Bessie Taylor, dying of a similar illness on Oc-

tober 22, 1902. This time it would come back to haunt Klosowski. An investigation into her death prompted the exhumation of the bodies of Mary Spink and Bessie Taylor. The evidence was clear. Tartar-emeric is a slow-acting poison, but also a preserving agent. When the authorities opened Spink's coffin, five years after her death, she looked relatively unchanged, and further tests showed that Klosowski had likely poisoned all three of these women. Despite this evidence, he was only charged with the murder of Maud Marsh.

On October 25, 1902, Inspector George Godley, a Detective Sergeant at the time of the Jack the Ripper murders, arrested Klosowski as George Chapman. As more was learned about Klosowski, the more police realized that he was a real villain, capable of almost anything. One man was released from prison because Klosowski had lied about evidence in his case. The police would also learn about the many aliases Klosowski had used throughout his lifetime. He was constantly watched for fear he would commit suicide. Klosowski was hung at Wandsworth Prison on April 7, 1903.

According to McCormick, the statements of Dr. Thomas Dutton, that Klosowski worked under the White Hart pub during the time of the murders are of great importance. According to McCormick, this information came from Wolff Levisohn, who verified that Klosowski had worked there. It was supposedly Levisohn who had spoken to Abberline about the Jack the Ripper case and advised him that Klosowski was not the suspect he was looking for, but rather that Abberline should be searching for a Russian who was handy with a knife. According to McCormick, this was a reference to Pedachenko. Under this theory, the police were investigating a barber working in the basement of George Yard. The police allegedly spoke to Klosowski, prompting him to flea to another barber's shop in Tottenham, walking distance from the White Hart pub, where Abberline eventually tracked him down. Before they could set up any police surveillance on Klosowski, he fled again, according to McCormick's theory. This is where the story of Levisohn advising Abberline that he was searching for the wrong man comes in.

The entire chronology is marred by a fatal flaw. Research performed by Neal Shelden has proven that Klosowski did not work as a barber under the White Hart pub until 1890. This evidence eliminates any surveillance of Klosowski at the time of the murders, while also canceling out the story that Wolff Levisohn informed Abberline of the Russian who resembled Klosowski. Another internal error from this story is that Klosowski did not move to Tottenham until late 1894 and that he did not take over this barber's shop until January of 1895.

There are no known surveillance reports on Klosowski or any suspect at George Yard during the times of the murders, let alone any suspect specifically watched by Inspector Abberline that fit these precise descriptions. Abberline is also supposed to have interviewed Lucy Baderski, the wife of Klosowski. But Klosowski did not meet Baderski until 1889.

Numerous aspects of the story told by McCormick, gathered from Dr. Dutton, are based upon inaccuracies. These inaccuracies originated from research performed by crime historian Hargrave

L. Adam. In 1930, Adam published *The Trial of George Chapman*. This book contained a number of historical statements that have been proven inaccurate. McCormick's heavy reliance on Adam's 1930 work seriously tarnishes his opinions regarding Klosowski.

Despite claims by McCormick, Severin Klosowski would not be mentioned in connection with the Jack the Ripper murders until the end of his trial on March 23, 1903. One day later a reporter from *The Pall Mall Gazette* interviewed Inspector Abberline for his thoughts on a suggestion made by *The Daily Chronicle* the previous day. From this statement to the reporter, it can be inferred that Abberline's suspicion regarding Klosowski did not develop until the Attorney General for Klosowski's trail had made his opening statement. Abberline's suspicions regarding Klosowski had not originated during the time of the murders, as erroneously stated by McCormick, who relied on the diaries of Dr. Dutton. This can be proven from an 1892 interview given by Abberline in *Cassells Saturday Journal*, in which he said that Scotland Yard was "lost in theories." There was no mention of Klosowski, or any suspect, for that matter. Dr. Dutton's diaries, or chronicles of crime, have never surfaced, and there is doubt as to whether they actually exist. Another interview with Abberline was conducted at the end of March 1903. Abberline emphatically stated, "Scotland Yard is really no wiser on the subject than it was fifteen years ago. It is simple nonsense to talk of the police having proof that the man is dead."

Born in Nagornak, Poland, in 1865, Severin Klosowski, alias George Chapman, was mentioned in 1930 and in 1959, but he was dismissed as a viable suspect by researcher Leonard Gribble in 1977, before being reconsidered in the 1990s as a viable suspect. Recent research has revealed a great amount of detail about Klosowski, allowing us to forever dismiss the deliberately misleading information offered by Donald McCormick. Researcher Philip Sugden, on the basis of the claim that Klosowski was Abberline's suspect, considers him one of the prime suspects. While Abberline knew almost as much as any man about the Jack the Ripper case, his suspicions were not aroused until Klosowski was on trial for poisoning Maud Marsh nearly fifteen years later.

In 2001 researcher R. Michael Gordon concluded that Klosowski was not only responsible for the murders attributed to Jack the Ripper, but was also responsible for the numerous torso murders that occurred within the same area and time frame. Gordon uses this multiple-murder, multiple-*modus operandi* theory to claim that Klosowski could have easily gone from decapitator and mutilator to serial poisoner. The murder of a woman in New Jersey, known as "Old Shakespeare," is also attributed to Klosowski. Klosowski was documented as having been in New Jersey during the time when Carrie Brown was murdered, yet Gordon's theory is seriously hampered by the number of murders he attributes to Klosowski without providing additional evidence. Gordon released a full-length book on the London torso murders the following year.

Klosowski was habitually cruel to women. This inevitably caused many problems with the women he lived with. Currently, there is no evidence that he was living with a woman during the time of the murders, and certainly no evidence he was living with the victims

of Jack the Ripper. When he married Lucy Baderski in October 1889, a pattern formed. Klosowski would use women until he no longer needed them or someone better came along. Then he simply discarded them.

After Annie Chapman left Klosowski, due to his chasing after another woman, she came back and asked for his help because she was pregnant. This could have been a serious problem for Klosowski's reputation. The easy thing to do would have been to murder her. Klosowski did not do that. Instead, he took her last name. He would be connected to her for the rest of his life, but he took no violent action against her. This could be what changed his mind toward women, as the next three women he resided with were all slowly poisoned. Severin Klosowski was thought to be very intimate at the beginning of all of these relationships, the opposite of what is believed of Jack the Ripper's relationships with women.

A slow poisoning would most likely not be acceptable for Jack the Ripper. By 1897 most thoughts of Jack the Ripper were nothing more than a fading memory, yet Klosowski waited months at a time to slowly poison these three women. Any number of "accidental" murders could have taken place. They did not need to be in the mold of the murders committed by Jack the Ripper.

Severin Klosowski possessed a violent nature and did commit at least three murders by poisoning women. He was in London at the time of the murders and is considered the preferred suspect of the man in charge of the ground investigation, Inspector Abberline, although conflicting newspaper interviews with Inspector Abberline do challenge this status. His age at the time of the murders (twenty-three), and his ethnicity (Polish) closely resemble Assistant Commissioner Robert Anderson's suspect. To this day Anderson's personal unnamed suspect is thought by numerous researchers to have been Jack the Ripper.

Adam, Hargrave L. *The Trial of George Chapman* (1930).
Begg, Paul, Martin Fido, and Keith Skinner. *The Jack the Ripper A–Z* (1996).
Gordon, R. Michael. *Alias Jack the Ripper: Beyond the Usual Whitechapel Suspects* (2001).
_____. *The Thames Torso Murders of Victorian London* (2002).
Gribble, Leonard. *True Detective* (March 1977).
McCormick, Donald. *The Identity of Jack the Ripper* (1959).
Shelden, Neal. *Ripperana* (October 1993).
Sugden, Philip. *The Complete History of Jack the Ripper* (2002).
http://www.casebook.org

VASSILY KONOVALOV

According to Donald McCormick, Vassily Konovalov was mentioned in a January 1909, secret Russian police bulletin, the *Ochrana Gazette*. This bulletin announced that Konovalov was now officially declared dead. Within this document, Konovalov is listed as wanted for the murders of one woman in Paris in 1886, one woman in St. Petersburg in 1891 and five women in the East Quarter of London in 1888. The latter is an obvious reference to the murders committed by Jack the Ripper.

The aim of the police bulletin was to obtain any outstanding information pertaining to Konovalov. It is this plea for information that connects Konovalov to the Whitechapel murders. The bulletin briefly provides some historical background information on Konovalov, including his birthplace and year, his physical characteristics and his final resting place. The bulletin does go on to give one more detail of importance— Konovalov's aliases, which included the alias Alexey Pedachenko.

Theorist Donald McCormick revived the Dr. Pedachenko theory, dormant since 1923, in 1959 by naming Vassily Konovalov as the true identity of Jack the Ripper. McCormick is solely responsible for sourcing the 1909 Ochrana secret police bulletin, where Pedachenko is listed among the aliases of Vassily Konovalov. McCormick's story develops and furthers the 1923 William Le Queux tale regarding Russian suspect, Dr. Alexander Pedachenko.

McCormick does not provide proper evidence for his source material, and coincidentally, not one of his sources has ever been traced. There are five basic sources from which McCormick claims to have drawn his information. The primary source is Le Queux's tale of Dr. Pedachenko. Le Queux, like McCormick, has never properly provided the necessary documentation of his research. This seriously damages the validity of his story, and McCormick's advancement of Le Queux's tale also suffers that weakness.

According to McCormick, the second of his sources was the January 1909, issue of the *Ochrana Gazette*, where the vital characteristics of Konovalov are laid out. This bulletin was never mentioned by William Le Queux, so it must be fully explained how it came into the possession of McCormick. McCormick states that he was shown a lithograph copy of this document by Prince Sergei Belloselski, a Russian exiled to London. This was supposedly shown to McCormick sometime prior to Belloselski's death in 1951. As McCormick's first book on Jack the Ripper did not come out until 1959, he obviously held on to this information for at least eight years. If Belloselski did have a copy of this untraced document, why did he not produce it earlier, when Le Queux first mentioned Dr. Pedachenko? The answer may be that Belloselski's involvement in this story was deliberately invented. McCormick mentions that Belloselski attempted to contact Le Queux regarding this Russian suspect but for some unknown reason, Le Queux never made use of this obviously corroborative information. In fact, Prince Sergei's own daughter, Marina, has stated that, if he had any documents pertaining to the identity of Jack the Ripper, she would have known about it. His circle of friends didn't seem to know anything about the document either.

McCormick is known to have frequented a bar also frequented by Belloselski, who carried around a scrapbook. It was in this scrapbook that McCormick was supposedly shown the Secret Police bulletin. Belloselski's daughter, however, claimed there were nothing but photographs of friends and family in this scrapbook. If McCormick had known Belloselski intimately enough to

be shown a lithograph copy of this bulletin, he would have also known that his treasured scrapbook contained only photographs. This was an apparent attempt by McCormick to link himself to Le Queux, through the use of Belloselski, an attempt that has ultimately come up short.

McCormick's third untraced source emanates from the three handwritten volumes of crime history authored by Dr. Thomas Dutton. Dr. Dutton lived at Aldgate, High Street, in the East End of London during the time of the murders, so he would have known a great deal about the history of the murders. After Dr. Dutton's death in 1935, Hermoine Dudley reported that she had been given the three volumes of work that constituted Dutton's *Chronicles of Crime*. According to Dudley, Dr. Dutton claimed to have assisted with the post-mortems on the victims. He also supposedly claimed to know the identity of Jack the Ripper. With regards to the murderer's identity, a brief description similar to another suspect, a "Dr. Stanley," was offered. Miss Dudley never produced these three volumes and, to this day, they still have not been unearthed.

McCormick bases his story of Konovalov on Dr. Dutton's three handwritten volumes of crime for his 1959 book, claiming that he was personally shown these volumes by Dr. Dutton in 1932. Two of the main claims of these mystery volumes are Dr. Dutton's close relationship with Inspector Abberline and a supposed 1888 search for the suspect Severin Klosowski, later known as George Chapman. It is imperative to clarify that McCormick mentions these passages from Dutton within his own theory so that he can claim that Dr.

Dutton thought Dr. Pedachenko was the exact double of Severin Klosowski. According to McCormick, the two suspects may have exchanged identities, or there may have been some confusion about who was really sought by Abberline.

McCormick however, uses this "evidence" to push for his own suspect, incorporating not only Le Queux's suspect, Dr. Pedachenko, but also Abberline's suspect, Severin Klosowski. McCormick uses Dr. Dutton to imply that Dr. Pedachenko may have been the more likely suspect. As these volumes have still yet to surface, it must be assumed that they never existed or that they did not contain the information stated by McCormick.

The fourth source McCormick used to argue Konovalov's guilt was a newspaper article from the *Glasgow Evening News,* published on November 27, 1947. In this article, an eighty-year-old criminologist, named Hector Cairns, is said to have a collection of documents on crime, one of which came from Rasputin and proved that Dr. Pedachenko was Jack the Ripper. The article was written by a "Cairns," but it happened to be "G. D. K. M'Cormick" who initially contributed the information to the paper. It is not known who G. D. K. M'Cormick actually was, but the similarities are apparent, and the omission of this name from Donald McCormick's citations leaves one to wonder if he is not the man who supplied the paper with this information.

The last of the McCormick sources was also a source possibly used by William Le Queux—Basil Thomson. If Le Queux did obtain any information from Thomson, then McCormick's use of a previously uncited letter by Thomson

would develop and advance the theory further. This appears to be McCormick's intention. The letter was written toward the end of Thomson's life, sometime around 1939, and was first mentioned in 1962, in McCormick's revised paperback edition of his 1959 book. This untraced and still un-produced letter evolved in another revised edition from McCormick in 1970. The 1962 account of the letter stated that Thomson had discovered from the French that Jack the Ripper was a Russian named Konovalov, who also used the alias Mikhael Ostrog. This was how Konovalov was known by Scotland Yard, as Mikhael Ostrog, yet they described him as a surgeon, while the French described him as a barber's assistant. It is noteworthy that McCormick never mentions Scotland Yard in connection with his preferred suspect. In 1970, when the updated version of McCormick's book was published, the Thomson letter the author refers to, still not produced, made no mention of the Mikhael Ostrog alias. Two years later, in the *History of the Russian Secret Service,* written by a "Richard Deacon," later positively identified as McCormick's pseudonym, Ostrog is repeatedly listed as an alias of Vassily Konovalov.

The entire scope of this source seems suspect. The Basil Thomson letter was written in 1939. Ostensibly, McCormick views the letter at some time between the writing of the 1959 and 1962 book. Thomson was the self-appointed Director of Intelligence during the time after the Russian revolution. He dealt specifically with the Bolsheviks, so he may have been privy to information such as this. Why, then, would Thomson state that he got the information regarding Jack the Ripper from the French? Le Queux originally stated that Rasputin's document on Pedachenko was in French. McCormick stated that Thomson learned the identity of Jack the Ripper from the French. Documentation does not exist for either story. In both stories, using the French is an attempt to gain credibility.

Thomson was a curious figure to incorporate into this story, but, looking at his own publishing history, we begin to see why he was used. In 1935, the year of Dr. Dutton's death, Thomson released *The Story of Scotland Yard*. In this book Thomson declares that the CID believed Jack the Ripper was an insane Russian doctor. When McCormick learned of the three named suspects contained within the MacNaghten Memorandum from Dan Farson in 1959, Thomson became the perfect tool to promote Ostrog as an alias for Vassily Konovalov, a task McCormick later performed under his pseudonym, "Richard Deacon."

And what would Donald McCormick need to invent this whole story? Merely developing the Le Queux story, McCormick's original source for his Konovalov-Pedachenko-Ostrog theory, would do nothing for him, so he would have to advance the theory to gain any recognition. A newspaper account is cited to back up the origins of the Le Queux story regarding Pedachenko. The Dr. Dutton volumes reinforce the Le Queux story and advance it by adding a known policeman from the case to foster credibility. The lithograph copy of the 1909 *Ochrana Gazette*, which states that Pedachenko was nothing more than an alias of Vassily Konovalov, allows McCormick to advance the Le Queux story. Now, McCormick had a newly named suspect which had supposedly come directly from his own writings and research. Finally, the letter by Thomson allows McCormick to connect his new suspect with a suspect actually mentioned by Scotland Yard. It must be restated that none of McCormick's sources were ever produced for public scrutiny.

Until proven otherwise, McCormick's story must be viewed as pure invention. His sources are not corroborated, and his foundations are extremely weak. McCormick's connection of a known suspect, Mikhael Ostrog, to his suspect, Vassily Konovalov, is based on sheer speculation. He attempts to verify and back the connection by mentioning it in another book, under a pseudonym. The suspect, Vassily Konovalov, is based upon the story told by William Le Queux in 1923. The Le Queux story appears to be a complete fabrication, itself. As a result, all evidence points to the conclusion that Vassily Konovalov is an invented suspect. He should therefore be eliminated from consideration until McCormick's documentation can be accurately traced. Unfortunately, Donald McCormick passed away in 1998 and took the secret to the grave.

Begg, Paul, Martin Fido, and Keith Skinner. *The Jack the Ripper A–Z* (1996).

Deacon, Richard (Donald McCormick). *History of the Russian Secret Service* (1972).

McCormick, Donald. *The Identity of Jack the Ripper* (1959).

Le Queux, William. *Things I Know About Kings, Celebrities, and Crooks* (1923).

Thomson, Basil. *The Story of Scotland Yard* (1935).

AARON KOSMINSKI

Extremely little was known about Aaron Kosminski until the mid–1980s, with only the most basic information presented at that time. It is not known where he was born, yet the year of his birth is either 1864 or 1865, making him approximately twenty-three years old at the time of the murders. His movements at the times of the murders have never been fully ascertained. In July of 1890, Kosminski was taken from his residence, where he lived with his brother-in-law, Woolf Abrahams, to Mile End Old Town Workhouse Infirmary for treatment. It is not specified exactly what this treatment was, but Kosminski was released three days later into the care of Abrahams. Upon admission, the register noted that he had been insane for two years.

The next couple of months in his life are another mystery. On the 4th of February, nine days before the murder of Frances Coles, Kosminski was readmitted to the Infirmary. Three days later, he was transferred to Colney Hatch Lunatic Asylum. He remained at Colney Hatch until April 13, 1894, when he was transferred to Leavesden Asylum for Imbeciles, having been deemed "demented and incoherent." Kosminski would remain at Leavesden for the rest of his life, eventually dying twenty-five years later in 1919.

In an attempt to learn more about the history and demeanor of this man, an examination of the register books and doctors reports were examined. The original notes from Kosminski's 1890 stay at Mile End prove of little use. The notes basically stated that Kosminski was insane but had, for some reason, still been released into the care of his brother-in-law. After he was readmitted to Mile End, Dr. Edmund Houchin examined Kosminski.

The medical certificate of Dr. Houchin described the plight of this man, stating that Kosminski believed he was guided and controlled by an instinct that informed his mind. Kosminski claimed to know the movements of all mankind and refused to take food from others, choosing to eat from the gutter. These were obvious paranoid delusions and aural hallucinations, as Kosminski seemed to believe that a higher power spoke to him and controlled the way he acted. A witness named Jacob Cohen provided details to Dr. Houchin about Aaron Kosminski. Cohen stated that Kosminski ate from the streets, did not wash, compulsively self-abused himself (masturbated frequently), and had not worked at a job for many years. Cohen also stated that Kosminski had threatened his own sister with a knife. From Dr. Houchin's examination and the statements of Jacob Cohen, Kosminski was declared of unsound mind and detained for treatment. This "treatment" would last for the rest of his life and apparently never cured him.

On the opposite side of the committal order, Maurice Whitfield, the Relieving Officer for the Western District of Mile End Old Town, made a few comments regarding Kosminski for the benefit of Colney Hatch. Whitfield reported the cause of Kosminski's illness as unknown. He stated that Kosminski's first attack of insanity occurred in July of 1890, when he was first admitted to Mile End. The present attack had lasted for the past six months. This statement is a mystery, as it would indicate that only a month after his first release from Mile End, this present bout of insanity began. Perhaps Mile End should not have released Kosminski after the staff first declared him insane back in July of 1890. Whitfield's final statement is of extreme importance. He specifically says that Kosminski was not dangerous to other people. This emphatic statement, addressed to the people who would now be taking complete care of Kosminski, indicates that Kosminski's insanity was deemed non-violent by an expert in the field.

The reports from Colney Hatch show Kosminski to be suffering from aural hallucinations, as Dr. Houchin had originally diagnosed. The notes add that he continued to refuse to work, that he objected to washing himself, and that his mental health was deteriorating. In all the reports on Kosminski from Colney Hatch, only one mentioned violence. Kosminski apparently grabbed a chair and made an attempt to strike an attendant. Most of the reports and notes on Kosminski describe him as incoherent. Some notes refer to Kosminski as excitable, but the statement made upon his transfer from Colney Hatch to Leavesden was that Kosminski was not dangerous. He was described again as incoherent. This was further supported by the order for Kosminski's admission into Leavesden, which declared him a harmless lunatic.

There are no more notes on Kosminsky's health or activity until sixteen years later in 1910. It can be assumed that these records have been lost. Case notes that have survived describe various aspects of Kosminski's final years. At that time in his life he had begun having health problems. Kosminski's weight slowly decreased, and he had problems with his bowels. His death in 1919 is listed as a result of gangrene of the left leg. Throughout his stays at any one of the three facilities mentioned above, Kosminski was never characterized as homicidal or as dangerous to himself or others. From what is known of this suspect, he appears to be a simple man who suffered from delusions and heard voices.

The first mention of the suspect Kosminski comes from the MacNaghten Memorandum, in 1894. It must be made clear that nowhere in any of the MacNaghten reports does the name, "Aaron," appear. The portions of the two known versions of the 1894 MacNaghten Memorandum that relate to Kosminski exhibit marked differences. MacNaghten's personal draft version stated that Kosminski was,

> a Polish Jew, who lived in the very heart of the district where the murders were committed. He had become insane owing to many years indulgence in solitary vices. He had a great hatred of women, with strong homicidal tendencies. He was (and I believe still is) detained in a lunatic asylum during March 1889. This man in appearance resembled the individual seen by the City P.C near Mitre Square.

The Scotland Yard version of the memorandum reads as follows:

> Kosminski, a Polish Jew, & resident in Whitechapel. This man became insane owing to many years indulgence in solitary vices. He had a great hatred of

women, especially of the prostitute class, & had strong homicidal tendencies; he was removed to a lunatic asylum about March 1889. There were many circs connected with this man which made him a strong suspect.

In comparing these two versions, one would almost have trouble deciphering which one was the version intended to further the goal of the memorandum—to challenge the claim that Thomas Cutbush was Jack the Ripper. The two versions start basically the same, with the Scotland Yard version being the clearer of the two. The main discrepancy between the two versions concerns the end statement. In the draft version, MacNaghten mentions Kosminski's similarity to a suspect observed by a city police constable. Neither the suspect nor the constable has ever been positively identified. The Scotland Yard version does not mention this identification, but does state that Kosminski was a strong suspect.

In 1895, the year after the Mac-Naghten Memorandum was filed at Scotland Yard, an article appeared in *Windsor Magazine*, written by Alfred Aylmer. It made the first public claim that Assistant Commissioner Robert Anderson had formulated a theory as to the identity of Jack the Ripper. Aylmer stated that Anderson had a "perfectly plausible theory that Jack the Ripper was a homicidal maniac, temporarily at large, whose hideous career was cut short by committal to an asylum." As this was a theory of Anderson's, it must be assumed that the murderer referred to is Kosminski, due to the later revelation that Kosminski was Anderson's "Polish Jew" suspect. Internal evidence exists, however, that does not correlate with known aspects of Kosminski. More

importantly, as early as 1895, Anderson knew of Kosminski.

In Arthur Griffiths's 1898 book he mentions the three suspects from the draft version of the MacNaghten Memorandum, omitting their names. The next chronological reference to Kosminski occurs in the year of Anderson's retirement, 1901. Anderson wrote a number of articles and books and made direct references to the Jack the Ripper case after his retirement. The 1901 article, entitled "Punishing Crime," reiterates that Jack the Ripper was "safely caged in an asylum."

Six years would pass before Anderson would again write about the murders. In his 1907 book, *Criminals and Crime*, he restated the thesis of the 1901 article at the beginning of the book. On subsequent pages, Anderson toyed with the possibility of a revelation in the case, but that never came. The following year Anderson wrote another article which would appear in *The Daily Chronicle*. He did not expand on the suspect.

The full scope of Anderson's theory would be released to the public in 1910. His reminiscences were serialized in *Blackwood's Magazine*. In Part VI of the serial article Anderson would let loose the full range of his thoughts. Anderson blatantly declared that the murderer was a low-class Jew, protected by his people, who were also low-class Jews. These people refused to hand him over to the police even though they knew of his guilt, according to Anderson. The final sentence of the footnote needs repeating:

I will only add that when the individual whom we suspected was caged in an asylum, the only person who ever had a good view of the murderer at once identified him, but when he learned that the suspect was a fellow–Jew he declined to swear to him.

Herein lies the first public mentioning of the two most important aspects of Anderson's theory, that Jack the Ripper was Jewish, and that a fellow Jew identified him as the murderer.

At the time, Anderson's remarks were met with harsh criticism by the Jewish press. Anderson stood firm. His 1910 book, *The Lighter Side of My Official Life*, modified his story in one very clear way. Rather than saying the murderer and the people who protected him were low-class Jews, he stated that they were low-class Polish Jews. The criticism from the Jewish press did not dissuade Anderson from stating what he had come to believe.

Until 1987, only Robert Anderson would attest to a suspect identification in writing. In 1987 the copy of Anderson's book that had been given to Chief Inspector Donald Swanson was revealed to the public. This book, along with other documents, had been passed along to Swanson's grandson in 1980. After repeated attempts to get these documents published, he succeeded in 1987. In Swanson's copy of the book, Swanson had made a number of penciled notes.

He began by writing in the margins of page 138. On that specific page, Anderson had written of the identification. Swanson backed up the man he called his "old master" by writing, "because the suspect was also a Jew and also because his evidence would convict the suspect, and witness would be the means of the murderer being hanged which he did not wish to be left on his mind." This is nothing more than restating what Anderson had written. Swanson also wrote, "And after this identification

which suspect knew, no other murder of this kind took place in London."

So Swanson believed the last murder in the series to be that of Mary Kelly, keeping, in part, with the theory of the "canon." Swanson also believed that the suspect realized he was being identified, which would indicate that he could have been face to face with the witness. Also, Swanson indicated that the suspect possessed enough of his faculties to be aware that the identification was taking place. This is inconsistent with what is known of Aaron Kosminski, who, as far back as possibly 1885, was suffering from aural hallucinations and a general incoherence.

On the book's endpapers, Swanson does what Anderson never did. He named this suspect. His endpaper comments are as follows:

...after the suspect had been identified at the Seaside Home where he had been sent by us with difficulty in order to subject him to identification, and he knew he was identified.
On suspect's return to his brother's house in Whitechapel he was watched by police (City CID) by day and night. In a very short time the suspect with his hands tied behind his back, he was sent to Stepney Workhouse and then to Colney Hatch and died shortly afterwards—Kosminski was the suspect.

This was the first public naming of Kosminski as the Polish Jew referred to by Robert Anderson.

However, there are numerous errors within Swanson's writing regarding Anderson's suspect. Swanson states that the suspect was identified at the Seaside Home. The first Seaside Home, common vernacular for the Convalescent Police Seaside Home, where suspect identifications would occasionally take place, was not opened until March of 1890. If one assumed that this identification took place as soon as the home opened, then that would still be seventeen months after the original witness sighting. Kosminski had not been committed until July of 1890, and he only remained there for three days. If the identification took place during this time, Swanson would have us believe that Kosminski was brought to Mile End Infirmary for treatment of insanity, then positively identified by a witness as Jack the Ripper, who then refused to provide testimony. So, rather than keeping Kosminski locked away, where it was noted that he was insane, he was allowed to go home. How easy would it have been for the police to keep the possible Jack the Ripper murderer locked up in an asylum? Considering these circumstances, it must be assumed that the identification took place after this July 1890, three-day committal.

The immediate problem with this theory is that Aaron Kosminski was committed again but never released after that. On February 4, 1891, Kosminski was re-admitted to Mile End Infirmary and spent the rest of his life in one of three asylums. So the identification could not have taken place after the February 1891, committal. The other instance in July 1890, must therefore be the date of the identification, except for the fact that police then allowed the man they had supposedly identified as Jack the Ripper to go free.

Swanson plainly states that the murderer knew he had been identified. After March 1890, and perhaps as far back as 1885 Kosminski had been incoherent. He was diagnosed as insane only three months after March 1890. Now

we're asked to believe that a man who was guided by voices knew the implications of such an identification? Unlike the actual date of the identification, this piece of information may be a little easier to believe, yet serious doubts still linger.

Swanson states that Kosminski was returned to his brother's house and was watched day and night by the city police. Henry Smith, who was Acting Commissioner for the City Police on the night of the double murder and who was still active after 1890, would have been aware of and involved in any suspect surveillance, especially one pertaining to Jack the Ripper. In his memoirs Smith attacks Anderson, saying that he made a "reckless accusation." Even if nothing had come of this surveillance, Smith likely would have mentioned that it occurred, but he does not. To believe that city police surveillance of a suspect took place without the knowledge of Henry Smith is an unfounded leap.

Swanson next stated that a short time later the suspect was sent to "Stepney Workhouse with his hands tied behind his back." This whole statement has factual errors. By "a short time later," Swanson must have meant a short time after the identification. With regards to Aaron Kosminski, "a short time" would have meant six months. However, in February 1891, Kosminski was sent to Mile End Infirmary, not Stepney Workhouse. In fact, Kosminski is depicted as consistently objecting to work, and it would seem that if Kosminski were identified as the murderer Mile End would have known about the identification. There is no evidence to indicate that Kosminski was taken by force or had his hands tied upon his re-admittance to Mile End. Kosminski was described as not dangerous to himself or others, so there would be no reason for such as precautionary measure.

The remark that he was then taken to Colney Hatch is the only statement that accurately depicts Aaron Kosminski, but within the same sentence, Swanson states that he died shortly thereafter. Aaron Kosminski did not die until twenty-eight years after his transfer to Colney Hatch. Swanson then positively asserts that Kosminski was the suspect.

All the information within the Swanson marginalia does not accurately describe Aaron Kosminski. This calls into question whether Anderson's suspect was really Aaron Kosminski. There seems to be only unsupported or non-factual material concerning Aaron Kosminski in Swanson's notes.

The case against Aaron Kosminski boils down to Kosminski's mental health. He was clearly insane and suffering from a number of schizophrenic symptoms. His insanity may have ranged as far back as 1885. A number of medical personnel recorded Aaron Kosminski as neither suicidal nor dangerous to people. A person who was clearly insane, but not dangerous, would most likely not have committed these murders with such ferocity and precision.

There is also the matter of Aaron Kosminski remaining at large until February of 1891. If a lunatic such as Aaron Kosminski committed the murders, told to do so by a higher power, then the murders likely would not have ceased with either Mary Kelly or Alice McKenzie. After McKenzie's murder, in July of 1889, a full eighteen months elapsed before Aaron Kosminski was committed for life, yet no other Jack the Ripper–type murder took place during that span.

Aaron Kosminski was nothing more than a feeble-minded imbecile who could not be a productive or useful member of society. The right decision was made to remove him, as no good would have come from allowing him to freely roam the streets of London. He was, however, non-violent and had the outward appearance of a vagrant, two characteristics not associated with Jack the Ripper. If what Anderson and Swanson state were the truth, then the Kosminski that Swanson announced as Anderson's suspect was someone other than Aaron Kosminski.

Anderson, Robert. *Blackwood's Magazine* (1910).

_____. *Criminals and Crime: Some Facts and Suggestions* (1907).

_____, Robert. *The Daily Chronicle* (September 1908).

_____, Robert. *The Lighter Side of My Official Life* (1910).

_____, Robert. *The Nineteenth Century* (February 1901).

Aylmer, Alfred (Arthur Griffiths). *Windsor Magazine, Volume 1* (January–June 1895).

Beadle, William. *Jack the Ripper: Anatomy of a Myth* (1995).

Begg, Paul. *Jack the Ripper: The Uncensored Facts* (1988).

_____, Martin Fido, and Keith Skinner. *The Jack the Ripper A–Z* (1996).

Evans, Stewart P., and Keith Skinner. *The Ultimate Jack the Ripper Companion* (2000).

Fido, Martin. *The Crimes, Detection and Death of Jack the Ripper* (1988).

Griffiths, Arthur. *Mysteries of Police and Crime* (1898).

Rumbelow, Donald. *The Complete Jack the Ripper* (1987).

Smith, Henry. *From Constable to Commissioner: The Story of Sixty Years: Most of Them Misspent* (1910).

Sugden, Philip. *The Complete History of Jack the Ripper* (2002).

LEOPOLD II (LOUIS PHILLIPPE MARIE VICTOR), KING OF BELGIUM

Born in Brussels on April 9, 1835, Louis Marie Phillippe Victor would enter the Belgian Army during his youth and be appointed to the rank of second lieutenant at the age of eleven. Nine years later in 1855, he would achieve the rank of general. At the age of eighteen he married the daughter of the Archduke of Austria, Maria Henrietta. Upon the death of his father in 1865, he would ascend to the throne, taking the name Leopold II.

Known during his reign as a philanthropist, Leopold II would form the International Association for the Exploration and Civilization of the Congo. Rather than civilizing the Congo, Leopold II exploited free slave labor to amass a personal fortune. In 1908 the Belgian Government made the Congo an official colony. The following year, on December 17, 1909, King Leopold II would pass away. His nephew Albert would succeed him to the throne.

While conducting research for theorist Daniel Farson, Jacquemine Charrot-Lodwidge devised a theory that King Leopold II may have been Jack the Ripper. His theory is based on two circumstantial pieces of evidence. The first of these is that, during his life, King Leopold II was surrounded by scandal that reached into his private affairs. The second was that, during King Leopold II's reign, Belgium retained possession of the African nation the Congo. Char-

rot-Lodwidge hypothesized that on his visits to the Congo, undocumented to this date, King Leopold II developed a sadistic nature while observing the Congolese rituals and cultural habits.

Scandal rocks many a leader, and I challenge anyone to find a historical leader who did not have some part of his or her private or political life involved in scandal. That is the nature of politics and royalty. Scandal can be manipulated to serve the political climate of the time. This is not to say that King Leopold II was a saint. In fact, the opposite was true. King Leopold II's private life has been compared with that of his political conquest of the Congo. He is described as barbaric and despotic. King Leopold II relinquished control of the Congo to the Belgian Government in 1908, but he had already amassed a personal fortune from his exploits in that region.

Most of Europe had colonized certain areas of Africa by the mid–1900s, with Belgium being one of the exceptions. Attempting to advance the status and resources of his country, King Leopold II employed the help of adventurer and explorer Henry Stanley and ultimately gained recognized possession of the Congo in 1884. His aim was to civilize this area, but what really happened was mass death and carnage, and the rape of natural resources.

Jacquemine Charrot-Lodwidge has

connected these circumstantial pieces of evidence, while also deducing that King Leopold II was the suspect described by the psychic Robert James Lees. Lees's daughter, according to Charrot-Lodwidge, believed the identity of her father's suspect was of much higher rank than a doctor, and it was thus determined by Charrot-Lodwidge that a house described in the Lees story must be the London residence of King Leopold II. Combining all this speculation, Charrot-Lodwidge arrived at the conclusion that King Leopold II was Jack the Ripper.

This "evidence" does not form the basis for any kind of a theory, let alone proclaim someone as a suspect. There is nothing tangible to link King Leopold II to Jack the Ripper. There is an added problem with Chorrot-Lodwidge's theory. It has never been proven that King Leopold II was in London at the time of the murders. If King Leopold II had a particular residence in London, which certainly would not be out of the question, it was not the one mentioned in the story attributed to Lees. Lees makes it crystal clear that the house belonged to an eminent physician. There appears to be no real basis for the suggestion made by Jacquemine Charrot-Lodwidge regarding King Leopold II.

Begg, Paul, Martin Fido, and Keith Skinner. *The Jack the Ripper A–Z* (1996).
http://histclo.hispeed.com/royal/bel/royalbell2.htm
http://www.bartleby.com/65/le/Leopo2Bel.html

ALONZO MADURO

Unfortunately, not much is known about Alonzo Maduro. Maduro was suggested as Jack the Ripper in a 1956 article from *True Magazine*. The article has distinct degrees of separation from its 1956 source. The story originated with a broker named Griffith S. Salway, who actually met Maduro on the night of the murder of Emma Elizabeth Smith. Maduro allegedly expressed to Salway his displeasure with all prostitutes. After the murder of Mary Kelly, Salway reportedly found surgical knives among the possessions of Maduro, and it was this that convinced him that Maduro was Jack the Ripper. He kept this knowledge to himself until just before he was about to die in 1952.

As Alan Hynd wrote the article published in *True Magazine*, he must have been told the story by Salway's wife, who seems to have waited another four years before divulging it. Since the 1956 article, a number of publications and books have referred back to this story, yet there are discrepancies, and no further information has surfaced about Maduro, or Salway, for that matter. Recently, Maduro has been suggested as the suspect arrested in Vienna, Austria, in 1892, Alios Szemeredy. Noting a similarity in the stories surrounding these suspects, Maxim Jakubowski and Nathan Braund made this suggestion in their 1998 book, *The Mammoth Book of Jack the Ripper*. As always, a lack of evidence should prohibit the researcher from forming that hypothesis.

The existence of Alonzo Maduro has not yet been proven, and logical errors occur within Salway's story. According to Salway, after finding surgical knives in Maduro's possession, he became convinced of his guilt, yet decided to remain silent for 64 years, then only telling his wife just before he died. Salway provides no further information regarding Maduro, and his story is highly questionable. With over 40 years of elapsed time since the publication of this story, no further information has come to light regarding Maduro. Alonzo Maduro is not highly regarded as a viable suspect.

Begg, Paul, Martin Fido, and Keith Skinner. *The Jack the Ripper A–Z* (1996).
Hynd, Alan. *True Magazine* (1956).
Jakubowski, Maxim, and Nathan Braund. *The Mammoth Book of Jack the Ripper* (1998).

JAMES MAYBRICK

Born in 1838, James Maybrick was a cotton merchant from Liverpool. By the 1870s he was traveling back and forth from England to America, flourishing, along with his creation, Maybrick and Company, Cotton Merchants. The American South had been almost utterly destroyed by the Civil War and Reconstruction. When Maybrick set up shop in Norfolk, Virginia, in 1874, the American South had begun a campaign of radical reconstruction. In this system Maybrick's cotton trading prospered.

The most critical year to James Maybrick's future may have been 1877. While in Virginia, Maybrick caught malaria. Malaria was and still is extremely rare in the United States but is prevalent in the Tropics. Currently, over one million children per year are killed as a result of malaria, many of the fatal cases coming from the continent of Africa. As few as ten years ago it was recognized as the single greatest disease hazard for travelers. The disease is transmitted by the bite of an anopheles mosquito. It transmits a parasite, which contains a single-celled organism, known as plasmodia. The basic treatment for malaria is a drug called chloroquine, in conjunction with other drugs like quinine. This is where the predicament arose for Maybrick. According to Shirley Harrison, the first prescription given to Maybrick was only for quinine. He was not told that this was supposed to be used in conjunction with chloroquine. As this disease was very rare in America, perhaps even rarer in the 1870s, the chemist may not have known about the full treatment for this disease. As it would happen, this first prescription did not work. The second prescription used arsenic and strychnine. This is the origin of James Maybrick's arsenic addiction.

Maybrick had met his wife, Florence, aboard the SS *Baltic* in 1880. She was a Southern debutante, all of eighteen years old, chaperoned by her mother, Baroness Caroline von Roques. Florence and her mother were on their way to Paris, while Maybrick was returning to Liverpool. The romance sparked immediately between James and Florence. It was only a six-day trip but, by the time they had reached Liverpool, James had already proposed.

Some years after Florence Maybrick's 1889 trial for poisoning James, a woman named Mary Howard gave a deposition to the American State Department in Washington, D.C. Howard had known James Maybrick in America while running a whorehouse. In her statement, she claimed that Maybrick had frequented her establishment two or three times per week. He was steadily running with whores, but it was never revealed whether Maybrick had a preference for a particular prostitute. The goal of Howard's deposition may have been to aid Florence. According to Howard, as far back as the late 1870s, James was "dosing" arsenic on a continual basis. His addiction to arsenic had hardened before he had met his future wife, Florence.

Recent research into the Maybrick diary has produced another woman from James Maybrick's past. This woman, Sarah Ann Robertson, had a far greater influence on the Maybrick marriage than Mary Howard. It has been reported that James kept a mistress for twenty years. This unnamed woman was supposed to be living in Liverpool during the time of Florence's trial. She had been mentioned in Alexander Mac-Dougall's 1891 book, *Treatise on the Maybrick Case*. She was apparently calling herself the real wife of James Maybrick. She had for some time been going by "Mrs. Maybrick," signing her name this way as a witness for a wedding in 1866. There has been no marriage certificate found. Separate sources state that there were illegitimate children from this relationship, possibly as many as five. No birth or death certificates have surfaced for these children, yet reports of their existence from separate writers indicate that the relationship between Sarah Ann and James might have continued from the time they had met in London, in the mid–1860s, until at least 1887. It can be inferred from the diary that this affair continued through 1888, possibly through the time of the murders.

Before James Maybrick's name had ever been associated with Jack the Ripper, two twentieth century writers on the Maybrick case stated that it was during 1887 that James and Florence began sleeping in separate beds, at Florence's insistence. This may have been when she first found out about the on-going relationship between James and Sarah Ann. Florence was no angel herself, as two indiscretions have been hinted at, one with James's younger brother, Edwin, and one affair made public, an affair with Alfred Brierley. She had met Brierley at a dinner party in 1887, yet their relationship was strictly platonic early on, as Brierley was invited to a dinner party at Battlecrease in mid–November. There were heated arguments between James and Florence during 1888, as well as 1889, but if James had suspected anything was going on between Florence and Alfred Brierley, why would he have invited him to a pre–Christmas dinner ball?

It would appear that intimacies

between Florence and Alfred Brierley began either at this party or immediately thereafter. The affair lasted for a couple of months until Brierley met with Florence in late March of 1889 and told her there was another woman. Despite this and despite Florence and James reconciling, it appears Florence and Brierley continued to meet and correspond. It was this affair with Alfred Brierley, and a letter written by Florence, which the prosecution would present as a motive for her murdering James. Her past indiscretions, with a man named Williams and with James's younger brother, Edwin, were not brought up at the trial.

During April of 1889, James's health steadily deteriorated. Adding fuel to the fire, Florence believed she was pregnant. The baby could only have one father, Alfred Brierley, as James and Florence had not been together since July of 1888. Florence still attempted to reconcile with her husband, but his health quickly worsened. He eventually stopped eating, and his only solace was his regular dosing. On May 9, 1889, James Maybrick passed away. A number of different causes of death were offered, including kidney failure and exhaustion from gastroenteritis, yet the mainstay was that of arsenic poisoning. From what is known today, reinforced by certain doctors at the time whose opinions were weighed and placed aside, James Maybrick did not die of arsenic poisoning. Due to the emergence of the Maybrick diary and the possibility that James Maybrick was Jack the Ripper, intense research has basically proven that Florence Maybrick did not murder him. Even before the diary surfaced, criminologists and writers examined the case of Florence Maybrick without

mentioning Jack the Ripper. Authors such as Nigel Morland and Trevor Christie have hypothesized that procedural improprieties occurred at the trial, suggesting that her innocence was not that farfetched.

For a full discussion of the mistakes made during Florence Maybrick's trial, there can be no better book than Alexander MacDougall's *Treatise of The Maybrick Case*. Interestingly enough, researcher Melvin Harris, who has stood firm in his belief that the Maybrick diary is a forgery, states that MacDougall's 1891 book is one of only two essential books needed to have accurately forged a diary.

The origin of the Maybrick diary has changed over the years. A former scrap metal dealer turned writer, named Michael Barrett, first brought it onto the scene in 1992. Tony Devereux, a friend of Barrett's, supposedly passed the diary on to him in a pub in May of 1991. Devereux passed away soon after, giving the diary to Barrett. Where Devereux obtained the diary was a mystery, but one that would be solved only a few years later. The diary did not contain the name of the author, but the author claimed to be Jack the Ripper. Barrett began investigating the diary. It eventually led him to James Maybrick.

Researcher Shirley Harrison was commissioned to write a book on her investigations into the Maybrick diary. Harrison's book on the diary and on James Maybrick would come out in 1993, published by Robert Smith. A year earlier Smith had secured the worldwide publication rights. Serialization rights were sold to *The Sunday Times*, a popular London newspaper. On September 19, 1993, *The Sunday Times* published a report claiming that the diary was a fake. One of the experts they had queried was Melvin Harris.

When Robert Smith bought the worldwide publication rights in June of 1992, producer Paul Feldman purchased the broadcast rights for a documentary planned on the diary. This would be important, because Feldman has amassed a great deal of research into James Maybrick and his descendants, as well as the descendants of most of the players involved in the diary. Feldman published his own book on Jack the Ripper in 1997.

While numerous scientific tests were being conducted on the diary, Mike Barrett came out with a full confession. On June 27, 1994, *The Liverpool Daily Post* printed the story that Barrett claimed to have forged the diary, starting in 1987. This did not help the search for the truth. The supporters of the diary did not believe this confession, but they still did not know where the diary had come from. Many of the "clues" from conversations with Barrett turned out to be red herrings, but ultimately the conversation led Feldman to what is now assumed to be the provenance of the diary.

Feldman sat down with Mike Barrett's wife, Anne. She stated that the first time she saw the diary was in 1968. After the death of Anne's father's second wife in 1989, her father had given her a pile of books that included the diary. Her father had received the diary from his stepmother in 1950. Anne told Feldman that the diary was left to her by her father's step-grandmother. It was Anne who gave the diary to Tony Deveraux, to give to her husband Mike. She thought it might help his writing career.

One of the main detractors of the diary's authenticity, Melvin Harris, has stated that Anne Barrett's announce-

ment on the provenance of the diary was in a way, "forced." Harris believes that Feldman's persistence compelled Anne's declaration. It took more than two years and the breakup of her marriage for Anne to reveal this part of the story to the world, and both Feldman and Harris dispute the truthfulness of her statements.

The immediate problem is that the diary still had to be given to Anne's father by someone who knew James Maybrick. Feldman connects dot after dot after dot in an attempt to trace lineage between Mike and Anne Barrett to James and Florence Maybrick. To list all the traces Feldman uncovers would confuse rather than clarify, as certain parts of Feldman's book certainly does. James and Florence had numerous children, both separately and together, possibly ten in all. Something like half of the population of present-day England may be traced back to this couple through some relation.

None of this answers the question of who possessed the diary after James Maybrick. While no real answer may ever come, the public might have to accept that that is the real answer. And this is only if the diary is genuine, and not a recent forgery.

To list the numerous experts who performed scientific tests upon the diary would also confuse rather than clarify. Experts on both sides of the issue use their individual findings to bolster their cases and the scientific community is still no closer to the truth.

Researcher Andy Aliffe has considered the possibility that the diary may not be a modern forgery, but an old forgery. He believes the forger would have had to possess an interest in both the Jack the Ripper and Florence Maybrick cases. Aliffe's nominee did indeed have both—the crime historian L. Forbes Winslow.

What must be thoroughly understood here is that since the emergence or re-emergence, of the diary, a wealth of historical information has been discovered and unearthed regarding both James and Florence Maybrick. Newspaper accounts, letters, and books were used in an attempt to prove the diary as genuine. This was done in the 1990s, and it took less than six years to establish these links. With all that has been destroyed or lost over the years, imagine how much easier it would have been to establish these links in the 1890s, the 1900s, or even the 1910s.

Another potential piece of the James Maybrick puzzle emerged in 1993. In July of 1992 Albert Johnson bought an old-style gold watch from Stewart the Jewellers of Wallasey, Cheshire. The jewelry store reported that the watch had been in its possession for the past five years. Approximately one year later, Johnson reported that he had found scratches on the inner portion of the case. These scratches turned out to be the signature "J. Maybrick," the words "I am Jack," the initials of the five canonical victims, and other assorted markings. These other markings have not yet been deciphered.

Tests were immediately performed on the watch. The scratches were viewed as compatible with a date of 1888–1889. However, the emergence of the watch so soon after the discovery of the diary has not been seen as merely a happy coincidence. When rumors began to surface that the diary was fake, the gold watch only reinforced those opinions.

Theorist Paul Feldman has used his genealogical research to link Albert Johnson to James Maybrick, despite Johnson's claims that he bought the watch from a shop in 1992. This is further proof that almost anyone in present-day England can be traced to anyone else in Victorian London.

There is nothing to have prevented a forger of any period from creating this diary. All that was required was an intimate knowledge of James and Florence Maybrick and of the Jack the Ripper case. Knowledge of the Maybricks, specifically relative to James, may have been obtained from any number of sources, including non-contemporary newspapers and MacDougall's 1891 book. Material relating to Jack the Ripper was not only available to certain writers throughout the years, but the members of the police force who actively worked on the investigation were also available to provide information about the case.

Without the benefit of a foolproof scientific test, the world may never know conclusively when the Maybrick Diary was written. Even if a date were established, this would still not rule out the possibility of the diary being a forgery.

During the Jack the Ripper murders, James Maybrick was having an affair with Sarah Robertson. With Robertson Maybrick had a sexual outlet after Florence had asked him to move out of their bedroom, so a frustrated sexual appetite could not be an excuse for committing the murders. The affair between Florence Maybrick and Alfred Brierley had not begun until mid–November of 1888. In the theory proposing that Maybrick was Jack the Ripper, Mary Kelly would have been the last victim, right before Florence's affair with Brierley began. The theory asks the public to accept that after Maybrick's wife began an affair with a man he called a friend Maybrick stopped murdering and mutilating prostitutes. One would think that Florence having an affair with Alfred Brierley would have caused even more violent murders.

Maybrick's health did not begin to seriously deteriorate until 1889, so the cessation of the murders cannot be blamed on James Maybrick's failing health.

Mary Kelly was similar in age, and possibly in appearance, to Florence Maybrick. This has prompted supporters of the diary to state that Maybrick was envisioning the murder of his wife while horribly mutilating Kelly. If this were the case, then why would Maybrick murder the previous four or five prostitutes, who had no similarities to Kelly in either age or appearance? If the reason for the murders had been to get revenge against his unfaithful wife, Maybrick could easily have found women who resembled his wife.

James Maybrick would have had to travel to London from Liverpool on the dates of the murders, which took three hours by train. News of the murders had reached Liverpool. James and Florence were engaging in heated arguments during the time of the murders. Their marriage was in jeopardy. If James had been away from his home in Liverpool on the specific dates of the murders, that would have aroused Florence's suspicions, as well those of his brother Michael, with whom James stayed when he visited London.

Michael would have been even more suspicious than Florence. Surely Michael would have noticed if James's visits coincide with the murders and his brother had no alibi for the hours when the murders were committed. The sup-

porters of the diary claim that Michael might have known about his brother, perhaps going so far as to murder Alice McKenzie to protect his brother's name.

The numerous theories provided to explain the genuineness of the Maybrick diary all have internal issues. For every theory or link suggested by a supporter of the Maybrick diary, a detractor has produced an argument to counter it. No test will fully satisfy either side, as personal opinions regarding the Maybrick diary seemed to have become hardened.

James Maybrick was an arsenic addict, a condition stemming from a mistakenly prescribed medicine in 1877. He was also a womanizer, and this particular trait goes farther back than the origins of his arsenic addiction. Despite claims of mental abuse, there were never any outward signs James physically abusing his wife, who may have had up to three different affairs. Due to his numerous business holdings within the cotton industry, on the other hand, James Maybrick did have an intimate knowledge of the East End of London and a readily available place to stay there in the apartment of his brother, Michael Maybrick.

Unfortunately, the horrible truth that no researcher or theorist wishes to address is that, irrespective of whether the Maybrick diary is a forgery, there still remains the possibility that James Maybrick may have committed the murders attributed to Jack the Ripper.

Begg, Paul, Martin Fido, and Keith Skinner. *The Jack the Ripper A–Z* (1996).

Christie, Trevor. *Etched in Arsenic* (1968).

Clayman, Dr. Charles B. *The American Medical Association Encyclopedia of Medicine* (1989).

Feldman, Paul. *Jack the Ripper: The Final Chapter* (1997).

Harris, Melvin. *The True Face of Jack the Rip-*
per (1994).
Harrison, Shirley. *The Diary of Jack the Rip-*
per (1993).

MacDougall, Alexander. *Treatise on The*
Maybrick Case (1891).
Morland, Nigel. *This Friendless Lady* (1957).
http://www.casebook.org

JOHN MCCARTHY

The final "canonical" victim, Mary Jane Kelly, lived at No. 26 Dorset Street. Her address could also be stated as No. 13 Miller's Court. The two addresses were one and the same. John McCarthy was the landlord, and his rooms were locally known as "McCarthy's Rents." On the morning of the November 9 murder in Miller's Court, McCarthy sent his assistant Thomas Bowyer to Kelly's room to collect back rent. Bowyer discovered the body as he looked through the broken window. Bowyer immediately went to get McCarthy. McCarthy saw the mutilated corpse and sent Bowyer to Commercial Street Police Station. He followed after Bowyer to the station, eventually returning with Inspector Beck and Detective Constable Walter Dew.

John McCarthy was first named as a suspect in 1988. On August 30 of 1988 the *Toronto Globe and Mail* reported that a Canadian group of researchers had gathered enough information to lead them to the conclusion that McCarthy was Jack the Ripper. The research done by this unnamed Canadian group has never been revealed. Merely stating, "research has led us to believe that McCarthy was the murderer" is pointless without the actual research and information to back it up. This group does

hold the distinction of being the first to name McCarthy as a suspect, but that is apparently all they have. It is noteworthy that their conclusion was announced on the 100th anniversary of the death of the first "canonical" victim, Mary Ann Nichols. It has recently been suggested that John McCarthy, born in France in 1851, was a relative of Kelly, possibly an uncle or a distant cousin.

What is known of Mary Kelly's life comes from the man she lived with up until mere days before her death, Joseph Barnett. Barnett states that Kelly was born in Limerick, Ireland, in either 1863 or 1864. This has been extremely difficult to trace. There is no record of a Mary Jane Kelly born in the town of Limerick during 1863 or 1864 but, thanks to diligent research performed by Nick Warren, a record of the birth of *a* Mary Kelly was found for 1864 at Castletown, County Limerick, Ireland. Mary apparently told Joseph Barnett that her father's name was John Kelly and that he was an iron works foreman. The Mary Kelly found by Nick Warren was born to John Kelly and Ann McCarthy. We do not know whether this Ann McCarthy was related to the John McCarthy who ran Miller's Court, but it is an important corroborative point that Barnett stated that Mary Kelly's father was named John. This may well have been the Mary Kelly of Jack the Ripper infamy. A blood relationship between McCarthy and Kelly may explain why McCarthy allowed Kelly's rent to go unpaid for approximately seven weeks. Research continues to potentially discover a blood relation between John McCarthy and Mary Kelly.

It has been suggested that sending his assistant to collect rent of the morning of the murder was a guilty action on McCarthy's part. Why that morning, if the rent had gone for at least seven weeks? Also, Inspector Abberline interviewed McCarthy on the morning that the body was found. McCarthy is the man responsible for breaking the door down to Mary Kelly's room, rather than using his key, which as the landlord he most likely would have possessed. This is another speculative point proposed to promote the guilt of John McCarthy.

From what is known of Jack the Ripper, it can be stated that he murdered at least four members of the "canon" and probably murdered Elizabeth Stride as well. A new theory has emerged. Since Mary Kelly was killed indoors, the only "canonical" victim who was, according to this theory, she may have been the victim of a copycat killer. In this scenario, Kelly's murder would be an isolated incident. Joseph Barnett was originally proposed as her murderer, and only hers. Now John McCarthy has been proposed as the solitary murderer of Mary Kelly, also. Some have suggested that either Kelly was McCarthy's mistress or that McCarthy was a regular client of hers. This would have allowed for the accumulation of such a large amount of unpaid rent. Her murder could be the result of Kelly possibly blackmailing McCarthy. Numerous re-

searchers, in passing, have suggested this theory, which has yet to be fully and conclusively investigated.

This hypothesis fails in advocating McCarthy as her murderer, since Joseph Barnett was living with her up until the end of October. As the rent was allowed to build up from mid–September, Barnett would most likely have been aware of anything going on between Kelly and McCarthy during the entire month of October. Barnett often stated that he would not allow Kelly to go out on the streets to earn money as a prostitute. According to this new theory, however, Barnett would have let her pay for their rent by sleeping with McCarthy.

John McCarthy had no traceable connection to the prior victims, but did have a real and possibly distinct connection to Mary Kelly. This would have been a severe departure from Jack the Ripper's *modus operandi*. Murdering Kelly in her room, and his own backyard, then sending someone to discover her would have been unlike the Jack the Ripper of the previous murders.

If John McCarthy and Mary Kelly were related, he would not have killed Kelly after helping her with her rent problems for the previous seven weeks. The original proponents of McCarthy as a suspect, the Canadian group, led by literary agent Helen Heller, have never produced their research. A recent statement from Helen Heller may reveal why McCarthy was viewed as Jack the Ripper. An unnamed prostitute was found murdered in Miller's Court sometime after the Jack the Ripper murders. Heller and this unnamed Canadian group of researchers appear to attribute that murder to John McCarthy, who remained in the East End of London for quite some time after the murders attributed to Jack the Ripper. This tenuous link may have convinced Heller that McCarthy could be none other than Jack the Ripper.

According to research performed by Neal Shelden, *a* John McCarthy died on June 16, 1934. This John McCarthy was described as a lodging-house keeper and very well could be the man who rented rooms in Miller's Court during the height of the Jack the Ripper scare. This John McCarthy had one son and five daughters, with not only real estate interests, but also a financial interest in a prominent London Music Hall.

John McCarthy's intimate knowledge of the East End, having lived there most of his entire adult life, has made McCarthy a target for theorists. These theorists, however, have not produced any research or documentation as to why they proposed McCarthy as a suspect. The November 9 murder in Miller's Court does present some interesting coincidences regarding McCarthy. Enough circumstantial links exist to keep John McCarthy on the list of possible suspects.

Begg, Paul, Martin Fido, and Keith Skinner. *The Jack the Ripper A–Z* (1996).
Jakubowski, Maxim, and Nathan Braund. *The Mammoth Book of Jack the Ripper* (1998).
http://www.casebook.org

"DR. MERCHANT"

In 1972 researcher and theorist B. E. Reilly examined the story of Police Constable Robert Spicer's Brixton suspect, a doctor. Reilly found who he believed to be the only man to fit Spicer's story, identifying him as "Dr. Merchant," a pseudonym. "Dr. Merchant" was the only doctor from Brixton, South London, to die shortly after the murders ceased.

Spicer wrote to the *Daily Express* toward the end of his life, in March of 1931, and outlined his experience with this suspect during the time of the murders. Only hours after the double murder of Elizabeth Stride and Catherine Eddowes, Spicer, twenty-two years old at the time, stated that he was on duty near Brick Lane, down Heneage Street. At the bottom part of Heneage Court, down and off to the right of Heneage Street, he observed two people, a man and a woman, sitting on a dustbin. Spicer immediately took this man in on suspicion. The man explained that he was a well-respected doctor and supplied a Brixton address. According to Spicer, the man, whom he commonly referred to as "Jack," had blood on his shirt cuffs and carried a black bag. At the station, where Spicer claims there were eight or nine inspectors on duty, the suspect identified himself and was allowed to leave freely, without so much as his black bag being searched.

According to Spicer, he was reprimanded for this arrest. He would see this man accosting women several times afterwards and always said something to him, which would make the doctor flee.

Spicer was discharged from the force in April 1889, for being drunk on duty. Forty-two years passed before his tale was told. Nowhere in the police records is there any verifiable proof that this arrest was made by Spicer and that a suspect, a noted Brixton doctor, was allowed to leave after providing his credentials. It appears that this event may never have happened.

There are a couple of points to ponder regarding Spicer's story. On the night of the double murder, tensions within both police departments were at an all-time high, as two grisly murders had been committed right under their noses. Any suspect brought in on suspicion would not only have been recorded, but also fully investigated, especially one who had bloodstains on his shirt cuffs. From Spicer's own account, the attitude toward his suspect was nothing like that.

Another point of controversy lies in Spicer's sighting of this man. He claims that while walking his beat, he came across a man and a woman sitting on a dustbin preparing to conduct business. This was not the *modus operandi* of Jack the Ripper, who would not have been in plain sight chatting with a prostitute after committing two murders on one night. The murderer had just eluded the walking beats of policemen at two separate locations, but now he is caught with bloodstains on his cuffs by a twenty-two year old rookie?

Spicer goes on to say that he witnessed this man accosting women after that night, but all he did was shout on each occasion at him. It seems unlikely that an officer who knew the murderer and saw him accosting women afterwards would yet do nothing about it.

B. E. Reilly admits that "Dr. Merchant" is a made-up name. A pseudonym for a suspect does not answer any questions regarding that murderer's identity. As with most cases regarding a theorist's use of a pseudonym, there appears to be not enough to establish a clear link between that suspect and Jack the Ripper. When a pseudonym is used, it appears the main goal is simply to propose a suspect rather than attempt to answer a question of identity.

Begg, Paul, Martin Fido, and Keith Skinner. *The Jack the Ripper A–Z* (1996).
Reilly, B. E. *City* (1972).
Sugden, Philip. *The Complete History of Jack the Ripper* (2002).
Warren, N. P. *The Criminologist* (Spring 1992).
http://www.casebook.org

FRANK MILES

Born in 1852, Frank Miles was a well-known painter, who was also color-blind, living in the West End of London. He was most noted for portraits of society ladies, including numerous sketches of the famous stage actress Lillie Langtry. Miles was awarded the Royal Academy's Turner Prize in 1880.

Miles was a friend and possible homosexual lover of the famous author

Oscar Wilde. Miles and Wilde lived together for a short period of time until a falling out occurred between the two men over Miles's sexual preference, including a fondness for underage girls, whom he occasionally flashed. Scottish theorist Thomas Toughill advanced Frank Miles as a suspect in the early 1970s through correspondence with crime historian Colin Wilson.

In 1887, Miles was confined to an asylum due to his deteriorating mental health. He remained at Brislington Mental Asylum until his death in 1891. This fact was discovered shortly before 1975, exonerating Miles as a suspect.

Begg, Paul, Martin Fido, and Keith Skinner. *The Jack the Ripper A–Z* (1996).
Jakubowski, Maxim, and Nathan Braund. *The Mammoth Book of Jack the Ripper* (1998).
Wilson, Colin, and Robin Odell. *Jack the Ripper: Summing Up and Verdict* (1987).
http://www.casebook.org
http://www.hurstmereclose.freeserve.co.uk/html/lillie_langtry.html

MORFORD

A September 24, 1888, article in *The Star* describes a search conducted for a man named Morford, who it was thought might be able to shed some light on the murders. Morford had lived on Great Ormond Street up until about the 10th of September but had disappeared since that time. A pawnbroker may have brought Morford to the attention of the authorities. The pawnbroker claimed to have recently done business with Morford, who had pawned some surgical knives at his shop.

Researcher Philip Sugden unearthed the article regarding Morford. Sugden argues that Morford may be one of the unidentified medical students referred to by Charles Warren, in the September 19 memo to the Home Office. In the September 24 article, it states that Morford was trained as a surgeon but that, through the abuse of alcohol, he had lost his standing in the community. The name "Morford" has not yet ap-

peared in any medical directories that would show he was formally educated as a surgeon. Sugden has taken the absence of the name Morford to mean that he may have been John Orford, who was the Senior Resident Medical Officer at the Royal Free Hospital.

There are apparent differences between what is known of the suspect, Morford, and the physician, John Orford. Morford was described as a fallen or disgraced surgeon, while in the same year of the murders John Orford held a position of standing in the medical community. From internal evidence it appears they were not the same person. Sugden acknowledges this point, adding that Morford and Dr. John Orford may have been related.

It has not been established that the suspect Morford ever existed. He is not mentioned in any police files and only appears in one solitary, unsupported newspaper article. Continued research has failed to establish the existence of this potential suspect. Until some documentation is presented that can verify that Morford was in fact a real person, he must be viewed as a non-suspect.

Begg, Paul, Martin Fido, and Keith Skinner. *The Jack the Ripper A–Z* (1996).
Sugden, Philip. *The Complete History of Jack the Ripper* (2002).

"MR. MORING"

In 1935 author R. Thurston Hopkins described a man whom he believed perfectly fit the description of the suspect seen by George Hutchinson with Mary Kelly on the night of her murder. This man, whom Hopkins named "Mr. Moring," was a poet addicted to drugs at the time of the murders. According to Hopkins, Moring was a personal friend of Mary Kelly, and his father was a successful tradesman operating in the East End of London. As "Mr. Moring" was a confirmed pseudonym, the status of this suspect remained dormant for over fifty years.

Researcher and theorist Martin Fido has tentatively identified Mr. Moring as the poet Ernest Dowson. There are distinct parallels between Hopkins's Moring and Ernest Dowson, discussed in detail by Fido. There are, however, some differences. Hopkins described the father as a well-to-do tradesman. Dowson's father was not rich, and his business was failing, prompting Ernest to leave college in 1888. Dowson was also never known to be addicted to any drug other than alcohol, which would not characterize him as a "drug addicted poet." The truth is that the public may never know who exactly "Mr. Moring" was, and there has been doubt cast on Hutchinson's eyewitness description. (*See also* Ernest Dowson)

Begg, Paul, Martin Fido, and Keith Skinner. *The Jack the Ripper A–Z* (1996).
Hopkins, R. Thurston. *Life and Death at the Old Bailey* (1935).
http://www.casebook.org

JOHN NETLEY

The coachman John Netley remains one of the more intriguing characters attached to Jack the Ripper lore. An obscure figure, Netley was first described as taking part in the Royal Conspiracy in the 1970s. His active part in the Jack the Ripper murders has changed and evolved over the years, as further advances have been made upon the Royal Conspiracy Theory to answer various challenges. The evolution of Netley's involvement, as well as the theory's basis, has led numerous researchers to scoff at the mere mention of any conspiracy theory involving the royal family.

An evolution of research regarding Netley's background also exists. John Charles Netley was born in May 1860. Differing sources place his birth in Kensington, a royal borough of England, or in Paddington, a Northwestern metropolitan borough of London, to the east of Kensington. The son of an omnibus conductor, Netley was one of a set of twins. In 1903, Netley was thrown from his horse-drawn carriage after it struck an obelisk. His head was crushed under the wheels, and death was instantaneous.

In the 1976 bestseller by Stephen Knight, John Netley's place in the Jack the Ripper case was cemented. Knight, working from an interview with Joseph Gorman Sickert, described Netley as an ambitious bisexual who attempted to ingratiate himself within the upper-class community by means of self-prostitution. The owner of his own carriage, Netley was allegedly the man responsible for secretly chauffeuring Prince Albert Victor between Buckingham Palace and Cleveland Street. This last job would prompt Netley's involvement in the royal conspiracy and the murders attributed to Jack the Ripper.

Because of Netley's firsthand knowledge of Prince Albert Victor's secret trips to Cleveland Street, his marriage to Annie Crook, and the illegitimate child produced by that marriage, Netley was recruited by Dr. William Gull. His job was to chauffeur Dr. Gull around the East End of London as the doctor silenced the four women engaged in a blackmail plot against the Crown. According to Gorman Sickert and Knight, Netley's main job was to dump the bodies after Gull had murdered them inside the carriage. Within this theory, Netley would not be Jack the Ripper himself. He would have, in fact, been Jack the Rippers' garbage man. Medical evidence at the crime scenes has seriously challenged the theory's notion that the victims were murdered in a carriage and then placed in the spots where they were discovered. That specific element of the royal conspiracy Theory has been disproved. Therefore, Netley's theoretical role as Gull's stooge would have been impossible.

But Netley's role as a lackey for Dr. William Gull has only been postulated for three of the five murders. The murder of Elizabeth Stride is solely attributed to Netley, supposedly because Stride was unwilling to enter the carriage with Dr. Gull. Netley is described as the man seen by Israel Schwartz attacking Stride at 12:45 A.M., just moments before her body was discovered. Walter Sickert stated that Netley was approximately five feet five inches tall, with broad shoulders. This description matches perfectly with Schwartz's description of the man attacking Elizabeth Stride. Sickert's description of Netley does not appear in the 1976 book by Stephen Knight. That description appears in the 1991 updating of the royal conspiracy by Melvyn Fairclough.

Fairclough added to Knight's theory by claiming that Netley also murdered Emma Elizabeth Smith, alongside Frederico Albericci. That murder has been addressed under the discussion relating to Frederico Albericci, but it warrants readdressing. Smith was attacked by three local youths, believed to be from a street gang, another element neatly explained away by royal conspiracy theorists. Smith was not murdered as a result of the attack. She died three days later of peritonitis. Emma Elizabeth Smith was not murdered in the fashion outlined by Melvyn Fairclough.

Until the 1970s Netley was mired in historical obscurity. There were no accomplishments or public acknowledgements in an otherwise meaningless life. He is depicted as a man who tried to ingratiate himself with those above him in any manner possible. Knight declared that Netley was responsible for two attempts on the life of Alice Margaret Crook, the alleged illegitimate daughter of Prince Albert Victor. Despite research proving that John Netley was not involved in those two specific accidents, they are precisely of the mode a man such as Netley would have used to stay in the good graces of the hierarchy. The Royal Conspiracy, of which Netley is a major character, has been disproved. Therefore, Netley's conspiratorial involvement in the murders attributed to Jack the Ripper must follow along those same lines.

Beadle, William. *Jack the Ripper: Anatomy of a Myth* (1995).
Begg, Paul, Martin Fido, and Keith Skinner. *The Jack the Ripper A–Z* (1996).
Fairclough, Melvyn. *The Ripper and the Royals* (1991).
Knight, Stephen. *Jack the Ripper: The Final Solution* (1976).
Rumbelow, Donald. *The Complete Jack the Ripper* (1987).

MIKHAEL OSTROG

Until the early 1990s, Mikhael Ostrog remained a mystery. Through the research efforts of D. Stuart Goffee, Philip Sugden, Nick Warren and others, a more complete history of Ostrog is known than was ever thought possible. Ostrog's early days are still mostly a blank, but his year of birth is probably 1833 or a couple of years after that. The first known report of Mikhael Ostrog comes from 1863.

The years 1863 to 1866 saw Ostrog jailed every single year. Incarcerated for a variety of offences, including theft and confidence trickery, the picture painted of Ostrog was that of a con man and petty thief who presented himself under a variety of false names. In 1866, for the charges of theft of books and robbery, Ostrog was sentenced to seven years in prison. This was an incredibly harsh sentence given the crime, yet it was well within the powers of the judge, who took into account Ostrog's history of crime and prior offenses.

Ostrog was released from Chatham Prison in May of 1873. Seven years of penal servitude apparently had done nothing toward rehabilitating Ostrog, as he stole a number of items from the Woolwich Barracks eleven days after his release. Ostrog continued his stealing ways until arrested in October of that year. The following January Ostrog was sentenced to ten years in prison, with an additional seven years of police supervision. Another harsh sentence but, taking into account Ostrog's recidivism, it seems no worse than the three-strikes policy employed in penal systems today. He would be released from prison on August 28, 1883, but would be in trouble again only two months later.

Ostrog was mentioned in the October 1883 police gazette for failure to report to the metropolitan police as part of the conditions of his release. Much is made of Ostrog having been mentioned in the October police gazette during the time of the murders. Ostrog had a prior history in the gazette, appearing back in October 1883.

His previous sentence had included police supervision which would have kept Ostrog under watch for two years past the murders, similar to what is now known as parole. While on parole, the parolee must regularly check in with his assigned parole officer. This also appears to be the situation with Mikhael Ostrog. He was written up in October of 1883 for failure to report, and there appears to be no reason why Ostrog's name printed in the police bulletin should be attributed to anything more than his failure to report.

In this earlier gazette bulletin, some details of Ostrog's life are revealed, including an estimate of his birthdate: 1833. After this bulletin Ostrog vanished until July of 1887. There is the possibility that he may have been incarcerated for this failure to report. No specific crime was committed in 1883, so there would be no trial to search the records for. An immediate return to prison might have resulted.

In July 1887, Ostrog was arrested under the alias "Claude Cayton." This time he was only sentenced to six months in prison. Ostrog was certified insane while in prison and then was released on March 10, 1888. This is the last known report of Ostrog until the October 26, 1888, police bulletin, in which "special attention is called to this dangerous man." Throughout all of Ostrog's crimes and scams, one theme recurs: the absence of violence. The only known violent incident involving Ostrog was when he tried to throw himself under a train while handcuffed to someone. This was an apparent suicide attempt by a man who had spent the bulk of his adult life behind bars. The fact that he was handcuffed to someone was nothing more than a side note, as he, himself, was the target. Why Ostrog was considered a dangerous man might have more to do with the climate at the time of the murders than anything specifically relating to Ostrog.

He continued his habitual theft and was sentenced to prison until 1904. There are no further records after this release. The common use of aliases throughout his lifetime makes it extremely hard to establish biographical data on Ostrog. During November of 1888, he may have been in a French prison under the name "Stanistan Sublinsky." The Home Secretary would corroborate this in 1894. The Home Secretary, Herbert Henry Asquith, was told that Ostrog had been released from the lunatic section of a French prison in November of 1890. If this incarceration related to the November 18, 1888, sentencing of Sublinsky, Mikhael Ostrog might be cleared as a suspect. If the sentencing took place on November 18, the actual crime must have taken place more than a couple of days before that. This would clear Ostrog of the Miller's Court murder and, therefore, revoke his suspect candidacy. Unfortunately, it cannot be positively stated that Sublinsky was Ostrog, so he cannot be officially exonerated.

After the 1888 police gazette Ostrog next surfaced in connection with the murders as the third suspect named by Melville MacNaghten in 1894. The draft version of the memorandum is as follows:

> No. 3. Michael Ostrog. a mad Russian doctor & a convict & unquestionably a homicidal maniac. This man was said to have been habitually cruel to women, & for a long time was known to have carried about him surgical knives & other instruments; his antecedents were of the very worst & his whereabouts at the time of the Whitechapel murders could never be satisfactorily accounted for. He is still alive.

The Scotland Yard version reads,

> (3) Michael Ostrog, a Russian doctor, and a convict, who was subsequently detained in a lunatic asylum as a homicidal maniac. This man's antecedents were of the worst possible type, and his whereabouts at the time of the murders could never be ascertained.

MacNaghten was commonly wrong in his conclusions regarding all three suspects of the 1894 memorandum. His information regarding Ostrog was no different. In his personal draft version, MacNaghten states that Ostrog was habitually cruel to women and was said to carry surgical knives. Both of these statements have never been proven and, from research performed on Ostrog, they appear to be totally inaccurate. Ostrog did pose as a doctor, among other things, so a doctor's bag might have been a necessary prop, but there is no mention of any surgical knives. There is also no known reference to Ostrog's cruelty toward any woman, let alone enough references to indicate that this cruelty was habitual. These characteristics were kept from the Scotland Yard version of the memorandum for perhaps the same reason outlined above: They were untrue and could not be proven.

Ostrog was given new life in 1962 when Donald McCormick quoted a letter supposedly written by former Assistant Commissioner of the Metropolitan Police Department, Basil Thomson. In this letter, which has never been produced, Thomson had supposedly learned from the French that one of the aliases used by Vassily Konovalov was "Mikhael Ostrog." McCormick proceeded to plant Ostrog in books as Konovalov's alias. McCormick worked closely with Dan Farson in 1959. He saw the Lady Aberconway version of MacNaghten's Memorandum. McCormick had total access to the names of the suspects, including the third suspect, Michael Ostrog. This is why Ostrog was never mentioned in McCormick's original to 1959 version of his book. A link between Ostrog and Vassily Konovalov, McCormick's personally invented suspect, gave a short-lived credibility to McCormick's theory.

The criminal history of Ostrog has never displayed any outright signs of violence. When placed alongside the murders committed by Jack the Ripper, one would never have connected the former to the latter. It is not easily explained how a career con artist and thief managed to incorporate the murders and mutilations of at least five women into his criminal activity. Ostrog's criminal activity after the time of the murders places him right back into the mix of stealing and habitually getting caught at it. So why was special attention called to this man?

It was stated earlier that Ostrog was considered dangerous because of the murders. Later in life, he certainly was not a physical danger to anyone other than himself. After the double murder, the police made checks and inquiries at all local lunatic asylums. With Ostrog recently released in March, as well as having been certified insane less than a year previously, Ostrog would have been singled out as someone to watch for. As Ostrog had not reported as part of his police supervision, he was mentioned in the police gazette again.

If Ostrog was not Stanistan Sublinsky, then it is true that Ostrog's whereabouts at the time of the murders have never been ascertained. Numerous theories, regarding a number of different suspects, have postulated changes in a criminal's mode of activity. These changes rarely involve a leap from minor offenses, such as theft, to a major crime like murder. Ostrog will remain one of the historically significant suspects in this murder case, despite an academic move away from viewing Ostrog as a viable candidate.

Begg, Paul, Martin Fido, and Keith Skinner. *The Jack the Ripper A–Z* (1996).
Deacon, Richard. *History of the Russian Secret Service* (1972).
Goffee, D. S. *Ripperana* (October 1994).
Jakubowski, Maxim, and Nathan Braund. *The Mammoth Book of Jack the Ripper* (1998).
McCormick, Donald. *The Identity of Jack the Ripper* (1959).
_____. *The Identity of Jack the Ripper* (1962).
Sugden, Philip. *The Complete History of Jack the Ripper* (2001).

DR. ALEXANDER PEDACHENKO

The first mentioning of Dr. Alexander Pedachenko, whether as a suspect or as just a recorded documentation of his existence, is in the book *Things I Know About Kings, Celebrities and Crooks*, by theorist William Le Queux. Le Queux wrote several books about Russia after the 1917 revolution. The first of these books was a biography of the infamous monk Grigori Rasputin, in 1917. In his next book, only one year later, Le Queux revealed that his biography of Rasputin, who died in 1916, had been written from documents among Rasputin's possessions. Le Queux claims the Kerensky Government, overthrown by Vladimir Lenin and the Bolsheviks in October 1917, sent these documents to him. Le Queux's early books on Rasputin make no mention of the suspect, Dr. Alexander Pedachenko.

Five years after publishing his 1918 book, *Minister of Evil*, Le Queux wrote a semi-autographical book, titled *Things I Know About Kings, Celebrities and Crooks*. The first question that arises is why he waited at least six years after receiving these documents to reveal the identity of one of the most sought-after murderers of that time. Le Queux states that he wanted to find corroborative proof of the existence of this man before revealing his name, yet he does not do so in his 1923 book. The story Le Queux writes regarding Dr. Pedachenko is even more intriguing.

When Le Queux finally revealed the name of his suspect, he stated that it came directly from a manuscript, ti-tled "Great Russian Criminals," typed in French, among the documents given to him by the Kerensky Government. While Rasputin did not speak or know the French language, Le Queux declares that Rasputin dictated the manuscript. However, it was never revealed who had typed it in French or why Rasputin wanted to put it in print. Rasputin's own daughter has claimed that her father never had any interest in Russian crim-inals and that there was no connection between Rasputin and A. T. Vassil'ev, the Head of the Russian Secret Police, known as the Ochrana.

The Ochrana is connected Le Queux's story through information sup-posedly obtained from two informants, Johann Nideroest and Nicholas Zverieff. This aspect of the story begins with Zverieff. Le Queux claims that Zverieff provided the name of Jack the Ripper to Nideroest while both men were in Lon-don. Le Queux never mentions how long Nideroest held onto this informa-tion but only that he ultimately reported this to the Ochrana. Le Queux makes mention of a 1909 Ochrana bulletin, relating to suspect Vassily Konovalov using the alias "Alexander Pedachenko." He does cite a comment from Raspu-tin to the effect that the Ochrana al-ready knew Nideroest's information. How Rasputin would have come across this information, how he would have known that the Ochrana found this in-formation amusing, becomes the key issue. As was stated earlier, there was no connection between Rasputin and A. T. Vassil'ev.

Nicholas Zverieff was described as an elderly anarchist but, to this date, he has never been proven to exist. Johann Nideroest, on the other hand, is docu-mented as having existed and was of German and Swiss origin. He supplied information to various journalists and is later mentioned in a known 1930 Och-rana document concerning the Siege of Sydney Street in the East End of Lon-don in 1911.

There appears to be no evidence that the document from Rasputin ever existed. This would imply that Le Queux invented the entire story. To sup-port this statement, the chronology and the people mentioned by Le Queux must be fully examined. For example, why would Le Queux use Zverieff and Nideroest to establish a link to Raspu-tin?

Evidence has been unearthed that documents Johann Nideroest's exis-tence. Le Queux claimed to have arrived at his suspect from the evidence in a document belonging to Rasputin. Now, he needed some link to Rasputin. Le Queux was a journalist working for *The Globe* in London during 1888. Along with two other newspapermen, he would report on and discuss the Whitechapel murders. As a writer and former jour-nalist, Le Queux would have known about the information peddler, Johann Nideroest. In 1905, Nideroest attempted to sell a story about anarchists building bombs in Whitechapel.

If Le Queux had invented Zverieff, the story of him as an elderly Russian anarchist would have worked perfectly to link him to information given to Nideroest. The next problem concerns Nideroest getting information to Rasputin. Thus, the use of A. T. Vassil'ev and, perhaps even more important to the chronology of the story, former Assistant Commissioner Basil Thomson.

Thomson had declared himself "Director of Intelligence" in 1919, taking charge of the "Special Branch" of the Metropolitan Police Department. Thomson's branch was primarily concerned with Russian Bolsheviks. There is Thomson's link to Russia and anarchists. Thomson also later gave support to the theory that an anarchist, named Peter Straume, was the infamous "Peter the Painter" connected to the Siege of Sydney Street, which involved a group of Russian anarchists in London. Finally, in 1930, A. T. Vassil'ev made the claim that Johann Nideroest had helped Peter Straume escape to Australia.

All the necessary links for Le Queux to construct his story were present. How did Rasputin receive his information? He learned it from Vassil'ev. Despite the claim that Vassil'ev already knew this information, it had to come from somewhere inside London, and that is where Nideroest enters the picture. Through a link from Thomson, Nideroest can be connected to Vassil'ev. The only remaining problem would be from whom Nideroest obtained his information. The link must have been someone who had connections within the anarchistic front and who was familiar with Russians in London, or, perhaps, a Russian himself. Most importantly, the link had to be someone who could not refute Le Queux's story.

Enter Nicholas Zverieff, an elderly Russian anarchist, who fits all the characteristics needed. The minor detail of Rasputin not having a direct connection to the Head of the Ochrana, Vassil'ev, can be easily justified. Rasputin's popularity with Tsarina Alexandria over the healing of her ailing son made him a constant figure of notoriety within the Russian Empire. This would have brought Rasputin in direct contact with the Head of the Secret Police. The lack of a public connection between the two of them would be reduced to a matter of secrecy. It would be something impossible to disprove.

But there are too many negatives regarding Le Queux's story. Most importantly, there has never been any substantial evidence that Dr. Pedachenko actually existed. Le Queux's story must viewed as nothing more than that, a story. For a time it was a cleverly interconnected story, but it has ultimately caved in on itself.

Theorist Donald McCormick revived the Dr. Pedachenko theory in the late 1950s by naming Vassily Konovalov, the "real" Dr. Pedachenko, as the true Jack the Ripper. McCormick claimed that "Alexander Pedachenko" was an alias of Vassily Konovalov, his own personal suspect. As McCormick expanded upon Le Queux's invented suspect, the question surfaced of whether McCormick had actually known that Dr. Alexander Pedachenko was, in all likelihood, an invention of William Le Queux.

Begg, Paul, Martin Fido, and Keith Skinner. *The Jack the Ripper A–Z* (1996).
McCormick, Donald. *The Identity of Jack the Ripper* (1959).
Le Queux, William. *Things I Know About Kings, Celebrities, and Crooks* (1923).
_____. *Rasputin the Rascal Monk* (1917).
_____. *Minister of Evil* (1918).
Thomson, Basil. *The Story of Scotland Yard* (1935).
http://www.casebook.org

PORTUGUESE CATTLEMEN

A clerk in the British customs statistical department, named Edward K. Larkins, presented theories regarding Jack the Ripper both during and after the murders. His first theory was that a model, named Antoni Prichi, was the murderer, due to his physical similarity with the suspect described by eyewitness George Hutchinson. Larkins' most famous theory, one that he will be forever remembered for, is his belief that members of a Portuguese cattle boat committed these murders.

Using research from his lists of shipping movements during the course of the murders, Larkins concluded that Manuel Cruz Xavier had murdered Mary Ann Nichols and that Jose Laurenco had murdered Annie Chapman. Larkins attributes the murders of Elizabeth Stride and Kate Eddowes to a combined effort by Jose Laurenco and Joao de Souza Machado. Jose Laurenco apparently jumped ship in October 1888, so the murder of Mary Jane Kelly was attributed to Joao de Souza Machado alone.

Larkins peddled this theory to the police, to magistrate Montagu Williams, and to London Hospital. Apparently, the only person who outwardly voiced their belief in Larkins' theory was Montagu Williams. Other officials, such as Robert Anderson, viewed Larkins and his theories differently. In a memorandum to the Home Office, Anderson described Larkins as a "very troublesome busybody." Larkins's theory continued to be sent to anyone who would listen, and to most who would not, until at least 1893.

The main reasoning behind Larkins's theory was that during the Peninsular War against France, which began in 1808, Portuguese peasants committed atrocities against their enemies. Therefore, according to Larkins, members of that specific ethnicity must have committed the atrocities in Whitechapel. Larkins checked the shipping logs and found what he believed to be viable suspects. When his suspects' personal movements contradicted the dates of the murders, he simply replaced that suspect with another who was in London at the time.

Edward Larkins's theory lacks any basic evidence other than the fact that his suspects were in London at the time of the murders. His theory is, regrettably, based on hatred and ignorance. The fact that peasants committed acts of savagery during a war in the early 1800s, does not mean three separate fisherman of that same nationality committed the murders attributed to Jack the Ripper.

Begg, Paul, Martin Fido, and Keith Skinner. *The Jack the Ripper A–Z* (1996).

Evans, Stewart P., and Keith Skinner. *The Ultimate Jack the Ripper Companion* (2000).

http://www.genexchange.org/historyreg.cfm?state=il&ID=434

OSWALD PUCKRIDGE

Oswald Puckridge was first identified in a September 19 Home Office memo from Commissioner Charles Warren to Henry Matthews's Private Secretary, Evelyn Ruggles-Brise, describing three men who were currently under investigation. The second of these men was Puckridge, who was described as a surgeon who had threatened to "rip" people up. Puckridge had been released from Hoxton House Lunatic Asylum on August 4, 1888. A search for this man, according to Warren, had commenced, but as of yet had been unsuccessful. Puckridge was brought back into the suspect spotlight by researcher Jon Ogan in 1990. In 1993 researcher Philip Sugden re-examined the case of Oswald Puckridge. While gathering important background details on Puckridge, Sugden theoretically dismissed him as a viable suspect.

Oswald Puckridge was born in Sussex, England on June 13, 1838, the fourth of five children. He married Ellen Puddle on October 3, 1868. Puckridge is described as an "apothecary," or pharmacological chemist, on his marriage certificate. He is never listed as a surgeon, as Warren claimed in his September 19 memo to the Home Office. On May 28, 1900, Puckridge was admitted to a workhouse, where he would die of bronchial pneumonia on June 1. Puckridge had by this time become a general laborer, and there is no listing in any medical directories for an Oswald Puckridge.

Puckridge was mentioned in that specific memo to the Home Office, but he was never brought up again in regards to the case. This may imply that Puckridge subsequently cleared as a suspect. Despite Warren's resignation on November 8, 1888, newly appointed Commissioner James Monro would have known about the suspect from Henry Matthews, with whom he was in close contact. Monro might have known that Puckridge amounted to nothing as a suspect, or he probably would have written something about the continued search for this man. There appears to have been no search for Puckridge after Monro was placed in charge. The reason may be that the police had found out all they needed to know about Oswald Puckridge.

Begg, Paul, Martin Fido, and Keith Skinner. *The Jack the Ripper A–Z* (1996).
Sugden, Philip. *The Complete History of Jack the Ripper* (2002).

FRANCIS CHARLES HASTINGS RUSSELL, 9TH DUKE OF BEDFORD

There is only one entry connecting Francis Charles Hastings Russell with the murders committed by Jack the Ripper. In 1962 Phillippe Jullien, biographer of King Edward VII, asserted that Prince Albert Victor was thought to be responsible for the murders attributed to Jack the Ripper. Jullien mentions, parenthetically, that the Duke of Bedford was also rumored to have been responsible for the murders. No outside documentation has ever backed up this passing claim by Jullien and, to this day, no researcher has taken up the case against the Duke of Bedford.

Francis Charles Hastings Russell was born on October 16, 1819, the first son of George William Russell and Elizabeth Anne Rawdon. Francis Charles ascended to the dukedom after the death of his cousin, William Russell, on May 26, 1872. William Russell had been the only son of the 7th Duke of Bedford. Francis Charles's mother, whose beauty and will were praised both in poetry and in conversation, schooled Francis Charles and his two younger brothers at home. On January 18, 1844, Francis Charles

married Lady Elizabeth Sackville-West, the daughter of the 5th Earl de La Warr. The couple had four children, both of their sons ascending to the dukedom in succession. Francis Charles Hastings Russell passed away on January 14, 1891. He was known for taking a great interest in the progress of society and for funding numerous projects relating to cremation.

Jullien never revealed *which* Duke of Bedford was rumored to be responsible for the murders. Francis Charles Hastings Russell was sixty-nine years old at the time of the murders. There has never been a record of the 9th Duke of Bedford having been seen in or around the East End of London during the times of the murders. It is entirely possible that Jullien's "rumor" applied to a later Duke of Bedford.

Jullien, Phillippe. *Edward and the Edwardians* (1962).
http://genealogy.milin.net/genealog/d764.html#P39269
http://pages.prodigy.net/ptheroff/gotha/bedford.html

George William Francis Sackville Russell, 10th Duke of Bedford

Born in London on April 16, 1852, George William was the eldest son of Francis Charles, the 9th Duke of Bedford. He married Lady Adeline Somers-Cocks on October 24, 1876. George William fits the profile of Jack the Ripper much closer in age and stature than his father. He ascended to the dukedom just short of his thirty-ninth birthday, becoming the 10th Duke of Bedford after the death of his father on January 14, 1891. He would have a short-lived nobility, as George William passed away on March 23, 1893. His brother, Herbrand Arthur, would succeed him as the 11th Duke of Bedford.

If Phillippe Jullien were referring to any Duke of Bedford other than Francis Charles Hastings Russell, the Duke at the time of the murders, it would have been George William, just as the problems occur with the suspect status of Francis Charles Hastings Russell, those problems also exist with George William. The major distinguishing factor between the two men are their respective ages, sixty-nine as opposed to thirty-six at the time of the murders, and the health issues resulting from their age difference.

As stated above with respect to George William's father, Phillippe Jullien did not mention specifically which Duke of Bedford was rumored to be responsible for the murders. No documentation or outside source links either the 9th Duke of Bedford or the 10th Duke of Bedford to any murders attributed to Jack the Ripper. The intimate knowledge of the East End possessed by both father and son, who were born and spent the bulk of their life in London, may have contributed to Jullien's assertion of a rumor that has never been positively sourced or traced to its origins.

Jullien, Phillippe. *Edward and the Edwardians* (1962).
http://genealogy.milin.net/genealog/d764.html#P39269
http://pages.prodigy.net/ptheroff/gotha/bedford.html

Dr. Jon William Sanders

Dr. Jon William Sanders has been recently suggested as a possible suspect by researcher Jon Ogan. There are three reasons that Dr. Sanders may have been proposed as a suspect: he was a doctor; his death occurred a short time after the cessation of the murders; and his name was very similar to the 3rd insane medical student described by Commissioner Charles Warren, John William Smith Sanders.

In a memo to the Home Office, Commissioner Warren described a search for three insane medical students. The first two were traced and subsequently cleared, while the third one, John William Smith Sanders, who was investigated at the time of the murders, had gone abroad but was still sought after. Dr. Jon William Sanders, having the same name as this insane medical student, may have been mistaken for him, although it is a matter of documented fact that they were two different people.

Born in 1859, Sanders achieved his M.B. in 1880. Sanders practiced in London, having a successful medical career. He belonged to the British Gynecological Society and became the Medical Superintendent for Croyden Fever Hospital. Dr. Sanders may have come under suspicion because of the obvious medical expertise displayed by Jack the Ripper and the preponderance of doctor theories that spawned.

Dr. John Sanders died of heart failure in January of 1889 while under anesthetic. His death so shortly after the final murder makes a nice fit for those who insist that the November 9 murder in Miller's Court was the final crime of Jack the Ripper. The need to explain the cessation of the murders is satisfied by the death of a preferred suspect.

Dr. Jon William Sanders has no evidentiary connection to Jack the Ripper, apart from his noted medical and gynecological skill. The naming of Dr. Sanders as a possible suspect appears to derive from an interest in just that, the naming of possible suspects rather than theoretical deduction from known research.

Begg, Paul, Martin Fido, and Keith Skinner. *The Jack the Ripper A–Z* (1996).
Ogan, Jon. *Ripperana* (Summer 1993).
http://www.casebook.org

JOHN WILLIAM SMITH SANDERS

The first indirect mention of John William Smith Sanders occurred in an October 19, 1888, report to the Home Office by Inspector Swanson. Swanson mentions three insane medical students who had attended London Hospital. The first two had been discovered and cleared, while the third one was found to have gone abroad. A number of memos were circulated regarding this person, identified only as the third, or one of three, insane medical students. It was not until a November 1, 1888, report by Inspector Abberline that this student was named. Two subsequent reports mention John Sanders, or "Saunders," and the inquiries pertaining to him. John Sanders was traced to No. 20 Aberdeen Place, and it was thought that a woman named Sanders had lived there with her son but had left the country two years previous.

Inquiries into Sanders continued. Today, it is known that Sanders's mother lived at No. 20 Abercorn Place. Inspector Abberline must have written the address down incorrectly, for, at the time, Mrs. Sanders was still listed as residing at No. 20 Abercorn Place. The information regarding her son was also not correct.

John Sanders had been placed in various asylums during 1887. It has recently been discovered that, during the autumn of 1888, Sanders was safely locked up in a private asylum in Kent called West Malling Place.

It is unknown whether the police ever traced Sanders to West Malling Place, but the interaction between the metropolitan police and the Home Office seems to lead that way. They may have found out what is known today, that John William Smith Sanders could not have been Jack the Ripper, as he was safely locked up during the time of the murders.

Begg, Paul, Martin Fido, and Keith Skinner. *The Jack the Ripper A–Z* (1996).
Jakubowski, Maxim, and Nathan Braund. *The Mammoth Book of Jack the Ripper* (1998).
Sugden, Philip. *The Complete History of Jack the Ripper* (2002).

WALTER SICKERT

The Victorian artist of Dutch origin is painted in several shades in relation to the Jack the Ripper murders. Walter Sickert's involvement in this case ranges from informant to co-conspirator, theorist to lookout, to co-murderer to solitary murderer. Sickert displayed a keen interest in the Jack the Ripper murders as far back as can be documented, either from his own stories or the reports of associates who he held numerous conversations with him pertaining to the murders. In the 1970s, Sickert's obsession with the Jack the Ripper murders came full circle.

In 1970 theorist Donald McCormick named Walter Sickert as a suspect, based on his sketches and paintings of the murders. McCormick's unsourced accusation snowballed into Sickert's eventual inclusion in the Royal Conspiracy. Since then, no researcher has denied that Walter Sickert displayed a more than keen interest in the Jack the Ripper murders, while some have stated emphatically that Sickert was solely responsible. The story of Walter Sickert begins much earlier than 1970.

Walter Richard Sickert was born in Munich, Germany, on May 31, 1860. In 1868 he moved to London as a result of his father's problems with the governing politics of their home country. Oswald Sickert's native home was torn by the effects of war between Austria, Prussia, and Germany. In 1864 the Sickert's nationality and citizenship became German, and Walter became fluent in speaking and writing the German language. When Oswald moved the family to England, he adopted his wife's English nationality for his ever-growing family, leaving both Denmark and Germany behind. Before the move he had earned his wages as a comic illustrator.

Walter was the eldest of six children, five boys and one girl. When Walter was only two years old, he had two operations, described by his biographer, Robert Emmons, as "unsuccessful," for a fistula on his penis. A fistula is an outdated medical term for an abnormal opening, canal, or passageway from an internal organ to the surface of the skin.

It appears that Walter suffered from hypospadia, which is a congenital defect in which the opening of the urethra is located on the underside of either the head or shaft of the penis. He may have also been suffering from a condition known as chordee, in which the erect penis curves in a downward direction. If chordee is not treated successfully, sexual intercourse may be very difficult to perform. There are operations today to correct this, but they are normally conducted before a boy reaches the age of two. As Sickert biographer Robert Emmons has stated, the two operations performed on Sickert at the age of two were not successful. The normal functioning of the penis and urethra was not available to him. Sickert was, however, operated on again in 1865 at the age of six and a half.

Sickert was exceptional at whatever he attempted, including teaching himself how to read and write in German. By the age of ten he was studying French, probably following from his father's influence and love of French art that would carry over to his own painting. As a teenager he invented a modified form of chess, called "Sedan," in which the King could be taken. He was enrolled at King's College in 1875 where he studied literature and languages. He was able to recite speeches in French with such perfect diction that it was sometimes mistaken for his native language. He graduated from King's College in 1877, earning First Class Honors and the Vice Master's Prize for German.

One of Sickert's first loves was the stage, a love that would remain with him forever. He pursued acting and organized a group of amateur actors called the "Hyps." They would often go to the famous Lyceum Theater to study the performances of Henry Irving and his acting troupe. Sickert and Irving would become friends and would later work together on the stage, with Sickert performing five different parts in one play, including a riveting portrayal of a French soldier. He would continue acting with Irving and his troupe until 1881, when his personal finances became tight. This would lead him toward his other love and what we know him best for today, his art.

After leaving Irving's acting troupe Sickert entered the Slade to study under Alphonse Legros, an English painter born in France who worked alongside many of the famous Impressionists, such as Whistler and Degas. It was a meeting with Whistler in an unnamed tobacconist shop that persuaded Sickert to leave the Slade and study under Whistler.

The year, 1885, would be bittersweet for Walter Sickert. His father, Oswald, would die, and he would marry the first of his three wives, Ellen Cobden. Ellen was twelve years his senior, and their marriage may have been one of convenience. Her family had considerable wealth, which allowed Sickert to continue his burgeoning career. There was a definite air about their marriage, as Sickert was considered a man about town, often staying out to all hours. They would stay together as man and wife until 1896, when they would separate over Sickert's "chronic independence" and finally divorce in 1899. Cobden would go on to write at least two novels under the pseudonym Miles Amber. In one of these novels, *Wistons*, the parallels to her own life with Walter Sickert are readily apparent. The male character is twelve years the junior of the heroine. He would be described as a womanizer, and he rarely shows any affection toward her.

The 1890s saw the height of Sickert's artistic enterprises. He painted, visiting Venice for the first time in 1895 and often displaying his sketches of various London music halls. He wrote articles and essays on art, which inevitably led to a breach in his friendship with Whistler. He opened an art school in 1893 with the help of his former master and began teaching evening classes. These three passions would remain with Sickert for the rest of his life.

In the summer of 1898 Sickert traveled to Dieppe, France, as he had done many years previously. This time he would remain out of London until returning full-time in 1905. There have been many speculations about why Sickert left England. One of the most popular reasons given was his separation and divorce from Ellen Cobden, which effectively cut off Sickert's money supply, forcing him to live a modest existence.

After a six-year stay in Dieppe, with numerous trips to Venice and, without doubt, Paris, Sickert permanently returned to London in 1905. Despite numerous claims that he did not return to London during the period he was living in France, there is circumstantial evidence that he attended the funeral of Whistler in London in 1903. In any case, he was back to stay in 1905.

After returning to London he acquired three studios, one on Fitzroy Street, another on Charlotte Street, which was an extension of Fitzroy, and the third at No. 6 Mornington Crescent in Camden Town. Sickert took the opportunity to form a number of artist groups, which one could say he led, the most notable one being the Camden Town Group, which officially began in 1911. This group would later be renamed the London Group. It evoked memories of his London in the 1890s when artistic geniuses like Whistler, Degas, Renoir, and, of course, Sickert, worked as a cohesive artistic group, learning from each other, while also teaching the art of drawing to others.

This Camden Town Period is when many of Sickert's paintings appear to have relevance to the Jack the Ripper murders. Sickert's paintings have been dissected ten times over. For a pro–"Ripper" analysis, you may read Stephen Knight or Jean Overton-Fuller. For a contrasting argument, you can read almost every other researcher who discusses Sickert's paintings, most notably Wendy Baron and Richard Shone.

In 1907, a little over two years after Sickert's return to London, a prostitute named Emily Dimmock was murdered in her bed at 29 St. Paul's Road in Camden Town. The case became known as the Camden Town Murder, but it showed similar characteristics to the crimes of Jack the Ripper. For one thing, Dimmock had her throat cut deeply from ear to ear. The man arrested for this murder was a Scottish music hall artist, named Robert Wood. He would stand trial and be found not guilty. Sickert would go on to paint a group of pictures, titled "The Camden Town Murders." Without analyzing the pro–Ripper or anti–Ripper significance of these paintings, it should be noted that Sickert lived in the immediate vicinity of the murder, knew Robert Wood and drew extremely vivid scenes representative of that particular murder.

Patricia Cornwell, a recent proponent of Sickert as Jack the Ripper, says that Sickert's pure hatred of women, coupled with the similarity of Dimmock's murder to those in the Jack the Ripper series, has led her to believe that Sickert murdered Dimmock. The Camden Town Murder remains one of the premier unsolved London murders. Cornwell cites Sickert's paintings as proof of his guilt in this case. His paintings are also what drew Cornwell to the possibility of Sickert being Jack the Ripper.

In 1911 the newly formed Camden Town Group began to flourish with Sickert as one of its leaders. During this time, Sickert continued to paint and exhibit his art, while also continuing at his two other loves—writing about art and teaching. It was in this year that he would also return to another of his loves—women.

In the beginning of July 1911, Sickert had an engagement broken off at the very last minute. The story goes that the woman he was going to marry had told another gentlemen to wait for her. The choice was reportedly between this other man and Sickert. The woman chose the other man, and Sickert was left at the altar, so to speak. This event did not weigh on his conscience for very long, as he married one of his art students, Christine Angus, seventeen years his junior, only twenty-six days after his original July wedding was to have taken place.

At the time of their marriage Christine Angus was thirty-four years old, while Walter was fifty-one. By the time of her death in 1920, he had grown to deeply love her. Her death would lead to a period of depression that would be compounded by the death of his mother, Eleanor, in 1922. It would be loyalty like that shown by Christine that would lead to Walter's third marriage, to longtime friend Therese Lessore.

Despite mourning the losses of his wife and his mother, Sickert continued painting and re-established a friendship with Therese Lessore in 1924. The two remained close. Sickert would receive a number of accolades and awards. In 1924 he became an associate member of the Royal Academy but resigned shortly afterwards. In 1925 he was elected an Associate of the Royal Society of Painters, Etchers, and Engravers. He would become President of the London Branch one year later. It was in 1926 that Sickert and Lessore married. Their renewed friendship had grown into love, and she would remain with him through the rest of his life. One year after their marriage, he would be elected President of the Royal Society of British Artists.

He continued to write, teach, and paint, displaying his work in numerous exhibits in which he was the main exhibitor, often the only one. In 1934 the Sickerts relocated to Margate, England, where, at the age of seventy-four, he still painted and gave lectures. Four years later they would move to Bath, in southwestern England. The ever-aware Sickert still enjoyed his passions to their fullest extent. The couple would remain in Bath, where Walter Sickert would pass away on January 22, 1942. In the year prior to his death, he would be honored with a one-man show at the National Gallery in London.

In 1915 Sickert had met and become friends with Osbert and Sacheverell Sitwell. It would be Osbert Sitwell who would later write on Sickert and relate a story about Sickert and Jack the Ripper. In Sitwell's 1947 work, *A Free House*, he collected an anthology of Sickert's writings on most subjects. Sitwell also told the story of the lodger at No. 6 Mornington Crescent. Sitwell claimed that Sickert told a story about taking a room in a London suburb a short time after the murders. The proprietor supposedly revealed to him that the previous lodger had been Jack the Ripper. She had described this man as a veterinary student who was eventually taken home to Bournemouth by his widowed mother, where he would die three months later. According to Sitwell, the name of this man was written in the margins of a copy of Casanova's *Memoirs*, which was later given to Albert Rutherston. Rutherston was reportedly not able to understand the scribblings made by Sickert. The book was lost during the bombings of World War II.

While Sitwell's intention in the book was to reproduce Sickert's vast writings on art and art criticism, including a number of writings regarding Hogarth, this anecdote was reproduced because Sitwell stated, point blank, that Sickert's conversations persistently returned to Jack the Ripper. Sickert thought he knew the identity of the murderer. It seems strange, however, that upon learning the possible name of Jack the Ripper, Sickert would simply scrawl it in the margins of a book and then give that book away.

After returning from Dieppe in 1905 Sickert had taken a room at No. 6 Mornington Crescent in Camden Town. It was in this lodging that the story of the suspicious landlady originated. At first glance, there are a number of problems with the story. If Sickert had first moved to that room in 1905, as has been vehemently argued by the anti–Sickert's out there, then it must be assumed the room was not rented for close to sixteen years. Another possibility is that Sickert had lodged there previously, at some time shortly after the murders. Perhaps he re-rented those lodgings upon his return to London. If this were the case, then it also may be assumed that the other two studios he occupied upon his return to London in 1905, which were on Fitzroy Street, a street running directly parallel to Cleveland Street, were also studios previously rented by Sickert in the late 1880s and early 1890s.

There are a number of other instances in which Sickert reportedly told meaningful stories about the activities of the Whitechapel murderer. Two prominent tales have been incorporated into full-length books discussing the possibility that Sickert was either solely responsible for the murders or that he worked in conjunction with other conspirators. As far as can be determined the first official "Ripperologist" (if you discount Walter Sickert from such a group) to link him to the murders was Donald McCormick. In the 1970 revised paperback edition of his *The Identity of Jack the Ripper*, he makes the following claim: "Yet another suggestion made is that Walter Sickert, the painter, was Jack the Ripper. The reason for Sickert being suspected is that he was believed to have made sketches and paintings of the Ripper crimes...."

McCormick made no mention of Sickert in his first version, the 1959 hardback copy, or the first revised edition, which came out in 1962. What this implies is that this knowledge came to McCormick at some time after 1962. Information regarding Sickert's fascination with Jack the Ripper could have easily been taken from the two books by Osbert Sitwell, *A Free House*, from 1947, and *Noble Essences*, from 1950. However, these are not the earliest books that reveal Sickert's fascination with the Jack the Ripper case. There is a story from Robert Emmons about Sickert having been called Jack the Ripper by a group of young girls while walking in Copenhagen Street during the time of the murders. This anecdote appeared in the 1941 book by Emmons and was readily available to Donald McCormick. There were numerous other anecdotes relating to Walter Sickert and Jack the Ripper, including an interesting parallel from a 1960 book by Lillian Browse. McCormick may have been able to mold his accusation from these sources.

Based on the information supplied by McCormick, Walter Sickert is briefly mentioned in Richard Whittington-Egan's 1975, *A Casebook on Jack the Ripper*. At the beginning of the book Whittington-Egan mentions a list of suspects who had come under popular suspicion. Among these suspects is Walter Sickert. Whittington-Egan's book did not propose a suspect, so his research was not biased toward any previously named suspect. He finds, like many researchers have, that there was no real reason for suspecting Walter Sickert of having been Jack the Ripper. Sickert's inclusion in this list was a direct result of the accusation made by Donald McCormick.

Just one year later Stephen Knight would publish his landmark work outlining the Royal Conspiracy Theory. Knight elaborated the tale told to him by Joseph Gorman Sickert, who claimed to be the son of Walter Sickert on a BBC television program in 1973. Knight included Sickert in a group of three Masonic killers. The Royal Conspiracy Theory outlined by Stephen Knight has been disproved. Therefore, the notion that Sickert was one-third of a gang of Masonic killers must also fail.

There are marked differences between the story told by Joseph Gorman Sickert in 1973 and the theory revealed to the world in 1976 by Stephen Knight. Some of the basic material from Gorman Sickert is obviously incorporated into the Royal Conspiracy Theory, but in 1973 Gorman Sickert had made no mention of the Masons, a blackmail plot or his father's part in the murders, three main staples of the Stephen Knight theory.

After the 1976 Masonic conspiracy Sickert's candidacy as a viable suspect was not endorsed until it was been resurrected by Jean Overton-Fuller in 1990. She had previously written about another suspect, Robert Donston Stephenson, relating the story of Vittoria Cremers in her 1965 book, *The Magical Dilemma of Victor Neuberg*. Her 1990 book, *Sickert and the Ripper Crimes*, tentatively suggested that Walter Sickert knew a little more than he should have and therefore, that he was Jack the Ripper. Fuller examines the art of Sickert, and discusses a longtime friend of Sickert's, Florence Pash. Pash had known Ms. Fuller's mother, Violet, and had told her that Sickert's artwork contained vital clues to the murders. Pash, who made these claims during the late 1940s, also stated that she personally knew Mary Jane Kelly, whom Walter had hired as a nanny for Alice Margaret Crook, the alleged illegitimate daughter of Prince Albert Victor, the Duke of Clarence. Pash claimed that, as far back as 1892, that she believed Sickert might have been responsible in some way for the Jack the Ripper murders.

The latest theorist to accuse Walter Sickert of committing the murders attributed to Jack the Ripper has been fiction novelist, Patricia Cornwell. Cornwell emphatically stated that she would stake her reputation on Sickert being Jack the Ripper. Her 2002 book examines the art of Sickert and theorizes that Sickert was responsible for as many as 20 to 40 murders. Her boastful claim that she would prove Sickert was Jack the Ripper has come up extremely short. Cornwell relies on the old "prove me wrong" tactic and fails to construct a strong case against Sickert.

Walter Richard Sickert remains a figure entrenched within the Jack the Ripper legend. The numerous theories relating to his suspect candidacy have fallen short of their ultimate goal. There are certain circumstantial pieces of evidence that connect Sickert to the murders. Sickert, however, is partially responsible for these connections and has evoked an eerie sense of possessing some secret knowledge regarding the murders.

There appears to be no middle ground between researchers who suggest Sickert was Jack the Ripper and those who vehemently contest his involvement. Researchers and theorists have displayed tunnel vision on both sides of the argument. There is a September 6, 1888, letter, written by Sickert's mother, that states Walter and his brother were out of London that day. This does not conclusively eliminate Walter Sickert, but it becomes an intriguing point of controversy that has not been addressed by those who think Sickert is Jack the Ripper. The opportunity to return to London on September 8 and murder Annie Chapman existed, yet an unbiased researcher must admit that this appears to be a major stumbling block.

One thing is for certain. The Victorian painter will forever be intertwined with the name Jack the Ripper. Joseph Gorman Sickert, the alleged son of Walter Sickert, recently passed away. Gorman Sickert may have taken the real truth with him to the grave.

Baron, Wendy, and Richard Shone. *Sickert: Paintings* (1993).

Beadle, William. *Jack the Ripper: Anatomy of a Myth* (1995).

Begg, Paul, Martin Fido, and Keith Skinner. *The Jack the Ripper A–Z* (1996).

Browse, Lillian. *Sickert* (1960).

Clayman, Dr. Charles B. *The American Medical Association Encyclopedia of Medicine* (1989).

Cornwell, Patricia. *Portrait of a Killer: Jack the Ripper: Case Closed* (2001).

Emmons, Robert. *The Life and Opinions of Walter Richard Sickert* (1941).

Fairclough, Melvyn. *The Ripper and the Royals* (1991).

Knight, Stephen. *Jack the Ripper: The Final Solution* (1976).

Lilly, Marjorie. *Sickert: the painter and his circle* (1973).

McCormick, Donald. *The Identity of Jack the Ripper* (1970).

Overton-Fuller, Jean. *The Magical Dilemma of Victor Neuberg* (1965).

_____. *Sickert and the Ripper Crimes* (1990).

Rumbelow, Donald. *The Complete History of Jack the Ripper* (1987).

Sitwell, Osbert. *A Free House* (1947).

_____. *Noble Essences* (1950).

Sutton, Denys. *Walter Sickert: A Biography* (1976).
Whittington-Egan, Richard. *A Casebook on Jack the Ripper* (1975).

http://www.casebook.org
http://www.wetcanvas.com/Museum/Artists/s/Walter_Sickert/

CLARENCE SIMM

A 1989 article in the *Weekly World News* stated that, in 1951, Clarence Simm confessed on his deathbed that he had murdered fourteen prostitutes as a teenager in London. His wife, Betty Simm, held this information for 38 years before selling it to a magazine that specialized in shocking headlines and was known for having more interest in selling issues than producing verifiable journalism. From the claim made by Clarence Simm, if, indeed, he made it, it is a safe assumption that he was referring to the Jack the Ripper murders.

A few points arise from this apparent deathbed confession. Clarence Simm claims to have been a teenager when he murdered those fourteen prostitutes. Most of the eyewitness testimony, however, places the murderer close to thirty years of age. It is extremely difficult, despite the darkness of the night, to confuse a teenager for a man of thirty. Born sometime in the early or mid–1870s, it is doubtful that Simm would have possessed the minimal medical skill or anatomical knowledge needed to remove organs like kidneys and hearts from his victims.

The next major point to consider is the number of prostitutes that Simm claims to have murdered—fourteen. If one discounts Emma Elizabeth Smith, who was attacked by three men (assumed to be a local gang), a generous count of women murdered in London within that time period only reaches eleven, and that includes the multiple torsos discovered in London during the time period. If Simm had been Jack the Ripper, he would have remembered the exact number of women he had killed. Fourteen appears to be an elevated number.

The last point is that his widow, Betty, waited 38 years to tell the tale regarding her husband. This occurred only one year after the 100th anniversary of the murders, when Jack the Ripper was still headlining newspapers all over England. There is no evidence that Betty Simm revealed her story before the 100th anniversary of the murders, despite carrying it around with her for so long. There is also no evidence to remotely connect Clarence Simm to Jack the Ripper.

Begg, Paul, Martin Fido, and Keith Skinner. *The Jack the Ripper A–Z* (1996)

G. WENTWORTH BELL SMITH

Smith came to London from Canada during 1888 in connection with the Toronto Trust, or possibly the Toronto Truss, Society. His entire connection to the Jack the Ripper case emanates from a solitary source, his former landlord Mr. Callaghan. The Callaghans rented Smith rooms at 27 Sun Street, in Finsbury Square. Mr. Callaghan eventually informed the police of his belief that Smith was Jack the Ripper. Later, crime historian L. Forbes Winslow took up the case, and G. Wentworth Bell Smith became his personal suspect, to whom Forbes compared a number of other proposed suspects over the years.

Extremely little is known about Smith. The main history comes from Mr. Callaghan. While renting the room from Callaghan, Smith was described as a religious fanatic, with a strong hatred of prostitutes. On the night of the Martha Tabram murder, Callaghan stated that Smith came home at 4:00 A.M. Soon thereafter, Smith allegedly told Callaghan that he had to leave England and return to Canada. Callaghan claimed that Smith often stayed out late, so why on this particular night was it suddenly peculiar? This is simply due to the circumstance of the murder of Martha Tabram.

Smith had come to rent the room from Callaghan in August, and according to Callaghan, left only days after the murder of Tabram to return to Canada. Callaghan states that he did see Smith back in the country the following month, but it is important to note that Callaghan acquired all these negative beliefs regarding Smith over the span of only ten days, at the most.

Callaghan claimed that he informed the police about the strange habits of Smith after the murder of Martha Tabram and that the police inquired about Smith. When the story of this man was taken up by L. Forbes Winslow, no one was able to find any evidence of this inquiry. Inspector Edmund Reid headed up the Tabram inquiry. Inspector Reid was the officer in charge of the Local CID and, as thorough a policeman as he was, if there had been an inquiry into Smith, he would have reported it in the files. When Winslow went to the police with this story, he showed Chief Inspector Swanson a statement written by Callaghan. According to Swanson, the date on the statement had been altered, from August 9 to August 7, so that it would fit the Tabram murder. It is not known who altered the date, but the obvious choice would seem to be Winslow. It may nevertheless have been Callaghan attempting to cover his own story.

Callaghan believed Smith was also the man responsible for accosting another woman. On nothing more than mere suspicion, Callaghan became convinced that G. Wentworth Bell Smith was Jack the Ripper. Callaghan's negative feelings toward this man fueled his desire to tarnish Smith's name, and Callaghan eventually acquired a follower in Winslow. For the rest of his life, L. Forbes Winslow believed that he had solved this case and continued to comment on his suspect without ever producing a single shred of evidence against Smith. As late as 1910, Winslow was defending another suspect, William Grant Grainger, due to his hardened belief in Smith. Twenty-two years after the murders, Winslow still could offer nothing new about this very strange suspect.

Winslow could never even come out with a simple history of his man. This may be because Winslow found out something regarding G. Wentworth Bell Smith that negated him as a suspect. Perhaps Winslow just latched onto a suspect in order to be forever associ-ated with this legendary case. As of yet, no documentary evidence of the existence of G. Wentworth Bell Smith has been unearthed.

Begg, Paul, Martin Fido, and Keith Skinner. *The Jack the Ripper A–Z* (1996).

Evans, Stewart P., and Keith Skinner. *The Ultimate Jack the Ripper Companion* (2000).

Jakubowski, Maxim, and Nathan Braund. *The Mammoth Book of Jack the Ripper* (1998).

http://www.casebook.org

HENRY ARTHUR GEORGE SOMERSET

Born on November 17, 1851, Henry Arthur George Somerset is most remembered today for his involvement in the 1889 Cleveland Street Scandal involving a male brothel. He was the third son of the 8th Duke of Beaufort. Somerset was the Equerry to the Prince of Wales, Albert Edward, and Superintendent of the future King's stables. He was also a close friend of the Prince of Wales's son, Prince Albert Victor, the Duke of Clarence. It has been suggested that, due to Somerset's friendship and ties to the royal family, most notably the Prince of Wales and the Duke of Clarence, he was allowed to flee the country when the scandal broke, to escape any prosecution for his crimes and, possibly, to prevent him having to divulge compromising information about the Duke of Clarence. Somerset would go on to lead an uneventful life, eventually passing away on May 26, 1926. He appears to have gained the bulk of his historical fame through scandal and birthright.

Melvyn Fairclough's updated Royal Conspiracy Theory of 1891 included Lord Arthur as one of the men involved in the plot to protect the crown. The exact role of Somerset's involvement was not clearly defined. His putative role was similar to that of the Earl of Euston, a lookout and secondary accomplice.

Somerset and the Earl of Euston were distant relatives, as Somerset's father had descended directly from the Fitzroy line. Their involvement in the Cleveland Street Scandal has made their names synonymous with homosexual scandal. Fairclough states that the Earl of Euston and Somerset were in the East End on the nights of the murders, yet there is no documentation or outside corroboration of this statement.

In order to include elements of the Cleveland Street Scandal, a case also worked on by Inspector Abberline, Fairclough and Joseph Gorman Sickert have involved a number of members of aristocratic society in their updated Royal Conspiracy Theory. Since the original theory has been disproved, and since no major updates were made by Fairclough, it seems logical to discount the elaborations of the updated theory. This would include the naming of Henry Arthur George Somerset as a co-conspirator.

Fairclough, Melvyn. *The Ripper and the Royals* (1991).
Hyde, Montgomery H. *The Cleveland Street Scandal* (1976).
http://www.gayhistory.com/rev2/events/1889.htm

"Dr. Stanley"

The first English language book to offer a suspect came out in 1929. *The Mystery of Jack the Ripper*, written by Leonard Matters, was based on two sources. While in Argentina, Matters had found a journal that contained the deathbed confession of a former East End doctor claiming to be Jack the Ripper. The second source was a woman known only as Mrs. North, who contacted Matters about a man she had entertained during the time of the murders. This man had spoken rather casually about the murders. According to Mrs. North, the man had gone so far as to state that he was Jack the Ripper.

In 1926 Matters wrote an article for *The People*, wherein he related the story of an unnamed student who made his way from London to Buenos Aires, Argentina, to visit his former teacher. The student was reportedly told by his teacher, a formerly well-respected London doctor, that his son had contracted syphilis from Mary Jane Kelly in 1886 and died as a result. "Dr. Stanley," as Matters called the father, murdered Kelly and her friends to avenge the death of his son.

After reading this article, Mrs. North contacted Matters, as she believed her former client to be the man Matters had described. This man had frequented the café where Mrs. North worked and had spoken about the murders. After failing to keep a date with Mrs. North, this man had showed up some time later, claiming to be Jack the Ripper and claiming there would be one more murder. This man, according to Mrs. North, had failed to keep his original appointment with her in order to visit the graves of his wife and son.

Matters combined these two sources to write his book in 1929. Historians of the case have expressed doubt regarding the veracity of the stories offered in Matters book. Neither of these two sources have been traced or documented. Matters named his suspect, "Dr. Stanley," a pseudonym, which has also drawn severe criticism. As his book was written in 1929, Matters would have had access to men and women who may have lived in the East End at the time, yet he chose to base his theory on these two sources only. Matters claimed to have searched through the Medical Council record books in search of any doctor whose name sounded like Stanley, but he apparently had found no listing.

There are numerous problems with this theory. Syphilis is a disease which takes between twenty and thirty years to kill someone, yet, by the doctor's own account, it was the syphilis contracted from Mary Jane Kelly in 1886 that had killed his son. Obviously, the syphilis must have killed him before the autumn of 1888, yet it seems to have had no adverse effects on Mary Kelly herself. There is also the problem of Dr. Stanley seeking his revenge by murdering at least four prostitutes before the murder of his intended target. It has not been ascertained whether Mary Kelly knew the other "canonical" victims. If Kelly was the object of Dr. Stanley's revenge, why wouldn't he murder her first? Then there would be no need to murder her

friends. Matters would have us believe that Dr. Stanley's line of revenge through the victims worked backwards.

From Matters' own statements, "Stanley" may have sounded similar to the real name of the doctor in question. Less than forty years after the murders took place, Matters might have had the time to fully research this doctor and connect a name to the story. Matters did not.

Matters's theory moves the investigative community no closer to Jack the Ripper's identity. Since the 1929 naming of Dr. Stanley, no researcher has been able to identify a real person who fits Matters's story that leaves us with a suspect who may never have existed.

Begg, Paul, Martin Fido, and Keith Skinner. *The Jack the Ripper A–Z* (1996).
Clayman, Dr. Charles B. *The American Medical Association Encyclopedia of Medicine* (1989).
Jakubowski, Maxim, and Nathan Braund. *The Mammoth Book of Jack the Ripper* (1998).
Matters, Leonard. *The Mystery of Jack the Ripper* (1929).
http://www.casebook.org

JAMES KENNETH STEPHEN

James Kenneth Stephen was born on February 25, 1859, in the city of London. He was the second son of Judge Sir James Fitzjames Stephen and Mary Richenda Cunningham. The Stephen family came from a humble background yet through their will and ambition were able to climb the societal ladder. Legal and academic excellence allowed James

Kenneth's father, brother Herbert, and two uncles, James and Leslie, to rise above their modest beginnings and ascend to knighthood. J. K., or "Jem," as he was commonly referred to, had more than academic and legal excellence in his family line. His uncle Leslie's daughter was a brilliant writer, J. K.'s first cousin, Virginia Woolf.

At the age of ten he attended a prep school for Eton College. James Kenneth would form a lasting friendship and relationship with a student at Eton who was three years his junior. This student would eventually write about a number of poets, including James Stephen. In 1911, Arthur C. Benson published his *The Leaves of the Tree: Studies in Biography*, in which he revealed a lot about Stephen. Benson stated that Stephen constantly surrounded himself with younger boys who held his interest. Benson, himself, was three years Stephen's junior and often stated that he was awed at the presence of the handsome, brilliant and muscular Stephen, so much so that he would listen rather than speak, for fear of having this older student think less of him. Benson also stated that Stephen loved close and intimate relationships and that, despite being an emotional person, Stephen often hid his feelings, doubtlessly from himself, as well as others.

Stephen began his college career in 1878 at King's College, Cambridge, earning a Bachelor of Arts degree in 1882. While at Cambridge he involved himself in many extracurricular activities. He was elected President of the Cambridge Union, a public political speaking forum, in 1880 and was a member of the Amateur Dramatic Society. One of his many passions was writing, and he contributed to many Cambridge journals. He won the "Members Prize" for his essay writing.

Another recurring interest would be law. Most of the male members in his family would go on to excel in the law. It seems that J. K. was driven along that path as well. The main courses he excelled in were writing and history. He was placed first in the first class of the History Tripos in 1881, an achievement that no student had accomplished over the previous two years. Law remained a constant, though, and Stephen was awarded the first Whewell Scholarship in International Law. He would go on to be called to the bar in 1884.

In 1883 he had been recommended as a tutor and companion to nineteen-year-old Prince Albert Victor, known as "Prince Eddy." During Prince Eddy's formal residence at Cambridge, Stephen handpicked his friends, a close-knit social circle that shared certain interests. He urged Prince Eddy to join clubs, mainly the clubs that interested Stephen. Prince Eddy was close to five years Stephen's junior, and he looked up to Stephen. Stephen used this to his advantage, at least initially.

After being called to the bar in 1884, he remained as tutor and companion to Prince Eddy. Prince Eddy left Cambridge in 1885, and Stephen accepted a fellowship at Cambridge, starting his long line of changing occupations. He remained at Cambridge for the next couple of years until an accident in 1886 at Felixstowe. Stephen was riding his horse while on holiday, when the horse shied backwards and Stephen's head was struck by one of the propellers of a windmill, which cut the back of his head. A variation of this story is that Stephen was attempting to climb the windmill and accidentally brushed the back of his head against one of the propellers. Numerous researchers have assumed that this severe blow to his head caused brain damage that ultimately led to his insanity and death.

This distinct event in Stephen's life is a difficult one to decipher. There was a noted history of mental illness in his family, particularly running in the male

Stephens. His father, James Fitzjames, had just suffered a breakdown in 1885 which would eventually lead to his going insane some years later. Yet, up until that point in J. K.'s life, he had showed no outward signs of insanity. His political public speaking had often been described as scintillating, and he was basically in charge of a secret society at Cambridge that included Prince Eddy, who followed Stephen around like *his* loyal servant.

Stephen recovered from his accident during 1887. Writing had always been his true occupational love, regardless of family pressure to remain in legal circles. Before his accident he had contributed articles to such newspapers as *The St. James Gazette, The Saturday Review* and, most notably, *The Pall Mall Gazette.* In the latter of these he had had a number of successful parodies published. Stephen's satirical side, exhibited in his early writing, developed into the founding of his newspaper, *The Reflector.* Writing and journalism seem to have remained constant in his mind, even during his convalescence.

First published in the beginning of 1888, *The Reflector* was a weekly journal that challenged the rules and procedures that, since the dawn of the age of journalism, had hampered writers. The newspaper was designed to provide political and literary insight while confronting the social issues that could not be questioned by other newspapers. Stephen's idea was that strong and intelligent writing should win out over simply reporting the news. The basics of everyday news could be found in any newspaper, this newspaper was meant to draw in and challenge the reader with skillful writing and analysis. This allowed Stephen to attract such challeng-

ing literary minds as his uncle, Sir Leslie Stephen. J. K. was still largely responsible for writing each issue.

The Reflector managed to last only seventeen issues, the last issue published on April 21 of the same year it had begun. His ambition had exceeded the literary consciousness of the time, yet the effects of what he was trying to accomplish can be viewed in journalism today on a global scale. His final issue included an attack on the Postmaster General that may have been truly intended for a different target. Researcher and theorist John Wilding has suggested that because certain duties attributed to the Postmaster General were under the direct control of the Prince of Wales, the attack was actually directed at the prince. Wilding goes on to propose that this attack may have come about because the Prince of Wales had impregnated Mary Jane Kelly.

After *The Reflector* folded in mid-April, Stephen is said to have abandoned all work-related activities. The failure of his literary dream weighed heavily on him, so his father stepped in and assigned him to the post of Clerk of Assize, South Wales Circuit, in the summer of 1888. His brother was appointed to the same post in the Northern Circuit one year later. Their records in office were distinctly different. J. K. was given this office by his father during the summer of 1888, partly due to its light workload, yet research has shown that Stephen was not an active figure in this position.

Stephen eventually resigned in 1890 and returned to Cambridge to lecture and teach. Writing still remained the main focus of his life's work. He published a pamphlet in defense of compulsory Greek, a language he had an affinity for. Poetry had always been an outlet for his hidden feelings and the two works for which he is known, *Lapsus Calami*, and *Quo Musa Tendis?*, were published, with added revisions and editions, during 1891. He also published numerous articles and poems in Cambridge University journals.

On November 21, J. K.'s brother, Herbert, took him to St. Andrew's Hospital, Northampton. This was a mental health asylum. Stephen would remain there for the rest of his life, which only lasted until February 3, 1892. There are detailed reports of his declining mental health. Researcher and theorist Dr. David Abrahamsen has transcribed these documented reports on Stephen. These reports reveal many different sides of a complicated man. They also indicate a lackluster will to continue living, a change from the man who had just written a profound and well-received analysis on the Greek language.

Stephen's disease has never been accurately diagnosed, so it is too easily described as insanity resulting from his accident in 1886. While a sudden attack is not out of the question, it seems that brain damage from an injury five years previous would have prohibited Stephen from performing some of his literary and academic duties in the time between his injury and his sudden mental collapse.

Reports from St. Andrew's Hospital show very different sides of Stephen. At least one report states that he threw a looking glass through his window and stood motionless in front of that window while completely naked. Another report states that he had regained his strength enough to take part in outdoor exercise, this occurring sixteen days after he had begun refusing food. Numerous

reports reveal that he believed someone was coming after him, that there was a warrant out for his arrest, and that he had committed some sort of crime. During these times he appeared excitable, but he was fully capable of verbally describing his fears.

On January 14, 1892, Stephen learned of the death of Prince Eddy. Before this, he had begun to recover, exercising regularly and taking visits from his brothers, Herbert and Harry. Upon learning of Prince Eddy's death, he refused all food. Twenty days later, on February 3, he would fall into unconsciousness after speaking with his two brothers, and die two hours later. Many have believed that his death resulted from starvation, yet that is not the case. While he was refusing food, the staff at St. Andrew's force-fed him through a tube three times daily. There is no report indicating that Stephen was undernourished. One report on January 30, sixteen days after he had stopped eating claimed he was maintaining his strength. On February 2, he began eating a little. The following day, the day of his death, Stephen continued to eat. The official cause of death, however, was the failure to eat, mania, and exhaustion.

The first public association of Stephen with the Jack the Ripper murders was made in 1972, by Michael Harrison, in his *Clarence: Was He Jack the Ripper?* Harrison rigidly assessed the article by Dr. Thomas Stowell in *The Criminologist* two years earlier. He formed a profile of Dr. Stowell's suspect, "S." From leading Ripper historian and writer, Colin Wilson, we know that Dr. Stowell's suspect, was in fact, Prince Eddy, yet Harrison's profile did not perfectly fit Prince Eddy. The naming of "S" was what really got Harrison researching, and he came across the tutor and companion of Prince Eddy, J. K. Stephen.

Certain characteristics of the Jack the Ripper suspect profile drawn from Dr. Stowell's article seemed to fit Stephen perfectly. Harrison conjectured that Dr. Stowell's original pseudonym for his suspect was the suspect's own initial, "S," rather than the "X" that *Criminologist* editor Nigel Morland is reputed to have talked Stowell out of. If Harrison was correct, the suspect's identification must have come directly from Dr. William Gull. Harrison then postulated that Stephen must have been a patient of Dr. Gull, who might have treated him immediately after his accident at Felixstowe in late 1886.

Many researchers have stated that after Prince Eddy left Cambridge in 1885, Stephen parted company with the royal family. While there is reason to believe that the relationship between Prince Eddy and Stephen might never have been broken off, there is no positive proof that Stephen was a patient of the royal physician, Dr. Gull. If he had been, this would be even more evidence that Stephen had not really parted with Prince Eddy. The nature of Stephen's injury, and his family history of insanity affecting the mind, would have made Dr. Gull the perfect choice of physician. Dr. Gull was an expert in diseases of the brain and mind and, having the requisite surgical experience, he may even have been brought in at the request of Prince Eddy to check on his friend, companion, and possible homosexual lover.

However, the theory that Stephen was the suspect conflicts with elements of Dr. Stowell's theory. Stephen did not take a tour of India in 1889, and he definitely did not suffer from syphilis, as medical records from St. Andrew's prove. These are two major identifying factors of Dr. Stowell's suspect that do not apply to Stephen. There are other characteristics that do not apply to Prince Eddy, of course, like the resigning of his commission at the age of twenty-four. Harrison has taken this detail to describe Stephen. Stephen was twenty-four in 1883, but he did not resign his commission. Rather, he took up a commission to tutor and become a companion to Prince Eddy.

The misogynistic aspect of Stephen's poetry is self evident, yet Michael Harrison was the first researcher to point out that this was an obvious aspect of an outward hatred toward women. Harrison applied this misogynistic attitude to a misinterpretation of Dr. Stowell's article to conclude that Stephen was Jack the Ripper. Harrison was also the first researcher to notice the special relationship between Stephen and Prince Eddy, and he used this fact to support his case for Stephen's guilt. Stephen's motive, according to Harrison, was jealousy. Unfortunately, the suspect named by Dr. Stowell was not J. K. Stephen, which severely discredits the theory of Michael Harrison.

Six years after the first naming of Stephen by Michael Harrison in 1972, Frank Spiering produced a work, entitled *Prince Jack: The True Story of Jack the Ripper*. Spiering's book reads more like fiction based on certain historical facts than a work of well-researched and documented nonfiction. In Spiering's "novel," he attributes the murders to Prince Eddy, but he includes Prince Eddy's lover, J. K. Stephen, as the author of the infamous letter and postcard that provided Jack the Ripper's moniker to the world.

Spiering's work is wrought with numerous errors, regarding both Prince Eddy and Stephen, but at no time does he state that Stephen was responsible for any of the murders. There are no sources to trace the information provided by Spiering other than basic historical facts, such as Prince Eddy's engagement to Princess Mary of Teck and his love for Helene D'Orleans. This, coupled with the decade's infatuation with the Royal Conspiracy, made Spiering's book a best seller.

In 1987 Keith Skinner and Martin Howells published *The Ripper Legacy*. Despite their interest in Montague John Druitt as a suspect, one of the more intriguing aspects of the work was their proof of a connection between Druitt and Prince Eddy. To demonstrate this, J. K. Stephen was used. One such connection lies within an alleged secret homosexual society at Cambridge called the "Apostles." The authors stated that Cambridge was where Druitt and Prince Eddy had met. If there is any truth in this statement, it is also true that Stephen introduced Druitt and Prince Eddy.

Another connection between Prince Eddy and Druitt, through Stephen, has to do with where Druitt kept his law offices. Druitt worked at No. 9 King's Bench Walk, while Stephen's brother, Harry, had chambers at No. 3 King's Bench Walk, and brother Herbert worked directly across the street at No. 4 Paper Buildings. Since his naming as Jack the Ripper in 1972, Stephen has gone from author of the letters to go-between and introducer.

In 1991 Melvyn Fairclough named Stephen as a co-conspirator in the Royal Conspiracy. It is not specifically distinguishable which women if any, were murdered by Stephen, according to Fairclough. Joseph Gorman Sickert described Fairclough what have come to be called the Abberline Diaries, wherein Stephen's name is mentioned throughout as taking an active part in the Royal cover-up. He did not show these diaries to Fairclough or, at the time, to anyone, though later he produced what he said were the diaries for view. Fairclough and Gorman Sickert do not add evidence that lends credibility to the suggestion that Stephen was involved in the Royal Conspiracy.

The following year Stephen was again accused of actively taking part in the murders. Through pure psychological theorizing, forensic psychiatrist Dr. David Abrahamsen postulated that Prince Eddy and Stephen conspired to commit the murders. Stephen's misogyny, as evidenced in his poetry, remains one of the aggravating factors, according to Abrahamsen. While there are a number of historical errors, Abrahamsen's book is important, as it produces the asylum notes recorded by the hospital staff at St. Andrew's. A large element of the book is a psychological re-evaluation of information derived from Michael Harrison's 1972 work on Stephen and Prince Eddy. Dr. Abrahamsen might have seen the parallels between Harrison and Dr. Stowell's works on Prince Eddy and Stephen and then made the leap that two men together they murdered the women attributed to Jack the Ripper. There appears to be no salient motive for Prince Eddy and Stephen to have conspired to commit these specific murders, and the lack of any new substantiation or external support severely hampers Abrahamsen's work.

Just one year later, John Wilding came out with *Jack the Ripper Revealed*.

Wilding believed Stephen and Montague John Druitt were the murderers. There are two reasons Wilding believed he had solved the puzzle. The first lay in anagrams constructed from the Goulston Street Graffito and the Liverpool Letter (first publicly mentioned in 1927 by J. Hall Richardson). Wilding rearranged the Goulston Street Graffito to form another secret message, informing Inspector Abberline that Druitt is the one solely responsible for the murders. According to Wilding, this implies that Stephen must have written the message. A number of problems arise out of this. The link from Druitt to Stephen can be made rather easily through either of Stephen's two brothers and, perhaps, through Druitt's look-alike, Prince Eddy. Why, then, would you implicate a co-murderer who can be so easily traced back to you?

Wilding also suggests that Mary Jane Kelly had become pregnant by the Prince of Wales, and that the murders were committed to protect the Crown. Stephen was allegedly told of the pregnancy and knew that certain prostitutes had to be silenced. Stephen chose Druitt because Druitt might have been the one Mary Kelly told of her pregnancy. Wilding uses the final issue of *The Reflector* as evidence against Stephen and Prince Albert Edward.

However, if Kelly had become pregnant by the Prince of Wales, and Stephen had discovered this in time for the April 21 issue of *The Reflector*, Kelly would have been in her eighth or ninth month of pregnancy at the time of her murder. This pregnancy has been debated since 1939, yet it has always been assumed that she would have been in the early stages of pregnancy. Certainly, it would have been obvious if she had been in the final month of pregnancy when she was murdered. Wilding's theory disintegrates under this deductive reasoning.

Andy and Sue Parlour relayed a story to Kevin O'Donnell that expands on the notion that the murders were committed by Stephen and Montague John Druitt. They also believe that the murders were committed because the Prince of Wales had impregnated Mary Kelly. In this updating of the story, the authors include Dr. Gull, as the man responsible for coercing Stephen to commit the murders. Stephen supposedly chose Druitt to help him, and clues were left that would implicate the Freemasons, including the Goulston Street Graffito, the placement of the bodies, and certain tools of the Masons, such as the mitre, the square, and the apron.

An oral tradition from Dr. William Gull's hometown, Thorpe Le-Soken, is the major impetus for the Parlour's theory, an advancement of John Wilding's theory without further factual documentation. What is apparently forgotten here is that Stephen disliked the Prince of Wales enough to risk imprisonment for making his veiled attack in print. Yet, he feels the need to protect the prince's name? It seems illogical at best. The 1997 effort by the Parlours is another rehashing of the Stephen Knight Royal Conspiracy Theory, with the major players switched around.

Much of what we know about J. K. Stephen comes from his brother, Herbert. Herbert wrote about J. K. and produced an updated version of his published poems, specifically *Lapsus Calami*. He perceived his brother as strong-willed and almost beyond reproach. After 1911, Herbert was still trying to cover his brother's possible faults or idiosyncrasies. In a letter to Arthur C. Benson, Stephen's biographer and friend, Herbert stated that in regards to J. K., they, Benson and Herbert, differed as extensively as two men could. Benson had challenged Herbert's portrayal of his brother. Benson perceived distinct character flaws in Stephen, even if his memories of his dear old friend were largely flattering.

In life J. K. Stephen was a brilliant student, excelling in history, writing, and law. He has been described as an excellent political speaker and was singled out for numerous awards and recognitions. As a teen he excelled in sports like the "Wall Game," a derivative of football. Later in life he wrote about his affinity for the sport of tennis. Most who wrote about Stephen were awestruck at his presence. His talent and ambition allowed him to achieve whatever he put his mind to. James Kenneth Stephen was truly a Renaissance man, who took on many tasks and occupations, succeeding at them all. Without any formal training, he took up drawing and painting in the summer of 1888 and was described by both Arthur C. Benson and his cousin, Virginia Woolf, as a talented and able painter. It appears there was nothing that J. K. Stephen could not accomplish.

Abrahamsen, Dr. David. *Murder and Madness: The Secret Life of Jack the Ripper* (1992).

Begg, Paul, Martin Fido, and Keith Skinner. *The Jack the Ripper A–Z* (1996).

Benson, Arthur C. *The Leaves of the Tree: Studies in Biography* (1911).

Clayman, Dr. Charles B. *The American Medical Association Encyclopedia of Medicine* (1989).

Fairclough, Melvyn. *The Ripper and the Royals* (1991).

Harrison, Michael *Clarence: Was He Really Jack the Ripper?* (1972).

Howells, Martin, and Keith Skinner. *The Ripper Legacy* (1987).

Jakubowski, Maxim, and Nathan Braund. *The Mammoth Book of Jack the Ripper* (1998).

Knight, Stephen. *Jack the Ripper: The Final Solution* (1976).

Parlour, Andy, and Sue Parlour. *The Jack the Ripper Whitechapel Murders* (1997).

Richardson, Joseph Hall. *From City to Fleet Street* (1927).

Spiering, Frank. *Prince Jack: The True Story of Jack the Ripper* (1978).

Stewart, William *Jack the Ripper: A New Theory* (1939).

Stowell, Dr. Thomas. *The Criminologist* (November 1970).

Wilding, John. *Jack the Ripper Revealed* (1993).

http://www.casebook.org

http://www.library.utoronto.ca/utel/rp/authors/stephen.html#notes

ROBERT DONSTON STEPHENSON

Robert Donston Stephenson was both a suspect and a theorist in the autumn of 1888. He wrote articles on the murders for *The Pall Mall Gazette*, while also writing to the police regarding graffiti found in Goulston Street on the night of the double murder. Stephenson remained a dormant suspect for approximately eighty-five years until researcher Richard Whittington-Egan reminded the world about him. One year prior to the 100th anniversary of Jack the Ripper, researcher Melvin Harris developed the theory against Stephenson to book length, making him one of the few prime suspects in this case.

Robert Donston Stephenson has been discussed earlier in regards to his beliefs that Dr. Morgan Davies was Jack the Ripper. Stephenson claimed Dr. Davies reenacted the murder of Mary Jane Kelly for a patient with whom later Stephenson shared a hospital ward. According to this patient, Dr. Davies had intimate knowledge of the actual murder. Upon learning from the editor of *The Pall Mall Gazette*, William Thomas Stead, that Mary Kelly had been sodomized, Stephenson's beliefs regarding Dr. Davies solidified. There is no evidence or documentation to support any part of this story. The report by Dr. Thomas Bond on Mary Jane Kelly revealed no signs of sodomy. The patient that Stephenson shared his hospital ward with is never mentioned in any files as corroborating the notion that Dr. Davies reenacted the murder of Mary Kelly. Finally, W. T. Stead, despite editing the newspaper that accepted Stephenson's articles, is not known to have passed the information to Stephenson that Kelly had been sodomized.

After he was released from London Hospital on December 7, 1888, Stephenson told this story about Dr. Davies to George Marsh, an unemployed ironmongery assistant. The two men began passing themselves off as private detectives investigating the murders. Their relationship quickly turned sour, and Marsh went to Scotland Yard to turn Stephenson in as Jack the Ripper. Inspector Thomas Roots took his statement, which clearly outlined Marsh's brief history with Stephenson.

It has been argued that Robert Stephenson intended to become notorious with the police. Proponents of Stephenson's guilt claim that, by making himself known to police as a possible suspect, the police would be less likely to suspect him. After eluding the police for months, leaving them with not a solitary clue, Stephenson decided he needed to promote himself as a suspect. This is the theory we are asked to accept.

Two days after George Marsh made his statement to Inspector Roots, two documents are written that connect this particular triangle. Stephenson went to Scotland Yard and explained his own theory to Inspector Roots, while also describing his brief partnership with Marsh. Stephenson provided a location to Inspector Roots where he could easily be found. In his statement to Roots, Stephenson expressed some contempt for Marsh, who may or may not have expressed a fear of Stephenson. Of course, Stephenson may also have known about Marsh's statement, which brings us to our next document. Inspector Roots submitted a report declaring that Stephenson was someone whom he had known for twenty years. Roots described Stephenson as a habitual drinker and possible drug addict. Despite these character flaws, Roots gave an overall account of Stephenson that indicated he did not believe Stephenson was Jack the Ripper. More importantly, Inspector Roots forwarded his report on Stephenson, as well as his reports of the statements of Stephenson and Marsh, to Chief Inspector Swanson.

While the missing suspects file has

been theorized to include material relating to Robert Donston Stephenson, it appears obvious from Swanson's later comments on the subject that there was not much of a case against Stephenson. Swanson never mentioned Stephenson in later recollections on the subject, but as material was forwarded to him naming Stephenson as a suspect, Swanson more than likely investigated the matter. Neither Inspector Roots, nor Chief Inspector Swanson, believed in the guilt of Stephenson. The beliefs and statements of George Marsh obviously did not have much impact.

Stephenson's early history is riddled with question marks, due mainly to a lack of documentation. The bulk of the information known about Stephenson comes directly from him. He was often described as an habitual liar and drunkard, so this history of this incredibly intriguing suspect must be viewed with extreme caution.

Robert Donston Stephenson was born on April 20, 1841, in Sculcoates, a parish in Hull, England, to parents who owned a lucrative mill. We know nothing of his childhood. Researcher and theorist Ivor Edwards has collected as complete a chronology of Stephenson's movements as was ever thought possible. When he was eighteen years old, Stephenson visited Paris and became friends with Lord Bulwer Lytton's son. Lord Bulwer Lytton later initiated Stephenson into the Freemason Lodge of Alexandria.

Stephenson may have served in Garibaldi's army as a surgeon. Garibaldi was an Italian revolutionary who invaded Sicily in response to the Franco-Austrian War of 1859. Recent evidence has shown that there is some truth to this claim. Stephenson did serve with Garibaldi from 1860 to 1863, before leaving for the coast of West Africa.

While in Africa Stephenson studied the art of witchcraft and honed what he believed to be his supernatural powers. In January and February of 1889, he wrote two articles for *The Pall Mall Gazette* about black magic and the cult mysticism of West Africa. In the February article, Stephenson claimed he had murdered a female witch doctor in West Africa in 1863. This brings up the earlier theory of a murderer making himself notorious to the police, but Stephenson's history of telling grandiose stories apparently outweighed any secret message he may have been sending to the authorities. As shall be discussed later, this would not be the only time Stephenson would write about murder around the time of the Jack the Ripper murders.

After his trip to West Africa Stephenson returned to London and took a position at the Customs House in Hull, England. He may have gotten this job through his father's connections. At the time his father was the collector of the Hull Corporation dues. In 1868 Stephenson was fired from his post at the Customs House because of associations with various prostitutes, from one of whom Stephenson contracted a venereal disease. In this same year Stephenson would be shot in the thigh. The circumstances surrounding this event are hazy, which has led some to the conclusion that the shooting was of a suspicious nature.

On February 14, 1876, a man named Roslyn D'Onston Stephenson married a servant girl named Anne Deary. This has been presumed to be Robert Donston Stephenson, but it has been recently postulated that Roslyn

D'Onston Stephenson and Robert Donston Stephenson were not the same person. No clear-cut answer has emerged on this issue. Yet, considering the frequent use of aliases in the Victorian Era, as well as Stephenson's affinity for the occult, it seems a strong possibility that these were, in fact, the same person. Anne Deary appears to have lived until at least 1886. After that date, there is no further documentation on her. There is also no record of her death. Portions of a woman were found in the Thames River on May 11, 1887. Some have theorized that these body parts came from the murdered corpse of Anne Deary and that Stephenson was the murderer.

According to Victoria Cremers, Stephenson may have had his heart broken by a woman, named "Ada," during his youth, an incident that ultimately led to his sour views on women. Cremers's putative knowledge of Stephenson's past comes from Stephenson's own veiled references to his past. If "Ada" was meant as a reference to Anne Deary, the chronology of the Cremers's events would be mistaken. Anne Deary could not have been the lover of his youth, as Stephenson was already forty-five years old in 1886. Even Stephenson's supposed marriage to Anne Deary didn't happen until he was thirty-five years old, again, hardly youthful.

On July 26, 1888, Stephenson checked himself into London Hospital. He remained in a semi-private ward in London Hospital for the next 134 days and was discharged on December 7, 1888. Stephenson was treated at the hospital for neurasthenia, literally, nervous exhaustion. The symptoms of neurasthenia include loss of energy, insomnia, depression, muscle pain, specifically occurring within the abdomen and the chest, and a general loss of concentration. Today, "neurasthenia" is considered an outdated term. Individual symptoms have been associated with specific illnesses.

In the 1880s, in a large metropolitan hospital like London Hospital, neurasthenia did not require a patient to be secluded from other patients, as is indicated by the fact that Stephenson stayed in a semi-private ward. It is not currently known who Stephenson's roommate was during his initial stay at London Hospital, or if there was more than one. It is quite possible that his condition was not taken as seriously as someone afflicted with an illness or disease that could be properly diagnosed and treated.

Stephenson's admission to the hospital, of course, detracts from the theory that Stephenson committed the Jack the Ripper murders. London Hospital was known for its security and inaccessibility during the 19 century. The other side to that coin is that an illness like neurasthenia simply required bed rest. Stephenson would not have been a high priority on the medical staff's list, so that he could have easily snuck out on the night of the murders, despite the suspicion it may have aroused if he were caught. There is no record of Stephenson having been caught out of his room on any night, much less the nights of the murders.

Stephenson would return to London Hospital on May 13, 1889. He would stay there for only seventy-three days and be released on July 25, 1889. The admittance form lists an acute case of chloralism, an excessive abuse of chloral hydrate. Chloral hydrate is a drug used on the elderly to treat insomnia. The same doctor, a Dr. Sutton, worked on

Stephenson during his two stays at the hospital. One theory behind Stephenson-as-suspect is that he faked his original illness, then had a genuine case of neurasthenia after the murders ceased, for which he was treated. But according to this theory, Stephenson would have been taking medication to cure an illness that he faked; then, while taking the medication, he came down with the actual illness the medicine was supposed to cure. The odds against this happening seem astronomical.

Stephenson's failing health due to an excessive use of chloral hydrate is supposed, in theory, to have ended the murders. This would indicate that, while actually in London Hospital, Stephenson was well enough to commit these acts of savagery and escape any detection but that, once he left the hospital he was no longer well enough to murder. This explanation seems backwards, so I shall reiterate it. Stephenson is sick enough to be in the hospital, but well enough to commit the murders; when he becomes well enough to leave the hospital, he is too sick to commit any more murders.

In 1890, Stephenson developed a relationship with Mabel Collins. She was the editor of a theological magazine called *Lucifer*. The two of them went into business with Vittoria Cremers. Their company folded in 1891, and Stephenson later took Collins to court over some stolen letters. Two years later, a reformed prostitute named Victoria Woodhull converted Stephenson to Christianity. Stephenson would begin work on his book, *The Patristic Gospels*, which was eventually published in 1904. After the book, Stephenson would disappear. There is no documented record of his death. One possible date of death

for Stephenson has been offered as 1912. This comes from the black magician, Aleister Crowley. Crowley's stories and flair for embellishment have become that of legend. The search for a record of Stephenson's death in 1912 has failed to find any documentation.

Ardent researcher Chris Scott has unearthed documentary evidence of a register chronicling the death of Roslyn D'Onston, aged 76, during the latter part of 1916 in the district of Islington. An often-used alias of Stephenson was Dr. Roslyn D'Onston, and it appears at face value that Scott has discovered the answer to a question which has eluded researchers for the last quarter-century.

Victoria Cremers later related a story about finding a box among Stephenson's things. According to Cremers, this box contained a number of ties with stains that Cremers believed to be blood. After this discovery, Stephenson supposedly told Cremers that Jack the Ripper had concealed his victims' organs under his neckties. This appears to be the primary reason for Cremers's suspecting Stephenson. She later either told the story to Aleister Crowley, who in turn spun the tale to the journalist, Bernard O' Donnell, or she gave the story to O'Donnell herself. Crowley told O'Donnell a similar tale, stating that Stephenson had personally given him the box of blood-encrusted ties before his death in 1912. The two main supporters of Stephenson's guilt, Melvin Harris and Ivor Edwards, have vehemently denied that Crowley knew or had ever met Stephenson.

The macabre air about Stephenson, which may have solidified Cremers's beliefs, was nothing more than Stephenson being himself. Cremers routinely states that she had some degree of fear of

Stephenson, but the whole group was into some pretty weird stuff. They were black magicians and cavorted with a group of occultists. Stephenson was probably no odder than Aleister Crowley. While it seems peculiar that an occultist like Cremers feared Stephenson, it may have been the result of Stephenson spinning yarns and making himself out to be more than he was. Stephenson was a drunk, a braggart, and especially a liar.

In 1929, a former model named Betty May published her biography. Within this tapestry of truth and fiction, Betty May revealed her deep contempt for Aleister Crowley. She was the first to publish Victoria Cremers's story regarding the box of blood-encrusted ties, and she attributed the presence of this box to Aleister Crowley. Betty May claimed to have asked Crowley about the box of ties, to which he replied that Jack the Ripper had personally given it to him. Betty May would later testify in court that she had fabricated the story of seeing the box of blood-encrusted ties. She had taken key elements of her story from an unpublished manuscript of Crowley's.

On November 30, 1929, the *East Anglican Daily Times* ran a story by Pierre Girouard about a "Baroness K" and her discovery of an unspecified number of ties encrusted with blood. The Baroness K is Victoria Cremers, and Girouard claims that she informed the other members of the theosophical society about her discovery. Then, supposedly, the society sent an unnamed doctor to America, where he eventually confessed his guilt. Girouard's article is a combination of the elements of Victoria Cremers's story and a story relating to the Norwegian sailor-suspect Fo-

gelma. Fogelma died in a New Jersey lunatic asylum and was said to have confessed the murders to an unnamed criminology student. The only connection between the unnamed "doctor" and the suspect Folgema is the alleged confession taking place in America. Other than the "Baroness K" reference, it cannot be positively stated that any element of this theory refers to Stephenson.

In 1951 author Denis Clark relayed a similar tale about Betty May discovering the box of ties in the possession of Crowley. Clark adds no new evidence or information regarding this story, and the name of Robert Donston Stephenson is never mentioned.

Theorist and author Jean Overton-Fuller wrote *The Magical Dilemma of Victor Neuberg* in 1965. Neuberg was an author and lyricist who worked alongside poet Dylan Thomas. One of his associates was Aleister Crowley. Fuller relates Victoria Cremers's claim that Stephenson was Jack the Ripper. Fuller, who chose to include the Cremers tale merely as an anecdote, does not offer an analysis of the case against Stephenson.

In 1975, Richard Whittington-Egan discussed Robert Donston Stephenson as a possible suspect. Whittington-Egan's book was designed to be a reference work and offered no bias toward the viability of any particular suspect. He merely called attention to a suspect that had languished for many years.

Thirteen years later, a researcher, theorist, and noted debunker of myth and hoaxes, Melvin Harris, seriously proposed Stephenson as Jack the Ripper. Harris added another book in 1994 to further the case against Stephenson. At the heart of Harris's case is his portrait of Stephenson as a criminal mastermind who taunted the police with letters and deliberately made himself notorious.

Melvin Harris's central argument for Stephenson as a suspect comes from Stephenson's own constant writings during the time of the murders. Stephenson wrote a number of articles for *The Pall Mall Gazette*, while also sending his thoughts on the murders directly to the police. While that may theoretically work in some cases, constantly writing about the murders would appear to be counterproductive in the case of a murderer who has left no clues behind, a murderer who is not even suspected. As at least three of the people who dealt with him considered Stephenson to be Jack the Ripper. Stephenson would have wanted to keep the police as far away from him as possible. But what does Stephenson do then? He acts in such a way that George Marsh believes he is the murderer, which Harris claims is exactly what Stephenson wanted. Then Stephenson goes to see the police himself and lets them know where they can find him. This is either the luckiest play by any serial killer in recorded history or the bumbling and bluster of a strange man.

In 2002 theorist Ivor Edwards published *Jack the Ripper's Black Magic Rituals*. This offering advances Harris's case with a number of geometric patterns and astrological indicators to explain the exact reason for the murders. Edwards's effort needs serious research to examine the theories and patterns put forth. These patterns do not perfectly conform to each other. There are inconsistencies, including the distances between the victims' bodies, which ranged from 930 yards to 950 yards apart. On face value, this appears to be nothing more than a selective use of known information to fit the eccentricities of a preferred suspect.

Other elements to the theory that Stephenson was Jack the Ripper include a hatred of women, possession of a hiding spot, or bolt-hole, and a macabre desire to wield his power. In theory all three of these elements can be justified, but in practical terms they can all also be debunked as purely speculative.

Robert Donston Stephenson was a known liar, habitual drinker and braggart. He was also deeply involved in the occult and the study of magic. Stephenson often wrote under aliases, such as "Sudden Death" and "Tau Tria Delta." He also, most likely, referred to himself as Dr. Roslyn D'Onston. His disappearance in 1904, after the publication of *The Patristic Gospels*, may have been simply Stephenson adding another alias to his repertoire. Certain researchers have placed Stephenson at the forefront of the suspect list. This can only help the advancement of the case, as much more factual material needs to be unearthed regarding this peculiar suspect.

Beadle, William. *Jack the Ripper: Anatomy of a Myth* (1995).

Begg, Paul, Martin Fido, and Keith Skinner. *The Jack the Ripper A–Z* (1996).

Clark, Denis. *Swordfish and Stromboli, Beachcombing round Sicily* (1935).

Clayman, Dr. Charles B. *The American Medical Association Encyclopedia of Medicine* (1989).

Edwards, Ivor. *Jack the Ripper's Black Magic Rituals* (2002).

Harris, Melvin. *Jack the Ripper: The Bloody Truth* (1987).

_____. *The True Face of Jack the Ripper* (1994).

Jakubowski, Maxim, and Nathan Braund. *The Mammoth Book of Jack the Ripper* (1998).

May, Betty. *Tiger Woman* (1929).

Overton-Fuller, Jean. *The Magical Dilemma of Victor Neuberg* (1965).

Rumbelow, Donald. *The Complete History of Jack the Ripper* (1987).

Symonds, John, and Kenneth Grant. *The Confessions of Aleister Crowley* (1969).

Whittington-Egan, Richard. *A Casebook on Jack the Ripper* (1975).

http://www.casebook.org

http://www.redflame93.com/JacktheRipper.html

ALGERNON CHARLES SWINBURNE

Born on April 5, 1837, Algernon Swinburne hailed from an aristocratic background. His maternal grandfather was the 3rd Earl of Ashburnham, and his father was an admiral in the Royal Navy. Swinburne's childhood was spent on the Isle of Wight. He was very close with his family, including his paternal grandfather, who taught him French and Italian.

Algernon's parents belonged to the Church of England, and he possessed a vast knowledge of the Bible's scriptures. In his writing, he would eventually oppose organized religion for its political involvements in Italy. While attending Oxford, Swinburne would explore nihilism, the rejection of meaning in human existence, before leaving in 1860. After leaving Oxford he mixed writing with bouts of alcoholism. One such episode in 1879 nearly resulted in his death. This may have changed his lifestyle, which at the time encompassed homosexuality, masochism, and possibly pederasty and bestiality. Progressing deafness in his later years decreased his visibility, and Swinburne eventually died of influenza in 1909.

In 1975 Richard Whittington-Egan mentioned Swinburne in his list of unlikely Jack the Ripper candidates. Included in this list were Walter Sickert and George Gissing, both of whom were first mentioned in a 1970 book by Donald McCormick. It is uncertain who before Whittington-Egan might have suggested Algernon Charles Swinburne as Jack the Ripper, but, as far as can be determined, Whittington-Egan was the first researcher to present him as a candidate.

Algernon Charles Swinburne was a very small man in stature. He stood just over five feet in height and had a slight build. His strength, as well as his overall health, has been described as frail. Eyewitness testimony places the murderer at approximately five feet seven inches in height, with an average to stout build. This was not Swinburne.

During the time of the murders Swinburne lived with his legal advisor, Theodore Watts-Dunton. It was Watts-Dunton who rescued Swinburne from an early grave due to alcoholism in 1879, so it seems that Watts-Dunton would have watched Swinburne for any peculiar behavior. Watts-Dunton's house was right outside London, so coinciding trips to London by Swinburne would have alerted and alarmed Watts-Dunton. There is no evidence that Theodore Watts-Dunton believed Swinburne was Jack the Ripper.

There is no particular theory as to why Algernon Charles Swinburne's name surfaced in connection with Jack the Ripper. Whittington-Egan's mentioning of Swinburne may be no more than simply that. Swinburne was a masochist and possessed an addictive personality. By the time of the murders, his health had deteriorated due to abusing alcohol. For a man of his fragile stature and diminutive size, he would have had to be in perfect health to commit the murders attributed to Jack the Ripper. Every indication is that Algernon Charles Swinburne was not in ideal health.

Begg, Paul, Martin Fido, and Keith Skinner. *The Jack the Ripper A–Z* (1996)

McCormick, Donald. *The Identity of Jack the Ripper* (1970).

Whittington-Egan, Richard. *A Casebook on Jack the Ripper* (1975).

http://www.photoaspects.com/chesil/swin burne/

ALOIS SZEMEREDY

The first full-length book to offer a suspect was published in 1908. A Dutch writer, named Carl Muusmann, reported on the efforts of the Austro-Hungarian press to implicate Alois Szemeredy in 1892. Szemeredy had been committed to a lunatic asylum in Buenos Aires, Argentina, after robbery and charges of murder were brought against him in 1885. He eventually returned to Vienna for a brief stay in 1889, but was apparently not detained by the authorities, despite the possibility that Szemeredy may have deserted from the Austrian Army prior to his incarceration in Argentina. During his nine-day stay in Vienna during 1889, Szemeredy stated that he was headed to America.

There is no documentation on Alois Szemeredy after from the time he leaves Vienna in 1889 until he returns in 1892. Upon his return, he was arrested again on suspicion of committing murder and robbery. While in the custody of the police, Szemeredy committed suicide. This led the press, most notably *The Daily Graphic*, to suggest Alois Szemeredy was Jack the Ripper.

Szemeredy described himself as both a surgeon and a sausage maker. No record of Szemeredy's military career has as of yet been discovered. His desertion from the Austrian Army could possibly explain his leaving the country for Argentina, but a crushing blow to that presumption is Szemeredy's return to Vienna in both 1889 and again in 1892. The Austrian police may not have known Szemeredy was in Vienna during his nine-day stay in 1889, but it is obvious that the police knew he returned in 1892, as he was immediately arrested. There were desertion charges brought against Szemeredy in 1892. On face value, it would appear that his desertion was not the reason Szemeredy left Vienna his Argentina.

While in Argentina, Szemeredy was placed in a lunatic asylum during 1885. The charges against him were robbery and murder. It is currently not known whether this asylum was a criminal lunatic asylum, similar to Broadmoor. Due to the extreme nature of the charges, I am inclined to believe that it was a criminal lunatic asylum. Since no record of Szemeredy exists until 1889, there is a strong possibility that he was incarcerated for the entire period.

Szemeredy spent nine days in Vienna during 1889. This is known because Szemeredy registered his address when he arrived. His return to Vienna implies that Szemeredy was not wanted in Austria at that time. The fact that he registered of his address should further back up that conclusion. The registering of his address does carry with it certain penal connotations. However, this would also signify that, most likely, Szemeredy did not escape from the lunatic asylum in Argentina but, rather, was released after serving out the designated sentence. It should also indicate that, upon returning to Vienna, Szemeredy was not concerned with secrecy or avoiding the authorities.

Another return to Vienna in 1892 should indicate that Szemeredy was not previously wanted in Austria for any crime. This is evident from the fact that Szemeredy actually committed a crime during the return in 1892. There is absolutely no reason to leave a country where you are not wanted to go to a country where you are wanted by the law, only to then commit a major crime. Szemeredy's 1892 arrest was identical to the charges in Argentina, murder and robbery. If Szemeredy could be said to have a *modus operandi*, this would be it.

However, none of the women from Whitechapel had enough money to justify robbery.

Szemeredy's suicide, while in custody, is the primary impetus behind his later connection to the case. When arrested on similar charges in Argentina, it has been shown that Szemeredy was placed in a lunatic asylum for an undisclosed period of time, which I have estimated at approximately four years. I have to believe the conditions in an Argentinean lunatic asylum during the 1880s could not have been that favorable. While no one will ever know the real reason Szemeredy killed himself, the act may have been committed to avoid returning to an asylum. There also remains the possibility that Szemeredy may not have committed suicide. The suicide story may have been provided to the press to conceal police misconduct.

The case against Szemeredy has been laid out above. His presence in London during 1888 has never been established. There is a strong chance he may have been incarcerated in Argentina. The offering of information about himself to the Austrian authorities does not fit the picture of someone who was eagerly sought. Szemeredy's return re-enforces the idea he was not worried about public knowledge of his location. Szemeredy's mode of criminal behavior also differs from that of Jack the Ripper.

Begg, Paul, Martin Fido, and Keith Skinner. *The Jack the Ripper A–Z* (1996).
Muusmann, Carl. *Who Was Jack the Ripper?* (1908).
http://www.casebook.org

OLGA TCHKERSOFF

The first female name to surface as a suspect was that of Olga Tchkersoff. In 1937, a former policeman named Edwin T. Woodhall proposed a Russian immigrant, named Tchkersoff, as the murderer. Woodhall claimed that her guilt was confessed to two Russian immigrants who moved to the United States. The two Russian immigrants had supposedly had their story regarding Tchkersoff published by an American journalist. According to Woodhall, Olga's younger sister, Vera, had died due to complications from an illegal abortion, so the murders were committed as an act of revenge upon Mary Jane Kelly, who had led Vera down the path to prostitution.

The major problem with Tchkersoff as a suspect is that this story, supposedly told to the American journalist, has never been found or documented. No trace of a woman named Olga Tchkersoff has been found matching the description of Woodhall's proposed female Jack the Ripper. Naming Olga Tchkersoff as Jack the Ripper is along the same lines as suggesting a Jill the Ripper. When a suspect is named who cannot be proven to have existed, that suspect cannot be seriously advanced as the murderer until proper documentation surfaces to verify her existence.

Begg, Paul, Martin Fido, and Keith Skinner. *The Jack the Ripper A–Z* (1996).
Jakubowski, Maxim, and Nathan Braund. *The Mammoth Book of Jack the Ripper* (1998).
Stewart, William. *Jack the Ripper: A New Theory* (1939).
Woodhall, Edwin T. *Jack the Ripper: Or When London Walked in Terror* (1937).

DR. WILLIAM E. THOMAS

An oral tradition, made public in 1993, held that Dr. Thomas would return home to Aberffraw, Wales, where his father resided, immediately after each of the "canonical" murders. After the November 9 murder of Mary Jane Kelly, Dr. Thomas suffered a nervous breakdown and was brought back to North Wales, where he remained until he committed suicide on June 21, 1889.

Dr. William E. Thomas was born in 1856, on the Isle of Anglesey in North Wales. He became a licensed apothecary and later a licensed physician. In 1884 Dr. Thomas was a practicing physician only a short distance from the East End of London. He remained in London until his nervous breakdown some time after the November 9 murder.

This oral tradition, which has passed from generation to generation for 105 years, can hardly be counted as reliable. Precise dates and events tend to change as one person tells a tale to another, so the degree of certainty questionable at best. Dr. Thomas' suicide in 1889 does present an intriguing coincidence for theorists who believe the cessation of the murders occurred as a result of Jack the Ripper dying. However, there remains nothing concrete to establish a link between Dr. Thomas and Jack the Ripper.

Begg, Paul, Martin Fido, and Keith Skinner. *The Jack the Ripper A–Z* (1996).
Jakubowski, Maxim, and Nathan Braund. *The Mammoth Book of Jack the Ripper* (1998).
http://www.casebook.org

FRANCIS THOMPSON

Thompson was born in 1859 to a doctor specializing in Homeopathic medicine and a Roman Catholic convert who had failed in her attempt to become a nun. Thompson's early school life is rich with stories of his affinity for fire. He burned his clothes, was reprimanded for an attempted arson attack on the church, and swung a device holding burning frankincense above his head. This passion for fire remained into adulthood, as Thompson burned his London lodgings in 1896.

His school, from which we have the numerous fire-related stories of Thompson's youth, was a seminary school named Ushaw College, which prepared young priests for their vows. When Thompson reached the age of eighteen, and the members of his class were preparing to take their Holy Orders, the president of the Seminary College advised Thompson's father that Francis should pursue another career. In the following year Thompson began studying medicine at Owen's Medical College and went on to become a surgeon.

Thompson's addiction to opium can be traced back to a lung infection in 1879. He was treated with laudanum, which was wine mixed with opium. Thompson's mother passed away the following year due to liver problems. In 1882 Francis Thompson suffered a nervous breakdown. He repeatedly failed the medical exams, so his father set him up with a job that he would be dismissed from after only one day. Thompson's opium addiction had begun to show, and he left home in late 1885.

Thompson continued writing poetry and worked odd jobs occasionally. Thompson's poetry was continually rejected and a suicide attempt and delirium followed. He finally had some writing published in 1888. Soon after, he published his first volume of poetry. Thompson has since enjoyed a cult following, and this inevitably led to his naming as a suspect.

In 1968, Thompson biographer John Walsh noted that he was living on the streets during the time of the murders and might have been questioned in connection with the Jack the Ripper investigation. Twenty years later, on the centennial of the Jack the Ripper murders, an article appeared in *The Criminologist* examining the suggestion made twenty years earlier by Walsh. The author, Dr. Joseph Rupp, titled the essay, "Was Francis Thompson Jack the Ripper?" Rupp came to the conclusion that Thompson was not the infamous murderer. The article received little notice, and Thompson was not taken seriously as a suspect until 1997, when Richard A. Patterson developed the suggestion that Francis Thompson was Jack the Ripper.

There are many facets to Patterson's theory, including Thompson's proximity to the murders, his background in medicine and surgery, his opium addiction and, mainly, the hidden meanings within the verses of his poetry. Another interesting connection made by Patterson was that poet Alice Meynell and her husband, editor Wilfred Meynell, housed Thompson after he set fire to his London lodgings in 1896. Meynell was a neighbor of Hilair Belloc, brother of Marie Belloc Lowndes. Lowndes wrote the 1911 novel *The Lodger*, the first fictitious novel based on the Jack the Ripper murders.

This novel attributed the crimes to a religious fanatic who had lodged at a certain residence, where his landlord became suspicious of his nocturnal activity. This in no way could apply to Francis Thompson, as he was living on the streets during the time of the murders. Any connection between Meynell and Belloc Lowndes would have nothing to do with Thompson.

With respect to his medical training, Francis Thompson never passed any licensing exams. While studying at Owen's Medical College for a number of years, Thompson never achieved enough skill or knowledge to pass these examinations. Whether he obtained enough anatomical knowledge or surgical skill to remove specific organs, such as the heart or kidneys, is open to debate, but his studies occurred at least six years prior to the murders. Throughout his education, there were also several events, including a lung infection, his mother's death, and a nervous breakdown, to distract him from his training.

Thompson was destitute and living on the streets, in the summer and fall of 1888, Thompson would have been a conspicuous figure roaming around the East End after the murders. This may have led to the speculation that Thompson was questioned at the time of the murders, but the police recorded no questioning of or investigation into Thompson. If Thompson had been found on the streets after any of the murders, he would have been questioned. If he was questioned, he must have produced some type of alibi, or there would have been a mention of his arrest or detention in the police files.

The suggestion has been made that Thompson was seeking out one particular prostitute, with whom he may have had a secret affair. As Thompson was living on the streets at the time of the murders, he would have known the prostitutes of East End to some degree, and they assuredly would have come to recognize him. If it were the case that Thompson was searching out this unfortunate and that the murders were committed as either a result or a byproduct, then one of two things must be true: the woman Thompson sought out was Mary Kelly, as she was the last "canonical" victim, or the woman sought was either Martha Tabram or Mary Ann Nichols, as one of their murders was the first in the series.

If Kelly were the prostitute sought after by Thompson, why would her murder be preceded by the unnecessary murders of at least three other women, all of whom looked nothing like Mary Kelly. It would not have taken Thompson ten weeks to find Mary Kelly on the streets of the East End. If the prostitute in question were Tabram or Nichols, then Thompson's mission would have been completed with one of their murders. There would be no reason to continue the murder spree unless Thompson had grown to love the act of killing. This could not be the case, as the murder of Mary Kelly appears to have ended the murder spree of Jack the Ripper, and Thompson lived on in London for many years after that murder. If Thompson were responsible for the murders of Alice McKenzie and Frances Coles, one would believe that Thompson had acquired an insatiable thirst for the kill. Why, then, would he let the entire year of 1890 go by without satiating his hunger?

One of the main arguments for Thompson as Jack the Ripper are the lyrics of his poetry. This argument has been used before to promote other suspects. The simple fact that Thompson's poetry could have reflected the murders does not mean that he was responsible for the murders. Thompson lived in the area at the time of the murders, so it seems understandable that the murders would have affected Thompson's writing.

The many arguments for Francis Thompson as a suspect are reflected in theories about other suspects, as well. They are basic arguments that have been used before and add nothing but a new name to the case. There has been no real motive established. Why Thompson would kill these prostitutes and then give up murder to focus on his poetry is a question that was never seriously answered by Patterson, quite possibly because there is no real answer.

Francis Thompson died in 1907 from a combination of tuberculosis and laudanum poisoning. By this time he had stopped writing poetry for a number of years, due to the depression and mental instability that accompanied his laudanum addiction. The addiction that was eventually a major part in his demise is reflected in his poetry with the angst and anger of this tormented man.

Walsh, John. *Strange Harp, Strange Symphony* (1968).
Rupp, Dr. Joseph C. *The Criminologist* (Autumn 1988).
http://www.casebook.org
http://www.geocities.com/athens/troy/2057/2002.html

Francis Tumblety

In 1993 researcher Stewart P. Evans purchased a batch of journalist George R. Sims's correspondence from Eric Barton, a collector of true crime and murder memorabilia. The batch included four letters, one of which reintroduced a suspect from the time of the Jack the Ripper murders. Upon this discovery, a great amount of research was undertaken. The search for another Jack the Ripper had begun.

Francis Tumblety was born in Canada, in either 1833 or 1838. While still a young boy his family moved to Rochester, New York. He was descended from an Irish father and was the youngest of eleven children. The earliest reference to Tumblety occurs at the age of fifteen. A canal boat captain named Streeter remembers Tumblety selling books and pamphlets on his boat between 1848 and 1850. After that, Streeter would not see Tumblety again until 1860. When Tumblety returned, he displayed the bawdy flair and style that would become one of his trademarks.

Tumblety turned up in Montreal in the year 1857, moving there in the autumn of that year from the United States. His apprenticing and learning the basics of medicine, perhaps with a focus on holistic and herbal healing, might explain the absence of seven years in Tumblety's recorded history. A childhood acquaintance of Tumblety's stated that he had run into him in Detroit and that Tumblety was studying and practicing medicine of a seedy kind, under the supervision of a "Dr. Lispenard." An 1881 newspaper article backs up this claim, stating that Tumblety had gained his knowledge of medicine from a Dr. Reynolds who ran Lispenard's Hospital. It is not known how long Tumblety was in Detroit, but it can be hypothesized that his medical knowledge was more holistic than surgical in nature. Tumblety soon found himself in trouble, arrested in Montreal for procuring an abortion. There was no surgery involved, just a box of pills and a bottle of liquid, and the case was eventually dismissed.

Tumblety began peddling his holistic medicines and became known as "the Prince of Quacks." At the time there was a movement toward holistic medicine that had been started by Samuel Thomson. These doctors were seen as "quacks," or "Indian Doctors," and were labeled as such in the press and the established medical community. These holistic healers offered an alternative to established medical practices through the use of herbs and roots, but the movement was also a rebellion against the orthodox religious practices of the medical community. Tumblety was a proponent and follower of the holistic movement.

Tumblety was practicing medicine in Toronto in 1858, but he would once again find trouble when he moved to New Brunswick, Nova Scotia, in July of 1860. He settled in Saint John, passing himself off as "a healer of ills and curer of diseases." This claim attracted a locomotive engineer named James Portmore. Portmore was suffering from a kidney disease, and Tumblety's medicines made him ever sicker. Portmore died on September 25, 1860. A coroner's inquest was held, which Tumblety attended to try to clear his name. When Tumblety realized this would not work he fled Saint John, never to return.

Years later, Tumblety was recognized by the Board of the Commissioners of Health in New York for his medicines, specifically his pimple cure. While this implies that the board recognized him as a member of the medical community, it also apparently handed him a copy of the state's health laws and ordinances, so there may have been some suspicion regarding Tumblety's practices.

Whether it was simply due to the nature of his medicines, or the board had information about his troubles in Montreal and Saint John, there was definitely a clear decision to provide Tumblety with guidelines pertaining to the accepted medical practices.

Tumblety would spend the next couple of years, off and on, in Washington, D.C., offering his services to General George McClellan and the Army of the Potomac. McClellan gave him papers that allowed him to freely travel throughout the country. His home base was Washington, though, where he partied and gallivanted with many officers of the Union. He had returned to his grandiose habits, parading around the city on a white horse or traveling around with two dogs. Tumblety became a noticeable figure and was parodied by a local acting troupe. Tumblety, as was his nature, sued the Music Hall that staged the farce.

Toward the middle of 1865 Tumblety's travels took him west to Saint Louis, Missouri. There, he would be arrested on a most serious charge—conspiracy to assassinate President Abraham Lincoln. He was imprisoned for a period of three weeks before his eventual release. This amounted to a case of mistaken identity. A known alias of Tumblety's was Dr. J. H. Blackburn. One of his medical assistants was a J. W. Blackburn, and the case of mistaken identity may have arisen from this. The man the authorities sought was a Confederate agent named Dr. Luke Blackburn. He had hatched a plot to infect the Union officers in the North with yellow fever by sending them contaminated clothing. Upon learning of this plot his arrest was ordered, and Tumblety was mistakenly taken in.

After his release Tumblety traveled to New York, Boston, and Saint Louis, practicing his holistic medicine, gaining considerable wealth from his pimple cure. It was during the later part of the 1860s that Tumblety first visited England. He would become a frequent visitor to London, traveling back and forth from the United States to many parts of Europe.

In 1873 Tumblety's mother died at the age of eighty-seven. The following year Tumblety was in Liverpool and had begun a homosexual relationship with the writer Henry Hall Caine. They had a stormy relationship. Tumblety wrote many letters urging Caine to visit him in both London and the United States. Tumblety's last letter to Caine, and the apparent end of their relationship, was in March of 1876. Caine was described as an attractive twenty-one years old, which illustrates Tumblety's distinct proclivity for younger men.

The next years of Tumblety's life have him back and forth from London to the United States. Much of Tumblety's history has been gathered from newspaper reports. Interviews with his acquaintances show a number of interesting character traits. He harbored a great hatred for women, arising out of a failed marriage, in which he had learned that his wife was a former prostitute. No marriage certificate has been found documenting Tumblety's marriage. The marriage may be nothing more than another one of Tumblety's fabricated tales.

Tumblety was present in London during the time of the Jack the Ripper murders. This has been documented, as Tumblety was arrested on November 7, 1888, and charged with four counts of gross indecency. These four counts occurred on July 27, August 31, the night of Mary Ann Nichols's murder, October 14 and November 2, indicating that he was living in London, or had continually traveled to and from London during the time of the murders.

The offenses that Tumblety was charged with were misdemeanors, not felonies. There were four separate counts. Tumblety theorists say the metropolitan police could not have kept Tumblety in custody for nine days for simple misdemeanors. There is, however, no record of Tumblety's release before November 9. The next recorded mentioning of Tumblety is on November 14, when he was remanded to custody. This must have meant that Tumblety had been free before this court appearance, even if only briefly. There is documentation regarding his November 7 arrest, his November 14 remanding, and his November 16 release on bail.

Tumblety fled the country, never to return. The "Special Branch" was following the movements of Tumblety, as is documented in known reports. Tumblety fled to Boulogne, France. On November 24, 1888, Tumblety made his way across the ocean to America on the steamer *Le Bretagne*, leaving from Le Havre. He boarded the ship under the alias "Frank Townsend."

When Tumblety arrived in America, he was under surveillance by the New York City Police Department headed up by Chief Inspector Thomas Byrnes. There was also an unnamed English detective in New York watching Tumblety. This detective may have followed Tumblety from England. Once the newspapers began mentioning that Tumblety was wanted in connection with the Whitechapel murders, it would not take long for Tumblety to resort to his old tactics. Tumblety's residence in

New York was watched until Tumblety apparently gave them the slip on December 6. The New York Police Department would not hear from Tumblety again.

After Tumblety disappeared, Inspector Walter Andrews was sent to the United States to conduct a search. The papers immediately connected Inspector Andrews's visit to America with the murders committed by Jack the Ripper. Andrews's primary mission was to conduct a search for and gather any information on Tumblety. This search failed, and Andrews returned to London.

Francis Tumblety passed away in Saint Louis, Missouri, on May 28, 1903, after three days of feeling severely ill and weak. He had spent the last couple of years living with his niece in Rochester, New York. His remains would be shipped back from Saint Louis to Rochester. The hometown Tumblety knew as a child would be his final resting place.

Francis Tumblety is viewed as a primary suspect today mainly due to the 1913 letter of correspondence between Chief Inspector John Littlechild and journalist George Robert Sims. I shall reprint the relevant section here:

> I never heard of a Dr D. in connection with the Whitechapel murders but amongst the suspects, and to my mind a very likely one, was a Dr T. (which sounds much like D.) He was an American quack named Tumblety and was at one time a frequent visitor to London and on these occasions constantly brought under the notice of police, there being a large dossier concerning him at Scotland Yard. Although a "Sycopathia Sexualis" subject he was not known as a "Sadist" (which the murderer unquestionably was) but his feelings toward women were remarkable and bitter in the extreme, a fact on

record. Tumblety was arrested at the time of the murders in connection with unnatural offences and charged at Marlborough Street, remanded on bail, jumped his bail, and got away to Boulogne. He shortly left Boulogne and was never heard of afterwards. It was believed he committed suicide but certain it is from this time the "Ripper" murders came to an end.

There are several historical errors within this letter. Littlechild stated that Tumblety was never heard of after he left Boulogne. That is incorrect. Tumblety's movements were well documented until December 6, when he gave the New York Police Department the slip. The name of the passenger steamship that Tumblety rode across the English Channel was known. The alias he used upon boarding the ship was known. His residence in New York was known and watched. This would hardly indicate that Tumblety was never heard of after leaving Boulogne.

The main segment relating to Tumblety offers the reminiscences of a well-respected officer who worked deep within the anti–Fenian and anti-terrorist movement. The position of Chief Inspector at the time of the murders appears to have been no more than that of an information collector. The historical errors display either Littlechild's fading memory or his low level of importance during the time of the murders. It is evidence of Littlechild's lack of knowledge on the subject that he did not know of "Dr. D," a clear reference to Montague John Druitt, misreported by MacNaghten as a doctor.

Tumblety theorists have claimed that the minor nature of his November 1888 offenses would have necessitated his release between November 7 and November 16. They have also argued that the Miller's Court murder was not a Jack the Ripper crime. Claiming that the police could not legally hold Tumblety on sexual offenses for nine days is pure nonsense. Tumblety was remanded on November 14, so he couldn't have been detained for the entire nine-day period, anyway. Yet, there is still no official record of his release on November 7 or November 8, in time to commit the Miller's Court murder.

Tumblety had a prior history of fleeing any area where he had been in serious trouble with the authorities, yet after his release, occurring between November 7 and November 14, he remained in London. Researchers who argue that Tumblety had to be released on November 7, affording him the opportunity to murder the Miller's Court victim, have a logistical and theoretical dilemma. The theory argues that after Tumblety was arrested for four sexual offenses, one going as far back as July 27, he was then released from jail within a day and, rather than quickly leaving London, he murdered one more woman. Then, rather than leaving London after that murder, he remained, only to be brought back to jail, all the while with the murders of at least four women hanging over his head. While not out of the question, the theory's flaws are readily apparent.

With regards to Francis Tumblety, there has been no real theory offered to explain why the murders were committed. Research has proven Tumblety's devious and shady characteristics, and a number of basic points should be examined.

Tumblety was believed to have kept specimen jars containing various internal body parts, including numerous uteri, as reported by Colonel Dunham when he knew Tumblety in Washington, D.C. Colonel Dunham attested to having seen these jars. The murderer took the uteri of Annie Chapman and Catherine Eddowes, after slitting their throats from left to right. Proponents of Tumblety as Jack the Ripper stress the connection, citing that his documented hatred of women indicated that Tumblety removed their uteri to de-womanize them.

Francis Tumblety is an extremely strange character. He did have an outward hatred of women. He was homosexual, but it is likely that this homosexuality was more of a pedophilic nature, indicating that it was about power and control rather than sexual desire. One of the four offenses for which he was charged took place on August 31, 1888, the day of Mary Ann Nichols's murder. If Tumblety is Jack, he would have been playing two very different sexual games that day, exerting power and control over a young man, then murdering and mutilating a woman. Tumblety was boastful by nature, a noted braggart and liar. Without direct proof, it would have been hard to accept anything Tumblety said, whether it was about something he did or about the prowess and skill he possessed. There is also no known record of Francis Tumblety acting out violently against women.

Tumblety's only proponent in the police department has made critical errors, although nowhere close to those in Melville MacNaghten's 1894 memorandum. An inferential analysis of the Littlechild Letter betrays the officer's personal beliefs rather than some insider knowledge. There are those researchers who accept Littlechild at face value, yet time has shown that an acceptance of a former police official's comments at face value may take a case down a path that eventually leads nowhere. While further debate regarding this case is of a generally productive nature, this does not sway the candidacy of Francis Tumblety one way or the other.

Begg, Paul, Martin Fido, and Keith Skinner. *The Jack the Ripper A–Z* (1996).
Evans, Stewart P., and Paul Gainey. *Jack the Ripper: First American Serial Killer* (1995).
http://www.casebook.org

CHARLES WARREN

Appointed as Metropolitan Police Commissioner by Home Secretary Hugh Childers, Charles Warren began his duties on March 29, 1886. Previously, Warren had been commanding troops in Suakim, a port on the Red Sea in the Sudan, a position that Warren had held less than two months. Childers was prepared to give Warren full autonomy, but six months later Childers would be replaced as Home Secretary by Henry Matthews. Matthews and Warren would not get along.

Warren's feuds were legendary. He feuded not only with Henry Matthews over autonomy of the police department, but also with Assistant Commissioner James Monro over a number of issues, including autonomy over the Criminal Investigative Division and the appointment of Melville MacNaghten to the post of Assistant Chief Constable. Warren had met MacNaghten in 1881 when MacNaghten had attempted to settle a dispute and was beaten senseless. Warren described MacNaghten as "the one man in India who had been beaten by Hindoos."

Warren also feuded with Richard Pennefather. Pennefather was the Receiver of the Police, responsible for the administration of police pensions. Warren was visibly and verbally displeased with the way Pennefather and the police administered their pensions. This would gain Warren the favor of the men working under him.

Warren's troubles with the press in London began in 1886. During the Lord Mayor's Show, a portion of the crowd got out of control. On June 21, 1887, the celebration of Queen Victoria's fiftieth anniversary as monarch, a Miss Cass was arrested and charged with solicitation. Miss Cass filed a wrongful arrest suit against the police and the arresting officer. Warren defended the arresting officer and the police. He was vilified in the press for his indiscreet actions. On November 13, 1887, matters would get even worse.

A demonstration formed at Trafalgar Square consisting of the unemployed people of London. Warren deployed troops to clear the square. The troops acted with swiftness and violence, causing the death of one man. This day would go down in history as Bloody Sunday, and the radical press crucified Warren, demanding his removal from office. A year later they would get their wish.

During the Jack the Ripper murders, Warren appointed Chief Inspector Donald Swanson to run the investigation, due to the absence of Assistant Commissioner Robert Anderson. Warren accepted the bulk of the criticism for the failed attempts to capture the Whitechapel murderer. Warren only visited one scene connected with the Jack the Ripper murders. This visit shall be discussed shortly, as it deals with Warren's candidacy as a suspect.

Warren tendered his resignation on November 8, 1888, the day before Mary Kelly was murdered. Warren's resignation was accepted and announced in the newspapers on the 9th, the day Kelly's body was discovered. This was also the day of the 1888 Lord Mayor's Show and the celebration of the Prince of Wales birthday. Warren's resignation had little to do with the overall failure of the police to capture Jack the Ripper. In a response to the press attacks during the Jack the Ripper crisis, Warren published an article in *Murray's Magazine*. The article defended the actions of the police and also broke an official rule requiring police officials to clear all writing before publication. Warren failed to do this and was severely reprimanded by Home Secretary Henry Matthews. The militarist and disciplinarian that Warren was, he had no choice but to resign his post as Commissioner of the Metropolitan Police Department. Researchers say that the written reprimand from Matthews was specifically worded to prompt Warren's resignation. Matthews would immediately replace Warren with his longtime friend and subordinate, James Monro.

Charles Warren was born in Bangor, England, in 1840 and educated at Cheltenham College. At the age of seventeen, Warren joined the Royal Engineers. The Royal Engineers began surveying Western Palestine around 1867. Their work is the basis for what is currently known regarding the landscape of Jerusalem. One of the more famous Middle Eastern archaeological discoveries, one conducted by Warren and the Palestine Exploration Fund, was the surveying of King Herod's Temple. Warren was given his own company within the Royal Engineers in 1869, eventually reaching the rank of lieutenant colonel.

After completing his stint in the Royal Engineers, for which an underground tunnel system was named after him, Warren was sent to settle boundary disputes in South Africa. He returned to England briefly in 1880 to teach surveying and cartography at Chatham. Warren was again sent to Africa to act as a diplomatic liaison regarding the territories possessed by England. At the beginning of 1886, Warren was given command of a garrison of troops at Suakim.

Freemasonry is at the heart of Charles Warren's suspect candidacy. Warren's ties to Freemasonry went back almost thirty years before the Jack the Ripper murders. Warren was initiated into the Lodge of Friendship, No. 278, at Gibraltar, on December 30, 1859. In 1861 Warren would enter the Grand Arch and was made a Knight Templar by 1863. His love and passion for Freemasonry earned Warren a lodge named after him in 1879 in Dutoitspan, site of a diamond mine in South Africa. He was elected the Founding Master of the Quatuor Coronati Lodge, No. 2076, on November 28, 1884. Due to Warren's absence from England, the lodge was not consecrated until January 12, 1886.

The Quatuor Coronati Lodge, No. 2076, was the foremost lodge dedicated to Masonic research in England. Warren was at the forefront of this research endeavor.

In 1976 researcher Stephen Knight implicates Warren in the Royal Conspiracy. Knight goes so far as to state that Warren may have been offered the post of Commissioner of the Metropolitan Police Department so that he could shield his fellow Freemasons from the consequences of the coming Jack the Ripper murders. Warren was offered the Commissionership in early 1886, so for this theory to have any basis, the Royal Conspiracy to protect the Crown would have begun prior to Warren's appointment. Knight does not address this issue, as it contradicts various other aspects of his theory regarding the Jack the Ripper murders.

In 1991 Melvyn Fairclough's updated Royal Conspiracy Theory named Warren as one of the Jack the Ripper *coterie*. As has been discussed throughout this book, Fairclough and Gorman Sickert do not offer further factual information regarding their numerous suspects's complicity in the conspiracy and murders. Warren's official involvement in the murders, according to both Knight and Fairclough, was that of an outside protector, whose job it was to control the police and protect his fellow conspirators.

The only murder site personally visited by Warren was Goulston Street, where a chalked message was left that was believed to have been written by the murderer of Catherine Eddowes. A small piece of Eddowes's apron was found directly under the message, which read, "The Juwes are The Men who will not be Blamed for nothing." Variations of the message exist, recorded by both Police Constable Alfred Long and Detective Constable Daniel Halse. The important word within the message is "Juwes."

The word, "Juwes," was a term that had not been used in English Freemasonry since approximately 1814. Researcher Paul Begg has emphatically stated that "it is a mystery why anyone ever thought that Juwes was a Masonic Word." Begg's argument self-destructs within the same paragraph. Begg also states that the word featured in British Masonic rituals until between 1814 and 1816, then he goes on to declare any connection between "Juwes" and Masonry to be a mystery. Begg does accurately state that the term, "Juwes," would not have been known to British Masons.

Warren, however, was a founder and leading member of the foremost Masonic research lodge in England. It seems logical that Charles Warren would have known the implications of the word, "Juwes." Warren is allegedly the man responsible for the erasure of the Goulston Street Graffito. According to this theory, Warren would have wanted the graffiti erased immediately, before any possible connection could be made to the Freemasons. This is not to say that the Freemasons committed the Jack the Ripper murders within the scope of the Royal Conspiracy Theory. In fact, logic points toward the opposite conclusion, that the Freemasons did not commit the murders. There would be no reason to leave a public message for a fellow Mason like Warren if he were involved in the conspiracy.

After resigning the Commissionership in November 1888, Warren would travel to Singapore to once again command troops. In 1891 Warren became District Grand Master of the Eastern Archipelago. As a lieutenant general, Warren was vital in winning an offensive during the Boer War. In 1904 Warren was promoted to general and involuntarily retired the following year. He would go on to be a major player in the Boy Scout movement, while continuing his passion and work with Masonic research and history.

Described as an evangelical Christian and an extreme militarist, his personality and background did not suit the political climate during the Jack the Ripper murders. His stubbornness and pride prompted his own resignation. Warren would pass away in 1927, leaving a grand legacy of archaeological discoveries, noted surveys of Biblical historical sites, and military encounters. He would be most remembered today as the Commissioner in charge of the Police force that was thoroughly beaten by Jack the Ripper.

Begg, Paul. *Jack the Ripper: The Uncensored Facts* (1988).
_____, Martin Fido, and Keith Skinner. *The Jack the Ripper A–Z* (1996).
Fairclough, Melvyn. *The Ripper and the Royals* (1991).
Fido, Martin. *The Crimes, Detection and Death of Jack the Ripper* (1988).
Knight, Stephen. *Jack the Ripper: The Final Solution* (1976).
Williams, Watkin W. *The Life of General Sir Charles Warren* (1941).
http://www.pef.org.uk/Pages/Warren.htm

NICOLAI WASSILI

In 1872, a number of prostitutes, at least five, were murdered in Russia. According to Nicolai Wassili, these women were murdered to "save their souls," and allow them to enter Heaven. Wassili, sometimes described as Nicolas Vassili, or Vassily, was caught and confessed to the crimes. He was sentenced to fifteen years' imprisonment. The last information known about Wassili was that he was released from an asylum in his hometown of Tiraspol, Ukraine, Russia, on or about January 1, 1888. After the murder in Miller's Court on November 9, the newspapers flooded the market with stories of possible suspects. From November 14 through the 16 at least three newspapers, including *The Manchester Guardian*, *The Evening Star*, and *The Ottawa Citizen*, told the story of Wassili murdering prostitutes in Paris during 1872, suggesting a connection to Jack the Ripper. In these newspaper reports it has been intimated that upon his release from the asylum in Ukraine, Wassili had been headed in the direction of London.

When describing the murders in Paris in 1872 attributed to Wassili the parallels to Jack the Ripper immediately surface. It must be stated first that these accounts of Wassili are entirely derived from newspaper articles of the time. There still remains no verifiable proof of the existence of Nicolai Wassili. These murders were committed in Paris. Therefore, Wassili's committal to an asylum must have taken place in Paris or someplace in France. However, Wassili's later release was from an asylum in his native Tiraspol, Russia. These two contradictions have been pieced together from various newspaper reports on Wassili. There remains no evidence to support any of this, either in France or in Russia. Records do get lost and misplaced; that is unfortunately a fact. That is not meant to say that Wassili ever existed or, contrarily, that he did not exist.

The murders attributed to Wassili are precisely the reason he has been suggested as Jack the Ripper, so let's examine them. Wassili was a highly religious man, leaving for Paris when the Russian Orthodox Church attempted to subdue the fanatical sect to which he belonged. While in Paris he tried to convert and reform prostitutes, but he fell in love with one of his attempted converts. Wassili eventually murdered her after she shunned him due to their conflicting religious beliefs. She was his first victim, and this apparently started Wassili on his murder spree.

Fifteen to sixteen years later, Wassili was released after he was "cured." After approximately eight to nine months out of an asylum, would Wassili have started the same cycle in London? This would suggest that Wassili knew his victims and murdered them after he was shunned by them. While that does not have to be the case, as certain serial killers have been known to change their *modus operandi*, someone who was perpetrating the murders based on fervent religious beliefs would tend to perform these murders in a ritualistic way, perhaps to make a religious statement. This was not the case with either the murders committed by Jack the Ripper or those attributed to Wassili in 1872.

The victims of the murders in Paris were not mutilated abdominally, nor were their throats cut from left to right in two separate adjoining incisions. There were mutilations and one woman was "hacked and slaughtered," according to the *Montreal Daily Star* of November 14. The connecting factor in Paris is that these women were stabbed in the back. While the Parisian women were not robbed, similar to the Whitechapel victims, they represented a different economic class of women. The bodies of the Parisian victims were found along with money and jewels, indicating a higher social standing than the women who were murdered by Jack the Ripper. Another characteristic difference in these murders is that the first murder attributed to Wassili, Madeleine, screamed out as her assailant fled the scene screaming himself. This is a far cry from the murders in Whitechapel, in which a quiet killer prowled the streets dispatching his victims in silence.

Begg, Paul, Martin Fido, and Keith Skinner. *The Jack the Ripper A–Z* (1996).
http://www.casebook.org

DR. WILLIAM WYNN WESTCOTT

William Wynn Westcott was born on December 17, 1848, in Leamington, England. Westcott's parents died before he reached the age of ten, so his uncle, Dr. Richard Westcott Martyn, adopted him. Westcott attended University College in London to study medicine. Westcott became a Freemason and a partner in his uncle's medical practice in 1871. While working alongside his uncle in medicine, Westcott met and married his wife, Elizabeth Burnett. The couple would have five children.

Two years after his uncle's death in 1879 Westcott was appointed Deputy Coroner for North-East London and Central Middlesex. He would remain in this position until retiring in 1918. He moved to South Africa in 1920, eventually dying there on July 30, 1925. His writing on medical issues encompassed alcoholism and suicide.

Westcott joined numerous Masonic lodges, rising up the ranks of each lodge. In 1886 he became a member of the Quatuor Coronati Lodge. This lodge was devoted to Masonic research. Among the lodge's members was Police Commissioner Charles Warren. Westcott would be appointed as the Worshipful Master for that particular lodge in 1893.

In 1887 Dr. Westcott and two others founded the *Order of the Golden Dawn*. It was a system of magic that was developed into an Anti-Masonic society based on Rosicrucian rituals and beliefs. The other two founding members have not been implicated as possible suspects. During 1887, Dr. Westcott became the Coroner for Central London. At the time of the murders Westcott was not mentioned in any suspect files or police notes, despite being both a doctor and part of a society that was based on the occult. It was more than 100 years before researcher Christopher Smith suggested Westcott as a possible suspect in a three-part series of articles in 1993.

Dr. Westcott based *The Order of the Golden Dawn* on the amalgamation of three separate mystical religions, Egyptian, Judaic Mysticism and Christian Mysticism. The mixture of these three religions takes the form of Rosicrucianism. Rosicrucianism has no direct meaning but can be best described as a movement or advancement toward spiritual truth, personal enlightenment, and a freedom of the mind, spirit, and soul. The creation of the Golden Dawn was done primarily out of a need to have an organization dedicated to the research and teaching of the occult. It is termed Anti-Masonic due to its departure from rituals and sacrifices in favor of study, teaching and the striving toward higher learning.

In 1896, due to political pressure, Westcott publicly stepped down from running the Golden Dawn, yet he remained a constant figure behind the scenes. He returned after the uproar had calmed in 1900, joining a rival branch of the Golden Dawn. This may be as a direct result of author and fellow mystic Aleister Crowley joining in 1898. The movement began to head in the direction of demonic magic. Westcott continued to write throughout his life, primarily on matters of the occult and religion

In 1897, Diana Vaughn, a Satanist viewed as the "High Priestess of Masonry," claimed that Westcott was a chief of the English Luciferians. She claimed to have visited Westcott's home and made copies of the order's rituals and practices. Vaughn engaged in a witch-hunt against Freemasonry in which many upright members were libeled.

Westcott had been a Freemason since 1871. He knew their rituals and history, yet it was a dislike of these same rituals that drove Westcott to form a society that devoted itself to the study and teaching of magic and the occult. His implication as a suspect is based on the precept that the murders were ritual sacrifices. In fact, it was rituals and practices such as these that Westcott rejected to form his own society. Even the man who suggested him as a possible suspect, Christopher Smith, not only implicates the society as a whole, but also makes clear that he still favors another suspect.

The naming of Westcott as a suspect arose because he had helped found a secret society, *The Order of the Golden Dawn,* and during the time of the murders he was the society's most familiar face. William Wynn Westcott dedicated himself to achieving and advancing in life, through the growth and development of his mind, spirit, and soul. It is highly unlikely that a man with these ideals would mindlessly murder at least five women using ritualistic practices that he had opposed during the latter part of his life.

Begg, Paul, Martin Fido, and Keith Skinner. *The Jack the Ripper A–Z* (1996).
Smith, Christopher. *The Criminologist* (Winter 1992–Autumn 1993).
http://www.casebook.org
http://www.golden-dawn.org/biowestcott. html
http://www.hermeticgoldendawn.org/Documents/Bios/Westcott.html

Index